Contents

To my mother,
MARGARET BURGESS

Foreword

My intention in this book is to account for the changing character of British society during a period when the pioneer of industrial capitalist development was coming under increasing pressure from foreign competitors. The emphasis is upon the changing position of labour in its relations with the wider society, especially as this has reflected and, in turn, affected the subsequent course of British capitalist development. The outcome of this process was to produce a recognisably 'modern' pattern of British social relations as began to emerge in the 1930s, marked by a growing acceptance of 'corporatist' solutions to problems of economic and social instability. A climate of opinion was consequently created that was conducive to the resolution of conflict, which survived until the late 1960s. My hope, therefore, is to have located 'paths to the present' in this survey of a period that has shaped British society as it is today.

My intention is also to inform the reader of the vast and increasing body of academic literature on this important period, much of which is contained in not easily accessible journals. I make no excuse, therefore, for the relative absence of references to materials of primary research. What I hope this work will achieve is to foster a critical understanding of basic issues often overlooked amidst the minutiae of academic scholarship. I am thus indebted to many people for making a study of this kind possible, as the references and bibliography indicate. I have also benefited directly from discussions with staff and students at the University of Glasgow, and deserving of special mention in this regard are my former colleagues, Roy Hay and Bob Holton, and Joe Melling whose forthcoming doctorate in the Department of Economic History breaks new ground in its analysis of the origins of modern social policy. I remain personally responsible, of course, for any errors of fact or omission as well as for any contentiousness in interpretation.

Keith Burgess
University of Glasgow

CHAPTER 1

The Accommodation of Labour, 1850s–70s

Introductory

The situation of labour in capitalistic society involves a complex network of economic and social relationships. The central dynamic of capitalism is the accumulation of surplus value, obtained by the buying and selling of labour power. Yet the importance of the forces of production in determining the character of labour's relationship with capitalist society at a given stage of its development should not reduce an analysis to the form of a crude economic determinism. Labour, by definition, is a creative act identifying man as a social animal. The sum total of creative acts assumed by labour in society implies that its role in production, distribution and consumption involves the exercise of imaginative and intellectual faculties. The latter affects, in turn, the character of labour's relationship with the forces of production. Thus any treatment of labour as a social relation should concern itself not only with those issues that are specific to it in strictly productive terms, but must also include the subtle interaction of associations, traditions, loyalties and ideologies arising from man's capacity to respond to and shape the material world. The situation of labour in a particular society necessarily requires, therefore, a conception of the total structure of that society. The historian's task is to explain why and how societies change over time, hence the task of the historian of labour is to explain its changing character in light of its developing relationship with the total structure of society.

The relationship of labour to the history of British society is of special interest because of Britain's position as the pioneer of modern capitalist development. This gave rise to a unique symbiosis, implying a mutually dependent but simultaneously antagonistic relationship. It is arguable that during the period between the middle decades of the nineteenth century and the 1930s the development of British capitalism led to a transformation of the forms of labour's symbiotic relationship with society as a whole, as the productive relations of the pioneer of modern capitalist development themselves underwent transformation. The outcome by the 1930s was a recognisably 'modern' network of associations, traditions, loyalties and ideologies. This successfully adapted British capitalism to conditions that were much less favourable to its dominant interests than those obtaining in the middle decades of the nineteenth century.

The Economic Context

An analysis of the developing relationship between labour and British capitalism from the mid-nineteenth century until the 1930s must begin with an examination of the forces of production at work in the 1850s and 1860s. The evidence of trends of prices and profits during the years 1850–73, for example, throws light on the general state of the economy in this period. This can no longer be regarded as an age of sustained price inflation making for the high profits and unlimited optimism commonly associated with it.[1] Prices did rise sharply during 1849–54 and in the early 1870s, but for the rest of the period they fluctuated around a plateau, interrupted temporarily by the disruption caused by the American Civil War. The causes of rising prices, at least in the period 1848–54, can be attributed to the impact of gold discoveries in Australia and California, and their effect in generating an international explosion of credit. The demand for goods was subsequently increased by the additional income created by mining activities. War expenditure in the Crimea, the USA and Western Europe was another contributing factor maintaining prices at relatively high levels during these years. It seems clear that prices generally rose faster than wages, yielding a greater return to profits, dividends and rents compared with returns to labour. It is also true that wholesale raw material prices sometimes moved ahead of prices of manufactured goods, thus squeezing the incomes of British capitalists, but these lags were generally short-lived and were more than offset by the continuing advances achieved in industrial productivity, which were especially striking during the years 1847/53–5–4/60 and 1861/5–66/74.[2]

What evidence there is suggests in the absence of a definitive study that profits were quite healthy during the period as a whole.[3] A general characteristic of the 1850s and 1860s that proved advantageous to British capital was the trend of price relations between finished goods exported and imported raw materials. Despite the rise in raw material prices, particularly during the American Civil War, the late 1840s marked an end to the secular decline in the ratio of export to import prices (and costs) that had caused considerable embarrassment to British manufacturers since the 1820s.[4] Thereafter, the price relation between imports and exports was relatively stable on trend, and moved distinctly in Britain's favour after the mid-1860s. This reflected the quasi-monopoly position enjoyed by British capitalists in overseas markets as other countries sought to industrialise by importing capital goods on an unprecedented scale. It is significant that the 'export proportion' of British industry rose more during the years between the late 1840s and 1860 than in any other period between 1814 and 1933.[5]

The sources of growth for British capitalism in the mid-Victorian period illustrate the forces of production at work during these years. The expansion of railways, for example, especially during the mania of the 1840s, marked a significant widening as well as deepening of the field for profitable investment following the crisis of 1839–42. Although the exact contribution of railways to accumulation and continued growth in the economy as a whole has been the subject of some debate, there is little doubt about their importance in stimulating the recovery of the late 1840s. In the quinquennium 1845–9, railway investment accounted for an all-time peak of 55% of all domestic accumulation in fixed capital.[6] The linkages between railway construction and the capital goods industries, including capital exports to finance railway-building overseas, implied that the domestic railway expansion of the 1830s and 1840s helped make possible the great export booms of the period 1850–73, as the waves of industrialisation centred on Britain spread throughout the world. Britain's lead in industrialisation made it possible for accumulation to be sustained without a massive injection of capital-intensive techniques that would have significantly raised the ratio of capital to labour—the organic composition of capital—and thereby impaired the prospects for continued accumulation.[7]

In the 1850s and 1860s, the trend of accumulation in major sectors of the economy like cotton textiles and engineering tended to a widening rather than a deepening of the investment field. The potential for economies of scale created by the expansion of the market, particularly overseas, had the effect of replacing and augmenting plant with more efficient equipment of an already familiar type. There was thus no marked shift in the capital-labour ratio, in contrast to the 1830s and 1840s when the bias of investment had been decidedly capital-using and labour-saving, resulting in an upward shift in the ratio of capital to labour.[8] This implied that during the period 1850–73 accumulation took place without leading simultaneously to a falling ratio of consumption to investment since the demand for capital and labour was in relative equilibrium. Unlike the 1830s and 1840s, therefore, when the capital-using and labour-saving effect of investment had raised the capital-labour ratio, with accumulation proceeding at the expense of consumption, investment in the 1850s and 1860s tended to be capital-saving and labour-using, creating as a result a steady growth of employment incomes although wages still lagged behind prices.

An analysis of the developing relationship between labour and British capitalism must, therefore, take into account the forces of production at work in mid-Victorian society that yielded some improvement in living standards, unlike the trends in the preceding period when the combination of static or declining wages and cyclical or structural unemployment had been a major cause of social unrest. The tremendous growth of Britain's overseas trade during the years 1850–73, including exports of capital as well as commodities, was primarily responsible for the changing pattern of domestic accumulation leading to higher wages and generally improved living standards. In 1853, for example, it has been estimated that one-half of all European investment in US railroad securities represented financial paper obtained in return for the purchase of British rails.[9] The result was that the amplitude of cyclical fluctuations, particularly slumps, was probably not as great after 1850 as it had been during the 1830s and 1840s. This would seem to be justified on theoretical grounds as the movement of the capital-labour ratio into relative equilibrium created conditions for greater economic stability.[10]

It is important to appreciate, however, that the more favourable conditions obtaining after 1850, particularly with regard to the demand for labour, were not enjoyed to the same extent by all members of the British wage-earning class. Given the shift from labour-saving to labour-using investment, it is to be expected that workers whose strategic position enabled them to take full advantage of the widening of the investment field would receive a comparatively large share of the wages from employment that the 'export economy' generated. These were not necessarily skilled.

workers in the strict sense of having served a formal apprenticeship, but would include groups like the fitters and turners in the engineering industry, the senior minders in cotton spinning, and the hewers in coal-mining, whose combination of aptitude and experience gave them a strong bargaining position. This was reflected not only in relatively high wages but the degree of control exercised by these groups over their own work situation, which included control over the less strategically placed operatives employed at the same stage of the labour process.

A factor related to the objective advantage enjoyed by these workers in relation to the mid-Victorian labour market was their subjective perception of the labour process. Market calculation had been slow to penetrate the pre-industrial skilled trades where craft consciousness had dictated a customary rather than market attitude to the wage bargain. This was part of the ambience of artisan small-scale production that had continued to employ the large majority of skilled workers during the first half of the century. By the mid-1850s, however, factory-based production and the extensive application of machine techniques had become commonplace in strategic sectors of industry like textiles and engineering. In the latter, capital was relatively unfettered by the limited supply of traditionally scarce craft skills, and the associated restraints on labour exploitation imposed by established customs and practices. The necessity of creating the new skills of the 'engineers' economy', for example, provided the opportunity for recasting the principles of wage determination on the basis of a calculation as to what market conditions justified. This affected, in turn, the attitudes of both employers and workers themselves. Thus the wage differential enjoyed by operatives like the spinning minders in relation to the earnings of the mass of unskilled labour in the cotton industry was the outcome of a calculation as to what the market might bear, arrived at according to the capitalist rules of the game:[11]

> Workers learned to regard labour as a commodity to be sold in the historically peculiar conditions of a free capitalist economy.

A striking development of the middle decades of the nineteenth century was not just that some workers were earning more than others but that this differential was obtained by 'playing the market', as the shift to labour-using investment implied that certain grades of labour came to acquire a scarcity value in their own right. This was to have a profound impact on the consciousness of the so-called 'labour aristocracy' as it affected their position in capitalist society.

While the growth of the 'export economy' in the 1850s and 1860s created a sellers' market for a privileged elite of workers, especially in the staple industries, the mass of labour lived at or little above subsistence level. The changing character of domestic accumulation was not able to absorb completely the industrial reserve army of labour brought into existence by the effects of technological displacement during the 1830s and 1840s. Moreover, the combination of rapid population growth and migration from rural areas, including Ireland, swelled the mass of casual underemployed workers in the large cities that acted as a drag on the unskilled labour market. Not only was the wage differential of skilled to unskilled somewhere in the region of 2:1, what evidence there is suggests that this widened in the period 1850–73. In the cotton industry, for example, the average weekly wages of senior minders rose by 8s 3d between 1850 and 1871, compared with an increase of 3s for unskilled (women) weavers.[12] In the building industry, labourers' wages rose by 25% between 1850 and the late 1870s while those of skilled workers increased by at least 50%.[13] In practice, this differential was even wider because of the unskilled labourers' greater vulnerability to unemployment. Unemployment among skilled trade unionists in the engineering, metal and shipbuilding industries only twice reached double figures in the period 1850–73—12.2% in 1858 and 10% in 1868.[14] Compare these figures with Mayhew's estimate that fully two-thirds of wage-earners in London were either in half-time (casual) employment or totally unemployed during this period.[15] In Edinburgh, the incidence of pauperism among building labourers was more than eight times greater than what it was for skilled masons and plasterers.[16] The economics of working-class differentiation was to have important implications for the informal associations, disciplines, ideology and politics of labour in the mid-Victorian period.

The Character of Class Relations

The increasing stability of British capitalism as an economic system in the 1850s and 1860s had an analogue in the changing character of social, ideological and political relationships during these years. The growth of the export economy created a new power bloc in British society, consisting of an alliance of dominant groups or fractions.[17] This included an increasingly numerous rentier bourgeoisie, enriched by the wealth that accrued to Britain as the hub of the international economy and centred in London and the south of England, having close contact with the central state apparatus. Another distinct although intimately related group were the big landowners, many of whom were also becoming rentier bourgeois in their own right (with the advent of limited liability), who benefited from the favourable trend of agricultural prices and rents in the mid-Victorian period, as well as rising income from urban property and industrial activities on their estates. They continued to occupy their traditional position, dominating the upper reaches of the state apparatus. There were also, of course, the industrial capitalists located primarily in north Britain who were steadily being accepted as members of the power bloc, although commonly only after they had acquired land or become rentiers. The fact that Victorian Britain was never totally dominated by businessmen–industrialists is crucial to an understanding of labour's developing relationship with that society. A final constituent of the power bloc was the 'urban gentry', the intellectuals who served the state at every level of administration, were members of professional associations and sat on Royal Commissions, and who articulated the prevailing ideology. Their closest affinities were with the landowners and rentier bourgeoisie, many urban gentry being drawn from families of these groups.

The concept of a power bloc should not be interpreted as denying the existence of conflict among its component parts. Nor as an alliance of groups did the power bloc always speak with one voice. The debates on issues like the franchise and labour legislation in the 1860s indicate keen differences of opinion on important matters. Yet the differences that did arise stemmed from disagreements over *how* best the rule of the power bloc as a whole could be maintained, unlike the situation in the 1830s and 1840s when the Corn Law agitation, for example, marked a struggle between industrial capital and the landed interest for control of state power itself.

The drawing together of the various constituents of the power bloc into a working alliance was the result of a complex interaction of factors. There was, above all, the increasing prosperity and stability of British capitalism during the period 1850–73, which helped assuage the hostility of industrial capital to the continued political dominance as well as social prestige of the landed aristocracy. The Lancashire cotton magnates, for example, who had seen their profit margins eroded in the late 1830s and early 1840s, as well as their very existence threatened by working-class unrest, were persuaded to accept a situation of power-sharing in the more stable conditions prevailing after 1850, especially in light of the repeal of the Corn Laws that had been the most obvious symbol of their discontent.[18] It is important to appreciate, moreover, that although the luminaries of the landed aristocracy continued to figure as leading members of the governing faction of the power bloc throughout the mid-Victorian period, the industrial bourgeoisie constituted the hegemonic faction in ideological terms, diffusing its own way of life and thought throughout British society.[19]

The ideology of the industrial bourgeoisie consisted of a number of closely related imperatives, often morally or religiously sanctioned, which amounted to a body of 'rational conduct'. This included social atomism, utilitarianism and possessive individualism. It was diffused throughout society in the following ways. In the localities, the agencies of hegemonic control like the town councils, Poor Law guardians and the press passed directly into the hands of the industrial bourgeoisie in the rapidly expanding manufacturing districts; while in the countryside landowners continued to govern in the sense that they came to be regarded as fit to govern. The ultimate test of fitness to govern rested with public opinion. It was in this respect that the urban gentry in articulating the dominant ideology had a crucial role to play. Drawing upon its affinities with the rentier bourgeoisie as well as the landed estate, the urban gentry functioned as a legitimating agent for the ideology of the industrial bourgeoisie, creating a climate of 'informed' public opinion by appealing to professional expertise. Although the latter was often critical of the precise means whereby power in society was allocated and exercised, it shared the prevailing outlook that held property-holding to be sacrosanct and celebrated the utility of possessive individualism. The urban gentry's critical inclinations were circumscribed, focusing on 'problem-solving' and rectifying 'abuses'. It was involved at various levels of activity, like the Royal Commissions and socio-scientific associations at national level and the civic improvement movement in the localities.

Conflict *within* the power bloc was thus reduced to questions of strategy and tactics rather than matters of principle. It is noteworthy that in contrast to the situation obtaining in the late 1830s and early 1840s, when the extent of social discord threatened to polarise

British politics along class lines, the character of party feuding in the 1850s and 1860s represented continually shifting alliances and allegiances cutting across the component parts of the power bloc. These reflected the rivalry between Whig landed magnates and Liberal industrialists on the one hand, and Tory landlords, brewers, bankers and miscellaneous 'respectables' on the other. Yet rivalry inside the power bloc was contained within an overall hegemony exercised by the industrial bourgeoisie and mediated in relation to society as a whole by the urban gentry of professional intellectuals.

The creation of a mid-Victorian power bloc, consisting of an alliance of dominant groups or factions, has a special significance in relation to the process of working-class differentiation. What needs to be explained is how the prevailing ideology confirmed the economics of working-class differentiation during this period. One possible link between economics and ideology has already been noted. It is argued that the widening wage differential enjoyed by the privileged elite of labour in the period 1850–73 was a result not only of the objective advantages attached to certain grades of skill and experience, in the context of the mid-Victorian labour market, but sprang in part from workers' perceptions of their relationship to the labour process. In particular, what enabled this minority to earn far more than the large mass of labourers was not just their objective situation in the labour market but their willingness to conceive of the wage bargain primarily if not exclusively in terms of a market calculation—to sell their labour to the capitalist for as much as the market might bear. Although the buying and selling of labour power according to market calculation necessarily implied conflict between workers and capitalists—with the worker seeking to sell the smallest amount of labour at the highest possible price and the capitalist endeavouring to buy the largest amount of labour at the lowest possible price—both capitalist and worker had to observe the rules of the game otherwise it would become unplayable. The constant stream of references appealing to the 'state of trade' in wage bargaining during the mid-Victorian period shows how the workers' perception of the capitalist-labour process was reified into an abstraction that was seen as somehow rational and universal.[20] This is not to suggest that the bourgeois imperatives of social atomism, utilitarianism and possessive individualism were adopted by workers without modification, but rather, a negotiated version of the dominant ideology was evolved that was compatible with their class situation.[21]

The upshot led necessarily to a considerable amount of tension if not ambivalence in workers' perceptions of their relations with the forces of production, as the frequently bitter industrial disputes of the period emphasise. Yet the privileged minority's ability to win wage increases during the period 1850–73 by 'playing the market' had, at least in part, a legitimating effect. There was, above all, a growing feeling that an amelioration of the workers' condition could be achieved within the existing structure of society. This is illustrated by the evidence submitted by the National Association of United Trades for the Protection of Industry (an organisation representing affiliated trade unions) to a Parliamentary Select Committee in 1856. Its first object was to secure a 'fair compensation' for 'industry, ingenuity and skill', or 'a fair day's wage for a fair day's work'.[22] This was an explicit recognition that a 'fair' deal for labour was obtainable in capitalist society, and the references to 'industry' and 'ingenuity' indicate that workers did not regard this as theirs as of right, reflecting an *a priori* claim by labour to the fruits of production, but looked upon it as something to be earned as a privilege wrung from the capitalist. In other words, it was labour's *utility*, especially its ingenuity, industry and skill, that *deserved* 'fair' dealing. This was a tacit admission that the interests of capital and labour were ultimately compatible. The association's second object made this more explicit: it argued that all disputes between employers and workers could be ultimately resolved by arbitration and mediation. When asked about the best remedy for strikers, its Secretary replied:[23]

If the diffusion of knowledge of the laws [of political economy?] and a good sound education could be given to the people, it would be an excellent means of learning [sic] them to be independent.

Working-class 'independence' could thus be obtained by self-improvement, within the existing framework of society. This is in striking contrast to working-class consciousness in the Chartist period when its concern with injustice and inequality had articulated a conception of society reconstructed along democratic and egalitarian lines. The economics of working-class differentiation created, therefore, a mechanism for transmitting a negotiated version of the dominant ideology to a privileged elite of labour during the third quarter of the nineteenth century.

Labour in the Workplace

The foregoing discussion of one of the links between economics and ideology illustrates the complex character of labour's developing relationship with mid-Victorian society. A more thorough treatment of the process of working-class differentiation requires elucidation at three distinct although closely related levels of analysis: labour in the workplace; labour in society, including its informal associations and disciplines; and labour's relationship with the political system. Taken together, these comprised the unique symbiosis enjoyed by labour in relation to British society as a whole in the period 1850–73. The subsequent history of labour tells how the antagonisms within this symbiosis intensified, as the relations of production in the pioneer capitalist economy underwent transformation, only to be reconstituted in the 1930s along quite different lines and under fundamentally altered conditions.

In the workplace, the real subordination of wage-labour to capital in the process of production itself was only finally achieved under factory conditions where the technical basis of machine manufacture realised in its ultimate form the unitary structure of capitalist enterprise. The latter posits that there can be only one source of legitimate authority within the firm: that which flows from the capitalist and his subordinates.[24] The unitary structure of capitalist organisation is an expression of an ideological as much as a technical relation between labour and the production process, and it has been argued that this forms 'the most important part' of the hegemony exercised by the industrial bourgeoisie over the working class.[25] Although factory production did not penetrate to all spheres of manufacturing in the 1850s, capitalist wage-labour had become typical, together with its ideological rationale—the unitary organisation of enterprise. Subsequent generations of workers thus became subject to the demands and regimen of wage-labour, where the adjustment of wages was determined by the operation of a free capitalist economy. An important difference, therefore, distinguishing the traditional craft sectionalism of the early nineteenth century from working-class differentiation in the 1850s and 1860s was the new context in which it took place. The fact that the widening wage differentials obtained during these years by a privileged minority of workers were won as a result of playing the capitalist rules of the game was just one aspect of the legitimacy this gave to the dominant ideology. Equally significant was the way it made the unitary structure of the firm tolerable if not positively acceptable, at least to those key workers in receipt of higher wages.

The pattern of authority and methods of wage payment typical of the mid-Victorian family firm were particularly important in legitimating its unitary structure. A striking characteristic of labour utilisation in this period was the extent to which authority and responsibility were delegated by the employer to key workers who were often subcontractors in their own right.[26] Throughout British industry, and especially in engineering, building construction, coal-mining and textiles, firms found that subcontracting enabled them to expand without having to raise large amounts of circulating capital since it tied the payment of wages directly to the completion of work. It also created 'incentives' for those workers chosen as subcontractors because any 'balance' remaining after the work was completed, and the operatives paid, was usually kept by themselves. Subcontractors thus had as keen an interest as the capitalist in ensuring that work was completed quickly and cheaply, in order to maximise their share of the total wage bill. Finally, subcontracting made it possible for firms to meet fluctuations in demand with the lowest possible overheads since their permanent wage bill included only those workers who as subcontractors possessed the skill and experience that could not be easily dispensed with, while the rest of the labour force could be more readily increased or diminished as market conditions fluctuated. This system took many forms in different industries. In engineering and building, so-called 'piece masters' and 'chasers' remained ubiquitous in the 1850s and 1860s, despite official trade union hostility, and in coal-mining and textiles, the practice of hewers and senior minders supervising work teams and paying wages out of a lump sum they received from the firm survived long after 1870. The extent to which subcontracting involved the delegation of the authority of the capitalist to a small elite in the labour force, who consequently enjoyed a comparatively privileged position, was part of the wider hegemony established by the industrial bourgeoisie during the mid-Victorian period.

It is not coincidental that trade unionism should have taken root among those workers who benefited most from the economic changes of the 1850s and 1860s.[27] In particular, the changing character of investment that became as much labour-using as labour-saving increased the demand for labour where skill and experience was required, especially in the staple industries, and the subsequent strengthening of its bargaining position gave birth to permanent trade unions. These sought to protect and augment the widening differential obtained by privileged groups like the fitters and turners, for example, at a time when the engineering industry was virtually unchallenged as 'the workshop of the world'. This was the formative period of the Amalgamated Society of Engineers—the first 'modern' trade union. Building workers too benefited from the construction boom caused by industrial expansion, population growth and migration, and rising incomes that led to suburbanisation around the big cities. Building employers were especially able to make concessions to labour in the guise of trade union recognition because of the favourable terms of trade, indicated by the falling price of building materials. The stability of building techniques preserved the integrity of traditional crafts, enabling skilled tradesmen to form sectional unions along 'amalgamated' lines. The completion of a basic rail network in the 1850s also created a coal industry increasingly integrated on a national scale, based upon regional specialisation, and the strength of export demand led to the growth of the first effective trade unions in the coastal coalfields of Northumberland and Durham. In cotton textiles, the relatively sudden and complete separation of workers from the means of production initiated the growth of 'modern' unions in the 1850s and 1860s.

During the third quarter of the century, then, the formation of permanent trade unions was generally confined to the more skilled and strategically placed workers, frequently subcontractors like the hewers in the coal industry and the senior minders in cotton textiles. This was bound to have a decisive influence on trade union policy and, moreover, on the relationship of labour in general with society as a whole since the organised minority also tended to be the 'natural leaders' in their respective industry. Although the efforts to establish trade unions were in direct response to the real subordination of wage-labour to capital in the production process, the character of these unions reflected positions of relative privilege that their members sought to protect and enhance. Hence trade unionism itself acted to confirm the process of working-class differentiation.

The ideology of trade unionism and the contents of union policy illustrate the tension if not ambivalence in workers' perceptions of their relations at the workplace. It is not strictly true that even the privileged elite of organised labour was 'bourgeois-minded' in the sense that it consciously articulated the prevailing ideology. The primary object of trade unions was to secure a minimum or 'living' wage for their members, which often brought them into conflict with employers who insisted on their right to pay any rate that their assessment of market conditions justified. By implication, this determination to guarantee minimum conditions of employment also extended to issues other than wages, especially the so-called 'managerial prerogatives' like hours of work, methods of wage payment (time versus piece rates or payment by results), apprenticeship ratios and manning levels. These could give rise to bitter disputes, like the 1852 lock-out in the engineering industry and the 1859–60 dispute in the London building trades, thus emphasising the practical difficulties encountered by employers in enforcing the unitary structure of capitalist enterprise.[28]

Yet the trade unions' very ability to defend their members' 'rights' and occasionally extract major concessions from employers meant that workers' consciousness rarely went further than a posture of sectional self-defence of the rights and privileges of the organised minority, despite rhetorical appeals to working-class solidarity. Thus prior to the 1852 lock-out in the engineering industry, for example, the workers' claim that certain machine tools should be operated exclusively by skilled mechanics led necessarily to a demand for the dismissal of many labourers or 'illegal men' from their employment.[29] Trade unionists consistently refused to entertain proposals that their organisations be open to all workers in a particular industry regardless of skill. In reality, the structure of the mid-Victorian labour market, containing as it did large numbers of casual underemployed workers, made this a hopelessly difficult task. This prevented trade unionists from developing a *class* analysis of the capitalist *relations* of production. The dominant ideology of self-improvement was renegotiated either in terms of the experience of the individual worker, when it emphasised the values of education, industry and thrift, or in terms of the group that by implication failed to develop a conception of the common interests of labour as a whole. In this respect, the provision made by many of the craft unions for friendly society benefits, like superannuation and unemployment payments, constituted another dimension of their sectional isolation.

An important advantage enjoyed by employers in resisting trade union demands was the legitimacy assigned to property-ownership by the dominant ideology, which served to justify their authority in the workplace. The sanctity of private property was a central tenet of mid-Victorian utilitarianism, and underlay the imperatives of social atomism, possessive individualism and the unitary structure of capitalist enterprise. As the employers' association declaimed during the engineering lock-out of 1852:[30]

> Ours is the responsibility of the details, ours the risk of loss, ours the capital, its perils and engagements. We claim, and are resolved to assert the right of every British subject, to do what we will with our own.

It was only occasionally during outbreaks of bitter industrial struggle that the prevailing ideology shared by employers with all property owners was made quite so explicit. What made it so constantly effective was the way Victorian evangelicalism imbued property rights with a moral if not religious authority, which made it such a powerful source of legitimacy for the subordination of labour to capital. This justified 'the social disciplines of dependence', succinctly expressed in the legal titles of Master and Servant.[31] For the great majority of workers outside the reach of trade unions, the reality of dependence upon employers was not only unqualified but was regarded more positively as protection against the sectional exclusiveness of the organised minority.

The transmission of the employers' ideology to the trade unionists themselves took a rather different route. Respect for property was disseminated in a negotiated form via the tracts of vulgarised political economy written for the literate working man. A list of books purchased by Edinburgh Trades Council in 1864, for example, included John Wade's *History of the Middle and Working Classes*.[32] As the title suggests, its main aim was to demonstrate the mutually dependent relations of capital and labour, regarding both as a legitimate form of 'property'. This view had a considerable ring of truth for the minority of trade unionists whose relatively privileged position gave them a degree of autonomy if not authority in the labour process. It is easy to understand, for example, how the many subcontractors employed in mid-Victorian industry could conceive of their labour as a form of 'property', including as it did not only access to control over productive resources but also supervisory powers over labour. In this respect, it has been argued that the concept of hegemony refers more to the mode of organising beliefs and values than to any particular set of beliefs and values.[33] The reformulation of labour as a form of property is a good example of the way a potentially dissident value could be transformed and incorporated within the dominant ideology, and consequently prevented workers from realising its class implications.

The formation of employers' associations during the third quarter of the nineteenth century, commonly in response to trade union pressure, created a forum for discussion as well as a focus of identity that helped clarify their ideology.[34] Formal organisation, the selection of spokesmen to submit evidence to Royal Commissions, and the publication of journals like *Capital and Labour* created new opportunities for organising beliefs and values and putting them into practice. In seeking to maintain their prerogatives, employers developed more refined formulations of the unitary structure of capitalist enterprise, drawing upon currently fashionable arguments that sought to justify the prevailing character of social organisation by analogy to the physical world of natural organisms:[35]

> The precise fact is that any great industrial organisation is a body in which there are many members. In this body the employer is the head, his capital is the circulating life-blood; the employed are the various organs of the body, its hands and feet. The promotion of harmonious relations between the two is, therefore, the promotion of health, ease, and comfort of the whole. Our objection to the interference of Trade Unions with the details of business management is only the protest of the whole body against the paralysis of its organs by the interference of an outside power...

This view reflected an important strand in contemporary business thinking that argued for a more positive approach in accommodating labour, in place of confrontation, including schemes for profit-sharing and welfare provision like workers' housing.[36] Yet, in practice, these attempts to evolve new forms of hegemonic control also included some degree of recognition of the right of workers to bargain collectively over wages and conditions of employment.

A survey of industrial relations during the 1850s and 1860s shows that employers became increasingly willing to grant bargaining rights to strategically powerful groups of workers who also happened to be members of trade unions.[37] Formal recognition legitimated their position as 'natural leaders', reflected not only in relatively high wages but in the degree of control they exercised at the workplace. Firms often found that the cost of any concessions incurred as a result was more than compensated by the disciplinary effect collective bargaining had on the rank and file, whether unionist or non-unionist. When union leaders were called in to help settle a dispute, employers frequently discovered that they had a moderating effect on local militancy.[38] This is not surprising especially when they were full-time officials since their lifestyle was distinguished from that of the average worker, exposed to the day-to-day subordination of labour to capital. In the major industries, the privileged minority of 'labour aristocratic' trade unionists usually performed managerial functions that in mediating conflict between capital and labour saved the employers considerable expense and trouble. Collective bargaining linked to union recognition served to formalise these arrangements.

Labour and Community

The symbiotic relationship of labour with mid-Victorian society also includes patterns of interaction outside the workplace. Forms of association like the co-operative store, friendly society and working men's club were particularly important in mediating labour's relations with the point of production. This *cultural* mediation of labour's *economic* experience has been identified as the key factor in accommodating organised labour to the conditions of industrial capitalism during the Victorian period.[39] The cultural milieu of the working-class community comprised another dimension of the process of differentiation within the wage-earning class.

As 'natural leaders' in their respective industries, the privileged minority of organised trade unionists also played a leading role in the cultural life of their local communities. A study of Edinburgh has shown that skilled manual workers were usually the moving force behind the establishment of friendly societies and savings banks, and they formed by far the most numerous category of members.[40] Their involvement in these associations, as well as in local recreational activities, brought them into contact with non-manual strata, especially petty bourgeois groups, and this interaction led to the reformulation of values like thrift and independence for consumption by a wider working-class audience. The transformation of co-operation from community-building to shopkeeping between the 1840s and the 1860s is a good example of how a scheme for restricting bourgeois-competitive society along co-operative lines was incorporated within the dominant ideology at the level of the working-class community.[41] Fully three-quarters of the membership of the Amalgamated Society of Engineers, for example, was said to have been believers in the co-operative principle in the 1860s; but the decision to pay dividends to individuals rather than accumulate funds for buying into industry and land on a collective basis implied that the ideal of community-building had given way to an emphasis on individual self-help.[42]

The growth of working men's clubs after 1850, before they threw off middle-class patronage in the 1880s, tells a similar story.[43] Formed ostensibly as social and recreational centres, they aimed to civilise labour in the image of 'respectability' and their object was avowedly class-conciliationist. The working-class community was thus not sealed off from contact with the wider society but contained transmitting points that assimilated the prevailing ideology for mass consumption. Moreover, the link between workplace and community was quite explicit because it was the rule for trade unionists to have their meetings in the local public house or club. In this way, the workplace and community experience of labour was interwoven at the cultural level. Analagous forms of working-class differentiation were reproduced in both spheres and tended to reinforce each other, hence the preference of many 'respectable' trade unionists for the new clubs established with middle-class patronage rather than the traditional public house.

The Victorian family made an especially effective contribution in mediating labour's economic experience at the cultural level. The family was central to the workers' world: it was the focal point for kinship, neighbourhood and friendship ties around which associations like the working men's clubs were constructed. Yet the relations of dependence linking wives, children and more distant relatives to adult male heads of household were themselves a powerful force for social discipline. For the organised worker, his role as 'natural leader' at the workplace and in the institutions of the community was reproduced in the hierarchical structure of the Victorian family. Role segregation within the household was highly organised, the adult males being sustained in their position as breadwinners by a kinship network of wives, relatives and elder children. This was especially marked in textiles where the relatively large numbers of women and juveniles employed frequently involved male heads of household arranging jobs for wives, relatives and offspring within the same or adjacent manufacturing establishment.[44] A lower but still significant incidence of patrimonialism in employment was also characteristic of the metals, building and coal-mining industries where the tendency for sons to follow their father's occupation rather than any other was striking.[45] This was reinforced by marriage patterns in working-class communities where research has shown that adult males expressed a definite preference for prospective spouses whose fathers were in the same or closely related occupation.[46] The authority of male trade unionists at the workplace extended, therefore, to overall responsibility for decision-making in the family context and, by implication, throughout the institutions of the community. Thus family structure internalised the dominant ideology of employers, manifest in the unitary character of capitalist organisation, by reproducing the forms of differentiated stratification at the workplace that were, in turn, analogous to the organised hierarchy of the family itself.

The expansion of areas of working-class settlement in urban areas was also the occasion for considerable investment in new housing built specifically for the 'labour aristocracy' whose relatively high incomes enabled them to rent or even purchase 'superior' accommodation.[47] This was hastened by the effect of slum clearance and new construction in city centres, which aggravated the general housing shortage and confined a large proportion of casual unskilled labour to notoriously 'rough' streets and districts. In this connection, it has been argued that the labour aristocracy's striving to get access to new housing not only reflected a desire to live in more comfortable surroundings but also to escape identification with the less 'respectable' inhabitants of the old central working-class areas, even when the newly-constructed accommodation to which they moved was badly built.[48] Districts so inhabited were distinctly lower-middle class in social composition, like Newington in Edinburgh and Plumstead in Kentish London. Their milieu accorded well with the high valuation assigned by the dominant ideology to domesticity and the integrity of family life. Particularly in this last respect, the labour aristocracy's new housing functioned as an essential support for the hierarchical structure of the Victorian family because it enhanced the status of male heads of household whose earnings capacity largely determined whether family life could be sustained in the sought-after accommodation, without the encumbrance of lodgers.

Less intrinsic to working-class communities but still affecting them in a profound way were the institutions and ideology of religious worship. Although the workers' alienation from organised religion has been noted, even in the context of the mid-Victorian period, there is no mistaking the extent of religious influences in society as a whole, illustrated by the statistics of attendance at church services and at Sunday schools.[49] In fact, what may be allowed to pass as the thoroughly secular character of the dominant ideology was deeply imbued with the notion of 'rational conduct' that reduced to moral and ultimately religious principles. The various branches of nonconformity, particularly the Methodists, had been especially active in providing 'sittings' in urban working-class districts and, as a result, their share of total church attendance had increased since the 1820s.[50]

There has been little agreement about the character of the relationship between nonconformity and working-class consciousness, but there is no denying that its influence was deeply felt.[51] One of its most important effects was to give impetus to the process of differentiation within working-class communities. Although the organisational forms that Methodism, for example, adopted in the coalfields were open and relatively democratic, which made it ideally suited to the expression of community solidarity, its impact ideologically upon the consciousness of individuals was more equivocal. Methodism was not a homogeneous lump—there were significant differences between Calvinist Methodism and the so-called 'Primitives'—but it was essentially individualistic, stressing personal salvation and the individual's contract with God. It thus gave religious sanction to social atomism, while the notions of 'predestination' and and 'elect' typical of the Calvinist sects implied a mode of personal conduct linked to self-improvement, temperance, punctuality and 'systematic' work and thrift.[52] This could be disruptive of community solidarity, at least as this affected workers' relations with other social classes. Devout Methodists tended not to discriminate between workers and capitalists but among individuals who were either God-fearing and 'respectable' or 'rough'; the latter condition implied a godless life of dissipation threatening eternal damnation.[53] They also tended to justify social mobility as proof of individual moral worth, which often meant isolation from if not conflict with the interests of 'community'. In the coal industry, for example, Methodists were heavily represented among the more highly paid face-workers, themselves often subcontractors, who owed their privileged position to the favour of a co-religionist employer.[54] Thus religious affiliation made a further contribution to the cultural mediation of labour's economic experience, creating a 'consensus' concerning norms and values that cut across class lines distinguishing workers from capitalists.[55]

Educational provision was an especially effective agent in disseminating religious influence, as well as acting as a powerful force for socialisation in its own right. Labour's experience of schooling during the mid-Victorian period was generally confined to elementary education, organised under the auspices of either the Established Church, the Catholic Orders or the various nonconformist denominations, and the religious purpose of education was made explicit in the Sunday school movement where biblical texts were often the only materials used to teach reading. The clergy and school inspectors, as members of the 'urban gentry', were concerned to see that elementary schools inculcated the values of obedience, deference, self-control and industry. Their role was not conceived in terms of a career escalator, but as a means of socialising labour to its preordained place in society. Thus the Report of the Newcastle Commission in 1861 claimed that it was neither possible nor 'desirable' to keep children at school after the ages of ten or eleven.[56] The structuring of educational provision along class lines, following the alienation of the old grammar schools and the rise of the so-called 'public schools', implied that the elementary system was designed to keep workers in their place. The pupil-teacher system where elder children could take charge of classes at the tender age of thirteen, and the practice of 'payment by results' introduced in the Revised Code of 1862, emphasised the mechanical drilling of the three Rs in an effort to reduce government expenditure on elementary schools.[57] This also represented a form of 'self-control' in working-class education since it meant that elementary teachers were invariably drawn from 'respectable' groups within the local community, including the elite of the working-class itself. These were among the 'subaltern intellectuals' of Victorian society, disseminating the dominant ideology for working-class consumption.[58]

More generally, the impact upon labour of the intellectual currents running through mid-Victorian society is difficult to assess. What is striking is the essential unity of the 'urban gentry' or what Gramsci has termed the 'organic' intellectuals, allied closely to the dominant classes, and the relative absence of so-called 'traditional' intellectuals less intimately tied to the power bloc and thus more able to develop a critique of society in a direction that would lead them to identify with the working class.[59] This might be explained with reference to the general character of the Victorian intelligentsia,

which has both an ideological and institutional dimension. Its unity
is readily understood in terms of the structure of educational provision that was narrowly elitist, effectively excluding the mass of the
population from post-elementary schooling, and confining its recruits to offspring drawn mainly from landowning and rentier
bourgeois families who had the leisure, income and inclination to
pursue a lengthy education. It has been suggested that the mid-
Victorians only valued education after wealth had been secured: self-
made industrialists, for example, sought it as a means of socially
advancing their children, regarding it as a symbol of 'gentility'.[60]

The prestige attached to gentility or 'gentlemanly' conduct reflects
the persistence of older cultural values, illustrated by the high status
Victorians continued to attach to landowning. These had an ambivalent relationship to the hegemony of the industrial bourgeoisie.
The fact that the mid-Victorian intelligentsia regarded themselves as
'gentlemen' above all else was central to their essential unity.[61] This
could produce critics of existing society like Arnold, Carlyle,
Kingsley and Dickens who in defending older 'cultural' values
attacked the competitive, commercialised and squalid character of
their age. Yet this criticism was couched in terms of an attack on the
evils of industrialism, rather than a critique of capitalism itself. The
mid-Victorian social commentators could thus develop at best only
a partial critique of their society, which was too easily reified into a
vague longing for some mythical 'Golden Age' or at worst lapsed
into sentimental moralising. They were unable to identify with
labour as a class and consequently their ability to challenge the
dominant ideology was impaired. In fact, it might be argued that
their very popularity, especially of Dickens, among literate working
men had a negative effect in preventing labour from evolving for
itself a total critique in opposition to the dominant values.

The institutional situation of the intelligentsia in mid-Victorian
society provided ample scope for the cult of the gentleman. A characteristic of gentility is the importance it assigned to leisure in enabling
the gentleman to take an 'objective' view of the world, analyse
its problems, and suggest remedies. An almost obsessive concern
with philanthropy has been isolated as the magnet that drew the
intelligentsia together during the 1860s.[62] The growth of professional associations like the National Association for the Promotion
of Social Science, and the various agencies that were expanding
within the state apparatus, gave institutional form to the phil-
anthropic inclinations of the urban gentry.[63] This had the effect of

drawing intellectuals into an 'organic' relationship with the dominant power bloc, thus making them generally less inclined to challenge its hegemonic faction—the industrial bourgeoisie. Attacks on
'abuses' there certainly were, and particular vested interests were
sometimes offended, yet in no sense did these lead to the development of a critique of the established order as a whole. The outcome
might be a more positive role for the state in regulating the most
obvious social evils of a free capitalist economy, hence the ever-
widening scope of the Factory Acts, but this did not threaten private
property or employers' prerogatives in any fundamental way. It
would appear that the ideological and institutional dimensions to
the behaviour of the mid-Victorian intelligentsia did more to
mediate labour's experience of capitalist society, by remedying some
of the most obvious of its abuses, rather than set in train an
interaction of thought and practice culminating in an assault on the
dominant ideology.

The role of the intelligentsia was especially important in the field
of social policy. Labour's experience of the Poor Law was particularly significant in this respect. It is widely believed that the Poor
Law Amendment Act marked a fundamental change in society's
attitude to the treatment of poverty. The criterion of 'less eligibility'
and the threat of the workhouse test sought in the interests of
economy to restrict as much as possible the state's responsibility for
maintaining the poor, leaving private charities to look after the
'deserving' as they saw fit. This has been interpreted as a practical
application of the social imperatives of utilitarianism, especially its
belief that man's worldly state is ultimately a reflection of his moral
condition.[64] Yet, in practice, this was not translated into policy
without modification. In fact, the local Poor Law guardians continued to dispense outdoor relief at times of distress caused by
cyclical unemployment or during a crisis like the Lancashire Cotton
Famine.[65] This apparently anomalous behaviour can be attributed
in part to the humanity of the local administrators as well as their
concern for economy—it cost less to distribute outdoor relief than
provide for a place in the workhouse. But this is not the entire
explanation. The urban gentry who ran the Poor Law Boards were
also worried that contact with confirmed paupers would have a
demoralising effect on the 'deserving' unemployed without work for
no fault of their own. They realised the disruptive effect that this
would have on the internal disciplines and cohesion of working-
class communities, especially their ideological and institutional

forms of 'self-control'. The extent to which they had absorbed older cultural values, like the paternalism of the landed aristocracy, meant that as 'gentlemen' they were obliged to act to prevent undue suffering, which if left unattended might endanger the entire fabric of society. The strict logic of the dominant ideology was thus not carried to its ultimate and perhaps fateful conclusion.

The Politics of Labourism

Labour's relationship with the political system constitutes the third and last-mentioned aspect of the unique symbiosis enjoyed by labour in relation to British society as a whole. Within the power bloc ruling mid-Victorian Britain, its governing faction or political voice acted with a considerable degree of autonomy, at least in Parliament, and was not controlled in any mechanistic way by the industrial bourgeoisie. The relative autonomy of the state apparatus indicated the continuing power of the landed aristocracy and the formative influence of traditional values on the urban gentry of intellectuals and administrators. In no direct sense did the industrial bourgeoisie control the government, especially at the centre. In the House of Commons, fewer than 25% of its members can be identified as 'bourgeois' (manufacturers, merchants, bankers), the large majority consisting of relatives, descendents or dependents of the aristocracy.[66] The latter also continued to dominate the Cabinet until the Gladstone ministries of the 1870s and 1880s, while in rural areas aristocratic influence prevailed even after the County Council Act of 1888.[67] The widening of the franchise realised by the 1832 Reform Act did not, therefore, lead to the political ascendancy of the bourgeoisie but consolidated the dominance of the landed estate in the context of rapid industrialisation and urbanisation.[68] Electoral behaviour continued to be determined by the characteristics intrinsic to particular constituencies as 'deference communities'. There was thus a 'real' base for the autonomy of the state apparatus in the mid-Victorian period. This helped in the reformulation of the dominant ideology for working-class consumption and also had significant implications for the development of labour politics.

The relative absence of the industrial bourgeoisie in Parliament is one aspect of the unique character of mid-Victorian politics. Paradoxically, the effect of the 1832 Reform Act in enlarging the electorate reinforced the political power of the landed interest by increasing considerably the cost of elections that few first-generation industrialists had either the time, connections or resources to contest. Most of the working class remained, of course, totally excluded from the franchise. The tensions between the landed aristocracy and the industrial bourgeoisie within the mid-Victorian power bloc were never entirely resolved, despite the extent of the ideological dominance that the latter had achieved. The resentment felt by the industrial bourgeoisie because of its exclusion from direct responsibility in political decision-making, which had reached crisis point during the Anti-Corn Law agitation of the 1830s and 1840s, continued to smoulder after 1850 and was aggravated by its sense of cultural isolation. There seemed little justification for the wealth and power that the great estates gave to their owners, particularly when they appeared to be the passive beneficiaries of the fruits of industrialisation rather than its active protagonists, and this resentment was given coherence by the writings of popular political economists who threw doubt on the contribution of rents in increasing the national income. Many industrialists, moreover, were also nonconformists outside the Established Church of the landed magnates, and this contributed to their sense of cultural isolation.

Within the Whig–Liberal coalition dominating mid-Victorian political life, the alliance of Whig magnates, professional urban gentry and businessmen was frequently subject to considerable strain, reflected in the debates on issues like church disestablishment, land reform and, above all, the franchise question. This coalition contained a small but vocal minority of 'militant' businessmen led by Radicals like Samuel Morley, Richard Cobden and John Bright, whose dedication to the cause of reform focused on the extension of household suffrage to the counties as well as the towns. This was linked to their determination to overturn once and for all the power of the landed aristocracy and its hold over the state apparatus. Although the Radical group comprised a minority even among the industrial bourgeoisie who were members of Parliament, its ability to mobilise demonstrations of support 'out of doors', i.e. among the disenfranchised masses totally excluded from the pale of the Constitution, secured a large popular following. From the 1840s, the Radicals had launched a succession of agitational campaigns designed to harness the energies of the working class in support of their programme for 'democracy', and led to the introduction in Parliament of a series of unsuccessful bills for extending the franchise.

The Radical conception of democracy was, however, quite different from the earlier Chartist vision. Household suffrage, hedged by qualifications including residence and rental or rated minima, replaced the Chartist demand for *universal* male suffrage that in the context of the 1840s had been almost revolutionary in its implications.[69] The demand for household suffrage was conceived of and posed as a test of 'respectability', a proof of the moral standing of the individual *deserving* the vote. Thus labour's claim to the franchise was formulated in terms of the dominant ideology. Household suffrage had an obvious appeal to the upper strata of the working class whose rising incomes during the 1850s and 1860s were enabling them to live in 'improved' accommodation and even aspire to the lifestyle of the lower-middle class. Yet the very extent of this improvement made their status as non-electors less and less tolerable. This resentment was the raw material of mid-Victorian Radicalism, making it possible for the disaffected among the industrial bourgeoisie to absorb the political aspirations of the working class and use them for their own ends.[70] Such are the origins of the class-collaborationist character of labour politics, which in the 1867 Reform Act achieved a signal victory. Few contemporaries were aware of the significance this legislation was to have for the subsequent development of labour's relationship with British society.

It is important to appreciate in the context of this period that the right to vote had a symbolic significance having far greater import than its appearance as a narrowly political demand might suggest. It was conceived as a test of 'manliness' and 'independence', its attachment to the possession of a household reflecting a reformulated version of the dominant belief in possessive individualism. At the same time, it was the rallying cry for traditional objects of class hatred like monarchy, the Established Church, aristocracy and militarism. Thus the demand for the right to vote did not necessarily represent a denial of class consciousness, even when limited to household suffrage.[71] Yet this ambivalence applies to the meaning of the demand in the abstract. Again, the realisation of hegemony refers more to the mode of organising principles of thought, and attitudes and values, rather than to their content when conceived in isolation from their social context. In this respect, Victorian Radicalism gave organisational expression to 'reform' that included a number of often contradictory elements, preventing class consciousness from developing into a comprehensive critique of capitalist society. Class feeling focused on particular aspects of power and authority, like the entrenched position of the landed aristocracy and the Established Church. The latter, while part of the mid-Victorian power bloc, was not essential in the long-run to the survival of its hegemonic faction, i.e. the industrial bourgeoisie. The task of the Radicals was, therefore, to mobilise class antagonism in support of a campaign for reform that in attacking the prerogatives of landed aristocrats—the demands for household suffrage in the counties, church disestablishment, 'free trade' in land—directed attention towards the popular manifestations of class power, but did not attack capitalism itself.

The demand for household suffrage was an ideal focal point for such a campaign. It appealed to 'respectable' elements in the working class, but was not revolutionary in threatening the power and authority of the industrial bourgeoisie. In the process, some of the most politically conscious representatives of labour, especially the spokesmen for the privileged minority of organised trade unionists, were incorporated into the Radical wing of the Liberal Party, under the charismatic leadership of William Ewart Gladstone. Yet the widening of the franchise was not achieved in a simple, straightforward fashion. The Radicals did not succeed in extracting household suffrage from the governing elite simply by sustained pressure, which subsequently created in a mechanistic way the 'hegemony' of the bourgeoisie in relation to the working class. The 1854 Reform Bill, for example, was a conscious response of the Whig magnates to pressure from below. It sought to offset the 'democratising' effect of widening the franchise by providing for a redistribution of seats, allocating 46 additional representatives to the rural-based counties where the disciplines of deference were still bound to operate.[72] This, in fact, was a model for future bills, culminating in the Reform Act of 1867. The Tories, led by Disraeli, could not either afford to ignore the issue of reform, for fear of losing their remaining credibility with the electorate, thus they too were converted to the cause of extending the franchise after 1857. Again, they sought to compensate for increasing the number of working-class voters in the towns by adding to county representation.

The very moderation of Radical demands, which always linked the right to vote to a specified household qualification, created the basis for an eventual compromise settlement. This is not to deny the continuing impact of agitation out of doors—the Hyde Park riots of 1866 and the May rally of 1867 in Hyde Park were seen as a serious threat to social order by the governing elite—yet by this time the

Radicals had at hand in the form of the Reform League a pliable instrument for realising their essentially limited aims.[73] The Reform League was, potentially, a force for class mobilisation since its membership was drawn primarily from among the most politically aware of the working class, but its leadership derived from the so-called 'Junta' of New Model union leaders who were tied financially as well as intellectually to the apron strings of the Liberal Party.[74] The extent of working-class differentiation in the preceding years implied that the leadership of the Reform League was not going to insist upon extending the vote to the 'residuum' of casual unskilled labour, and the fact that it hedged its demands for manhood suffrage with the qualifications 'registered' and 'residential' carried great weight with contemporary politicians.

It was in this context that the party rivalry of Liberals and Tories, Gladstone versus Disraeli, eventually carried the day in favour of a significant albeit limited widening of the franchise. The 1867 Reform Act enfranchised householders paying the poor rates, and all lodgers of one year's residence and paying an annual rent of ten pounds in the boroughs, but in practice the latter were excluded because of registration difficulties.[75] In the counties, the granting of the vote to owners of land of five pounds annual value and to occupying tenants paying twelve pounds yearly rental had little effect in undermining the power of the landed interest in deference communities, where voting was still open to public scrutiny, and especially since the attached redistribution of seats clause clearly over-represented rural areas. The net result was that at best only 30% of adult males in urban working-class constituencies were enfranchised.[76]

The effect of objective constraints contained within the provisions of the 1867 Reform Act, together with the extent of working-class differentiation at the workplace and in the associations of civil society, combined to legitimate the power structure of mid-Victorian society. The extension of the franchise was unlikely anyway to lead to the creation of a mass working-class party because the subsequently massive rise in electoral costs gave effective control of local politics to agents and registration bodies that owed their existence to the munificence of either the Liberals or Tories. Parliament rejected a proposal for election costs to be defrayed from the rates, and its opposition to the payment of members postponed for at least a generation the entry into party politics of working men entirely free to pursue the interests of their class.

Yet despite the significance of objective factors in preventing the formation of an independent working-class party in the 1870s, the impact of labour's total experience of its relations with mid-Victorian society in structuring its *response* to these objective constraints remains of decisive importance. In the 1868 General Election, for example, the Liberal agents were themselves surprised at the limited ambitions of the labour leaders in the Reform League, and the relative ease with which they could be persuaded to accept the offer of a very unequal partnership with the Liberal Party, especially since an alternative strategy for a genuinely independent working-class presence in Parliament *was* available.[77] The governing elite was itself acutely aware of the degree to which the political leadership of the 'labour aristocracy' had been fissured by the dominant ideology, regarding the election of 'good' men more important than the creation of an independent working-class party at Westminster.[78] Hence the government's apparently remarkable willingness to enact the labour legislation of the 1870s, which gave to trade unions an unprecedented degree of legal protection, in the face of substantial opposition from employers in their evidence submitted to Parliamentary inquiries.[79] Clearly, the state would have been unwilling to grant such concessions if it had conceived the moderation of the working class as arising exclusively from objective constraints that alone guaranteed compliance with the existing hierarchy of class relations. The subsequent election of a small number of working-class 'representatives' sitting as Liberal MPs was the outcome of a complex process of incorporation, which created the unique symbiosis enjoyed by labour in relation to mid-Victorian society as a whole.[80]

Notes

1. R. A. Church, *The Great Victorian Boom 1850–1873* (London: Macmillan, 1975), especially pp. 13–16.
2. Ibid., Table 4, p. 48.
3. For example, a profit of $12\frac{1}{2}\%$ has been estimated for the cotton trade in the 1860s despite the losses incurred as a result of the 'Cotton Famine'—see ibid., p. 50.
4. Werner Schlöte, *British Overseas Trade from 1700 to the 1930's* (Oxford: Blackwell, 1952), Diagram 12, p. 76; A. D. Gayer, W. W. Rostow, A. J. Schwartz, *The Growth and Fluctuation of the British Economy, 1790–1850* (Oxford: University Press, 1953), p. 653.
5. Schlöte, *Overseas Trade*.
6. Church, *Victorian Boom*, p. 32.
7. For a classic statement of the theoretical problems see Karl Marx, *Capital*

(London: Lawrence & Wishart, 1970), vol. I, pt VII; for a more recent discussion see Joan Robinson, *The Accumulation of Capital* (London: Macmillan, 1956), pp. 171–2.

8. See, for example, M. Blaug, 'The Productivity of Capital in the Lancashire Cotton Industry During the Nineteenth Century', *Economic History Review*, 2nd series, XIII (1960–1); Keith Burgess, *The Origins of British Industrial Relations* (London: Croom Helm, 1975), pp. 25 ff., shows a similar trend in the engineering industry.

9. P. L. Cottrell, *British Overseas Investment in the Nineteenth Century* (London: Macmillan, 1975), pp. 23–4.

10. See Robinson, *Accumulation of Capital*, where the potential instability associated with a rising capital–labour ratio is discussed.

11. E. J. Hobsbawm, 'Custom, Wages and Work-load in Nineteenth Century Industry' in the same author's *Labouring Men. Studies in the History of Labour* (London: Weidenfeld & Nicolson, 1968), p. 114; see also Burgess, *Industrial Relations*, Chs. 1–2, for further details.

12. E. J. Hobsbawm, 'The Labour Aristocracy in Nineteenth Century Britain' in *Labouring Men*, p. 293.

13. Harold Perkin, *The Origins of Modern English Society* (London: Routledge & Kegan Paul, 1969), p. 417.

14. B. R. Mitchell, P. Deane, *Abstract of British Historical Statistics* (Cambridge: University Press, 1952), pp. 64–5.

15. Henry Mayhew, *London Labour and the London Poor* (London, 1851), p. 322.

16. Robert Q. Gray, *The Labour Aristocracy in Victorian Edinburgh* (Oxford: Clarendon Press, 1976), Table 4.4, p. 50.

17. Robert Gray, 'Bourgeois Hegemony in Victorian Britain' in Jon Bloomfield (ed.), *Class, Hegemony and Party* (London: Lawrence & Wishart, 1977).

18. D. C. Moore, 'The Corn Laws and High Farming' in Peter Stansky (ed.), *The Victorian Revolution. Government and Society in Victorian Britain* (New York: Franklin Watts, 1973).

19. Gray, 'Bourgeois Hegemony', p. 77.

20. Burgess, *Industrial Relations*, especially p. 311.

21. Gray, *Labour Aristocracy*, p. 6.

22. Parl. Papers, *Masters and Operatives* (*Equitable Councils of Conciliation*): *Report and Minutes of Evidence*, 1856, XIII, C. 343, p. 23.

23. Ibid.

24. Alan Fox, 'Managerial Ideology and Labour Relations', *British Journal of Industrial Relations*, 4 (1966).

25. Gray, 'Bourgeois Hegemony', p. 84.

26. Hobsbawm, 'Labour Aristocracy', pp. 297–9; much of the detail in the following discussion is taken from Burgess, *Industrial Relations*, especially pp. 39–40, 116–17, 159–60, 239–40.

27. Burgess, *Industrial Relations*.

28. Ibid., pp. 21–4, 108–11.

29. Keith Burgess, 'Trade Union Policy and the 1852 Lock-out in the British Engineering Industry', *International Review of Social History*, XVII (1972), pt 3.

30. E. Vansittart Neale, *May I Not Do What I Will With My Own?* (London: John James Beezer, 1852), cited pp. 3–4.

31. W. L. Burn, *The Age of Equipoise* (New York: W. W. Norton, 1965), pp. 241–3.

32. Ian MacDougall (ed.), *The Minutes of Edinburgh Trades Council 1859–1873* (Edinburgh: T. & A. Constable, 1968), pp. 143–4; John Wade, *History of the Middle and Working Classes* (London: Effingham Wilson, 1842).

33. Gray, *Labour Aristocracy*, p. 6.

34. See Burgess, *Industrial Relations*, for a detailed discussion of the formation of employers' associations in the engineering, building, coal-mining and cotton textile industries.

35. *Capital and Labour* (March 1874), p. 51.

36. R. A. Church, 'Profit-sharing and Labour Relations in England in the Nineteenth Century', *International Review of Social History*, XVI (1971).

37. Burgess, *Industrial Relations*.

38. Parl. Papers, *Labour Laws: Reports and Minutes of Evidence*, 1875, XXX, C. 1157-I, evidence of James Wilson, Leeds building employer, p. 68.

39. Gray, *Labour Aristocracy*, p. 2.

40. Ibid., pp. 121–4.

41. Sidney Pollard, 'Nineteenth-century Co-operation: from Community Building to Shopkeeping' in Asa Briggs and John Saville (eds.), *Essays in Labour History* (London: Macmillan, 1967).

42. Parl. Papers, *Royal Commission on Trade Unions: Reports and Minutes of Evidence*, 1867, XXXII, *First Report*, evidence of William Allan, Secretary of the Amalgamated Society of Engineers, p. 44.

43. Richard Price, 'The Working Men's Club Movement and Victorian Social Reform Ideology', *Victorian Studies*, XV (1971).

44. Michael Anderson, *Family Structure in Nineteenth Century Lancashire* (Cambridge: University Press, 1971), especially Table 18, p. 58; Burgess, *Industrial Relations*, pp. 243–4.

45. Burgess, *Industrial Relations*. See also S. J. Chapman and W. Abbott, 'The Tendency of Children to Enter their Fathers' Trades', *Journal of Royal Statistical Society*, LXXVI (1912–13), Table I, pp. 599–600; Table II, pp. 601, 603–4.

46. John Foster, *Class Struggle in the Industrial Revolution* (London: Weidenfeld & Nicolson, 1974). Appendix 2, pp. 262–3, 268–9, for marriage indices of association in Oldham and South Shields, 1846–56.

47. See Gray, *Labour Aristocracy*, pp. 14–15, 95–9, for evidence in Edinburgh; see also Seàn Damer, 'Property Relations and Class Relations in Victorian Glasgow', *Discussion Papers in Social Research*, no. 15 (Department of Social & Economic Research, University of Glasgow, July 1976), pp. 8, 23–4, 26.

48. Robert Q. Gray, 'Styles of Life, The "Labour Aristocracy", and Class Relations in Later Nineteenth Century Edinburgh', *International Review of Social History*, XVIII (1973), pt 3, pp. 434–5; Geoffrey Crossick, 'The Labour Aristocracy and its Values: A Study of Mid-Victorian Kentish London', *Victorian Studies*, XIX (1976), no. 3.

49. Burn, *Equipoise*, p. 270; Foster, *Class Struggle*, p. 215.

50. Foster, *Class Struggle*, p. 214.

51. David Kynaston, *King Labour. The British Working Class, 1850–1914* (London: Allen & Unwin, 1976), pp. 84–5, 92–4, contains a useful survey of the literature.

52. Robert S. Moore, *Pit-men, Preachers and Politics* (Cambridge: University Press, 1974), pp. 109–10.

53. J. Hutchinson, 'Leisure in the South West Durham Coalfield, 1880–1914', unpublished MA thesis, University of Edinburgh, 1970, p. 23.

54. Moore, *Pit-men*, pp. 73–4, 86.

55. Robert S. Moore, 'Religiosity and Stratification in England', *Sociological Analysis and Theory*, IV (1974), no. 3, contains a general treatment of this argument.

56. Derek Fraser, *The Evolution of the British Welfare State* (London: Macmillan, 1973), pp. 244–5.

57. Brian Simon, *Education and the Labour Movement 1870–1920* (London: Lawrence & Wishart, 1974), pp. 114–20.

58. Gray, 'Bourgeois Hegemony', p. 89.

59. John Saville, 'The Ideology of Labourism' in R. Benewick, R. N. Berki, B. Parekh (eds.), *Knowledge and Belief in Politics: the Problem of Ideology* (London: Allen & Unwin, 1973), p. 223.

60. Burn, *Equipoise*, pp. 254–7; F. Musgrove, 'Middle Class Education and

Employment in the Nineteenth Century', *Economic History Review*, 2nd series, XII (1959–60), no. 2, p. 111.

61. Noel G. Annan, 'The Intellectual Aristocracy' in J. H. Plumb (ed.), *Studies in Social History* (London: Longmans, 1955), p. 247.

62. Ibid., pp. 244 ff.

63. O. R. McGregor, 'Social Research and Social Policy in the Nineteenth Century', *British Journal of Sociology*, 8 (1957); Perkin, *Origins*, pp. 319 ff., 428–9, estimates that the professional occupations trebled in size between 1841 and 1881, compared with a two-thirds increase in the general population.

64. Calvin Woodard, 'Reality and Social Reform: the Transition from Laissez-Faire to the Welfare State', *Yale Law Review*, 72 (1962), no. 2, especially pp. 298–300.

65. M. E. Rose, 'The Allowance System under the New Poor Law', *Economic History Review*, 2nd series, XIX (1966), no. 3; see also the same author's 'Rochdale Man and the Stalybridge Riot. The Relief and Control of the Unemployed during the Lancashire Cotton Famine' in A. P. Donajgrodzki (ed.), *Social Control in Nineteenth Century Britain* (London: Croom Helm, 1977).

66. W. L. Guttsman, *The British Political Elite* (London: Macgibbon & Kee, 1965), p. 41.

67. W. L. Arnstein, 'The Survival of the Victorian Aristocracy' in F. C. Jaher (ed.), *The Rich, the Well Born and the Powerful: Elites and Upper Classes in History* (Chicago: University of Illinois Press, 1973), pp. 210, 213.

68. D. C. Moore, 'Concession or Cure: the Sociological Premises of the First Reform Act', *The Historical Journal*, 9 (1966), no. 1; and the same author's 'Social Structure, Political Structure and Public Opinion in mid-Victorian England' in Robert Robson (ed.), *Ideas and Institutions of Victorian Britain* (London: G. Bell, 1967).

69. This was not achieved without difficulty; see, for example, Frances Elma Gillespie, *Labor and Politics in England 1850–1867* (Durham, North Carolina: Duke University Press, 1927), especially p. 94, for the early difficulties of the Radicals in organising a united front for reform in the 1850s.

70. Foster, *Class Struggle*, pp. 207–10, where the beginnings of this process are discussed with reference to Oldham.

71. Gray, *Labour Aristocracy*, pp. 158–64.

72. Francis B. Smith, *The Making of the Second Reform Bill* (Cambridge: University Press, 1966), p. 38.

73. A detailed discussion of these events and their significance is contained in Royden Harrison, 'The Tenth April of Spencer Walpole: the Problem of Revolution in Relation to Reform, 1865–67' in the same author's *Before the Socialists. Studies in Labour and Politics, 1861–1881* (London: Routledge & Kegan Paul, 1965).

74. Royden Harrison, 'The British Working Class and the General Election of 1868', *International Review of Social History*, V (1960), pt 3, pp. 433 ff.

75. Smith, *Second Reform Bill*, pp. 236–7.

76. H. F. Moorhouse, 'The Political Incorporation of the British Working Class: an Interpretation', *Sociology*, 7 (1973), no. 3, pp. 344–5.

77. Royden Harrison, 'The British Working Class and the General Election of 1868', *International Review of Social History*, VI (1961), pt 1, especially pp. 105–9.

78. Harrison, 'British Working Class', pp. 438 ff.

79. Burgess, *Industrial Relations*, for example, pp. 38, 112–27.

80. For an interesting study of this development in Salford see John A. Garrard, 'Parties, Members and Voters after 1867: A Local Study', *The Historical Journal*, 20 (1977), no. 1.

CHAPTER 2

The Challenge of the 1880s

The New Economic Environment

The commercial crisis of 1873 initiated a new phase in the development of British capitalism. Traditionally, the years 1873–96 have been identified as the period of the 'Great Depression'. Much debate has centred on the accuracy of this characterisation of the period, and difficulties of definition and specification have recently led one authority to question whether there ever was a 'Great Depression' at all during these years.[1] What is clear is that this period was not one of depression in the conventional sense of a downturn in the trade cycle. If any one factor gives these years unity it is the massive and almost continuous decline in prices. Between 1871–5 and 1894–8, the fall in price of products with a low value added was in the order of 40%, and the price of a strategic commodity like raw cotton fell even more—by 54%.

The problem of explaining this phenomenon is a difficult task. While monetary factors were emphasised by contemporaries at the time, the focus of attention in this context will be upon how prices reacted to changes in the 'real' economy. Again, as in the case of the mid-Victorian period, the changing character and direction of investment flows seems to have been particularly important. During the years 1850–73, the tremendous increase in the export of British capital and manufactures had been primarily responsible for the shift from labour-saving to labour-using investment, which meant that the demand for inputs of capital and labour per unit of additional output had been in relative equilibrium. The boom preceding the crisis of 1873 had led, however, to rapidly rising production costs, especially labour costs, at a time when the extent of industrialisation in Western Europe and the USA was creating greater self-sufficiency and even competition for British capitalists. The combination of rising production costs and a less expansive market environment overseas was the underlying cause of the commercial crisis of 1873. The latter was essentially a crisis of confidence in the continuing capacity of overseas markets to absorb the huge amounts of capital and goods the British economy was generating, at a rate of profit sufficiently high to offset the steep rise in production costs. The effect of the 1873 crisis was, therefore, to upset the fruitful interdependence of overseas and domestic expansion that had marked the growth of the British economy during the mid-Victorian period.

The origins overseas of the commercial crisis of 1873 led investors naturally to concentrate on the home market. Yet domestic investment was not that profitable, despite the fact that the rate of accumulation at home was almost as high in the period 1875–94 as it had been during the years 1855–74.[2] There was consequently downward pressure on both prices and profit margins. The spread of railways and steam shipping had opened up new and cheaper sources of supply abroad and had significantly reduced freight rates. Yet in the context of a less expansive and increasingly competitive environment for the output of Britain's staple industries, firms took advantage of cheaper raw materials after 1873 to cut their prices in an effort to maximise their share of the market. Thus the downward spiral of prices and profits was diffused throughout the economy. Moreover, the decline in calls for new portfolio investment overseas during the 1870s cheapened considerably the cost of raising capital.[3] The effect of cheaper credit was to persuade manufacturers to re-equip and expand in order to reduce their unit costs of production during a period when prices generally, including the prices of their own manufactures, were moving lower.[4] Yet this served only to reduce prices even more. And, more significantly, profits too came under pressure: the rate of profit in the UK that had reached a peak in 1871 fell steadily until 1878, and there was no sustained recovery in the 1880s until 1887.[5] As a spokesman for the Glasgow Chamber of Commerce explained in 1886:[6]

> The depression of trade complained of is not so much a decrease in the amount or volume of trade, as a great falling off in the market value of the manufactures produced and still more in the margin of profit, which in many cases has disappeared altogether, and has not infrequently been followed by a serious loss; and, further, that this state of matters has arisen mainly from an excess of production at home and abroad ...

This view was confirmed by employers from other districts.[7]

The problem of falling profitability was to have a profound impact on the overall development of the British economy after 1873. Investment in manufacturing that remained remarkably buoyant throughout the 1870s fell dramatically during the 1880s as profits failed to revive.[8] This was largely offset in aggregate terms by the lucrative opportunities for investment in the trade, transport and service sectors that continued to sustain a relatively high rate of domestic capital formation in the economy as a whole. Yet this failed to resolve the predicament facing the staple export industries, the vitality of which had played such a major part in accounting for the growth and stability of the mid-Victorian economy. The average annual rate of growth of British industrial production, excluding building construction, fell from 3.6% in the period 1861/5–66/74 to 2.1% for the years 1866/74–75/83, and it reached a low of only 1.6% during the period 1875/83–84/9.[9] The timing of this check to investment in industry was especially ominous because it coincided with the beginnings of a new phase of world capitalist development, characterised by increasing concentration and large-scale innovation.[10] It seemed to contemporaries that during a period when the prospects for industry were beginning to deteriorate, labour was starting to require *and* demand a greater share of the wealth created by the British economy.

The new economic environment confronting British capitalism after 1873 affected the character and interrelations of the groups or factions composing the mid-Victorian power bloc. The groups particularly affected were the landed interest and the industrial bourgeoisie. Rural communities in the south and east suffered especially from imports of cheap wheat and flour as new sources of supply were opened up in the Americas and Australasia: prices fell by one-half between 1870 and the mid-1890s, and rents had to be reduced by as much as 50% or more.[11] Increasingly, the great landowners had to look for non-agricultural sources of income to maintain their position, including revenue from urban property, mineral rights and fees from company directorships. Yet if the richest and more fortunately situated landowners were able to hedge their bets or diversify into pastoral farming where demand and prices were more resilient, the plight of smaller estates and tenant farmers with holdings of about 50 acres or less was often extreme indeed. The effect of the Great Depression was thus to polarise the landed interest along class lines, isolating a small group of the 'super rich' from the predicament of a much larger number. A similar process was also affecting the industrial bourgeoisie as profits began to fall away after the commercial crisis of 1873. An analysis of the distribution of profits returned under Schedule D for the years 1850–1 and 1879–80 shows that the incomes of the wealthier bourgeoisie had risen most, in comparison with the lesser bourgeoisie.[12] Like the greatest landowners, the *haute bourgeoisie* were able to hedge their bets, investing in urban property, government issues or overseas securities when the profitability of industrial enterprise came under pressure. In fact, it has been argued that by the 1880s the super rich among the biggest landowners and bourgeoisie were beginning to coalesce as a new 'plutocracy', drawn together by common interest, family ties and a shared ideology.[13]

This process implied that the industrial bourgeoisie as the hegemonic faction of the power bloc was beginning to lose its distinctive character. Its cutting edge as the most active protagonist of capitalist development became blunted in the context of changing economic and social conditions. There has been considerable debate about the quality of entrepreneurship in the late Victorian period, yet although there were some outstanding examples of the species active during these years—Lever, Beecham, Harmsworth—it is noteworthy that large-scale innovation was generally absent in the staple industries, particularly after 1880, despite their continuing importance in the economy. It is no simple task to explain the slackening of entrepreneurial drive in British industry, the success of which had given such effective support to the dominant ideology of the mid-Victorian period. Part of the problem can be related to the organisation of industrial enterprise where the direction of firms passed from the first to the second and third generation of family control, despite the spread of limited liability.[14] The fact that this often coincided with increasing economic difficulties after 1873 might well explain the British investors' preference for securities bearing a fixed rate of return, either domestic or overseas, rather than high-risk investment in new areas of manufacturing where, potentially at least, the highest rates of return could be expected.[15]

Yet attention should also be directed to the unique historical and social context in which British industrialists functioned. In this respect, the rentier bourgeoisie centred in London and the south of England that had formed one faction of the mid-Victorian power bloc strengthened its position of wealth and power after the 1870s. Until at least the First World War, the really wealthy in Britain (i.e. millionaires) tended to be merchants, bankers, shipowners and stock and insurance brokers, usually in the City of London, rather than manufacturers and industrialists.[16] And the former retained the ear of central government via the connections between the London financial houses, the Bank of England and the Treasury. There was during the late nineteenth century, moreover, a shift in the activities of major provincial industrialists like the Tennants of Glasgow to the metropolis. The continuing wealth, power and prestige of the tired of the trials and tribulations of factory, office and shopfloor. who in the face of a less expansive market environment was growing tired of the trials and tribulations of factory office and shopfloor.

The coming together of economic interest was only part of this development. Intermarriage and a similar educational background provided by the rapidly growing public schools were also eroding the sense of cultural isolation that had given the mid-Victorian industrialists not only much of their entrepreneurial drive but a determination to impress their ideology on society as a whole.[17] Their subsequent conversion to the values of aristocratic culture undermined the entrepreneurial ideal. Status-seeking in the form of a political career was deemed more desirable than a life wholly devoted to business.[18] The late Victorian plutocracy thus possessed a considerably greater degree of homogeneity than the mid-Victorian power bloc. But this implied an increasing resistance to innovation—a life devoted to the commercial application of applied science was not regarded as socially prestigious—and the price paid was probably a lower rate of economic development.[19] This was not auspicious in the context of the 1880s when labour was seen to require as well as itself demand a greater share of the country's wealth.

An analysis of labour's relationship with late Victorian society must take into account the less favourable economic environment, as well as the consequences of the coalescing of ruling groups into a new plutocracy, which together combined to produce a slowing down in the rate of industrial development after 1873. Money wages reached a peak in 1874, after a long period of slow but almost continuous advance, but they fluctuated thereafter around a slightly lower plateau until 1888–9.[20] The late 1870s were marked by a spate of disputes in the major industries that commonly ended in wage reductions as employers sought to cut production costs in the face of increasing competition.[21] Again, the surviving wage data are of rates of the 'aristocratic' minority of workers organised in trade unions who were generally less affected by unemployment or short-time working. The latter had a much greater impact upon the earnings of the unskilled and unorganised majority. In the summer of 1878, for example, as economic conditions worsened, some engineering firms in Glasgow were paying their men as little as 22–4s per week, far below the rate of wages nominally recognised in the district.[22]

In real terms, the differential distinguishing the standard of life of the privileged elite of labour from the experience of the majority of workers probably reached its widest point in the mid-1880s because the downward movement of prices after 1873 benefited only those groups who could maintain their money wages and remain in regular employment.[23] The declining trend of wages as a proportion of the national income is an indication of the combined effects of wage reductions, unemployment and short-time working during the years 1873–85/6.[24] On the other hand, a survey of the period 1859–1903 shows that the capitalists' share of total industrial output rose most between 1869–79 and 1880–6.[25] Increasing money inequalities were just one facet of this development. As the world market became more competitive, the opportunities for continually extending productive capacity ran up against the problems associated with a rising capital–labour ratio (the organic composition of capital) and a falling rate of profit. Employers sought to adopt the characteristic capitalist response to falling profitability by increasing the productivity of existing capitals, since lower profits did not encourage the substitution of labour by new capital-intensive techniques. Thus it became common for employers to intensify the utilisation of labour in combination with existing production methods.[26]

Rising unemployment was a corollary of the increasing rate of labour exploitation, particularly since the low level of domestic investment in industry during the 1880s was failing to create new job opportunities, commensurate with the rising numbers seeking employment. It was acknowledged by a leading engineering employer, for example, that the introduction of new forms of piecework or payment by results increased labour productivity but at the cost of diminished employment.[27] Even for the privileged minority of trade unionists, unemployment reached double figures in three years during the period 1875–90: 11.4% in 1879, 12.6% in 1883 and 10.2% in 1886.[28] Estimates contained in the evidence submitted by employers and trade union officials to the Royal Commission on the Depression of Trade in 1886 suggest that the *general* level of unemployment was especially heavy in centres of staple export industry. John Scott, the Greenock shipbuilders and marine engineers, stated that 36–7% of the 'whole trade' was without employment.[29] Even in a relatively 'sheltered' sector like building construction, about one-third of the skilled bricklayers in Liverpool were said to be without jobs in 1886.[30] The growth during this period of categories of casual labour like dock work implied that the proportion of the labour force most vulnerable to seasonal as well as cyclical or structural unemployment remained large. It is significant in this respect that the word 'unemployed' first appeared in the Oxford Dictionary in 1882 and 'unemployment' in 1888.

The impact of unemployment in the 1880s is related to a larger question that thrust itself into public debate during this period—the extent of poverty. Problems of definition make it difficult to measure poverty, which is not just synonymous with a lack of the basic necessities of life. An assessment would also have to include an appreciation of those things recognised to be necessary for a minimum standard of life at a given stage of a society's economic and social development. An understanding of poverty in an urban-industrial society, for example, would have to start from the assumption that most of life's necessities have to be purchased in the market, in contrast to the opportunities for exchange in kind and relative self-sufficiency in traditional rural societies. In this respect, it is important to realise that by the 1880s Britain was the world's most industrialised and urbanised country, with an estimated 75% of the population dependent exclusively on wages.

Poverty was not, of course, new in the 1880s. An estimate based on criteria developed in the late nineteenth century shows that 35.5% of Britain's families were in poverty in 1867.[31] Yet the mechanisms containing poverty in the mid-Victorian period, like the relief of distress on an informal basis that was possible when face-to-face contact still counted, could no longer function in a society increasingly dominated by large urban conurbations, especially London. Moreover, the flexibility in the implementation of the Poor Law during the 1850s and 1860s, which had allowed extensive distribution of outdoor relief at times of exceptional distress, could not be expected to cope with conditions of persistent and deepening depression in the late 1870s and 1880s. The onset of this period of high unemployment had, in fact, led the authorities to tighten up the administration of the Poor Law, in a vain attempt to deter the 'able-bodied' pauper and keep government expenditure within bounds.[32] The number of paupers relieved out of doors steadily declined during the years 1870–85, despite rising unemployment, yet those relieved in the workhouse dramatically escalated.[33] Particularly for the 'respectable' unemployed, the harshness and humiliation of the workhouse test seemed to justify any amount of poverty and suffering, especially in light of the rising expectations associated with the mid-Victorian period. But the depth and persistence of the depression was testing labour's capacity for self-help to the breaking-point.

There is abundant evidence demonstrating the extent of poverty in late Victorian Britain. The first volume of Charles Booth's *Life and Labour of the People in London*, published in 1889, showed that earlier writers had underestimated the extent of poverty in the metropolis, which he found was the condition of one-third of its population. Outward manifestations of poverty were not difficult to find. Malnutrition if not absolute want of sustenance continued to afflict the large majority of workers earning less than 30s per week as late as the 1890s, despite the reduction in wholesale prices since the 1870s.[34] Bad housing was another sign of poverty. This was the result of a number of factors including population growth, the demands of industry and commerce for building space, slum clearance that failed to make good condemned accommodation, and the need of most workers to live near their place of employment. All these combined to produce the highest density figures of the century in the major cities, particularly in London.[35] A related aspect of poverty was the fact that mortality rates remained significantly higher in the towns than in the countryside.[36] Thus the interaction of low wages, malnutrition, bad housing and infirmity, especially in old age, created a seemingly ever-increasing culture of poverty in Britain's large cities; and this was becoming virtually self-perpetuating. More precisely, it was the effect of irregular employment resulting from casual labour that has been identified as the single most important cause of poverty among the working class.[37] There was no more ominous a sign of the decline in profitability and the falling rate of industrial accumulation in the British economic system during the 1880s.

The extent of poverty in the midst of glaring inequalities affected the prevailing attitude to the treatment of the poor. In the mid-Victorian period, the belief in the inevitability of material progress had been central to the hegemony of the industrial bourgeoisie. What could not be ignored in the 1870s and 1880s was that despite rising wealth the poor not only showed no signs of disappearing but appeared to be increasing in concentrated masses in the expanding working-class districts of the large cities. The sharpening of geographic segregation along class lines was particularly striking in London which grew in size from two million inhabitants in the 1850s to more than five millions by the end of the century. In light of the deteriorating economic situation, the task of getting to grips with the threat of 'suburbanism' was given a new urgency. A spokesman for the National Association for the Promotion of Social Science observed in the depression year of 1879:[38]

One of the most important aims of this country and in this generation is to supply the want of social unity in the English people.

A growing preoccupation with the need for social unity began to undermine the credibility of the accepted solution to poverty based on individual self-help. In particular, there was the large number of casual underemployed poor who could not be easily fitted into the established categories of 'deserving' or 'undeserving'. Poverty could no longer be explained solely in terms of individual moral failure, which could be corrected by temperance, sexual restraint, diligence and thrift, but had become an economic problem rooted in the physical and social environment of the poor.[39] This marked a significant departure from the dominant ideology of the mid-Victorian period and threatened the hegemonic control that had reconciled labour to its situation in a free capitalist economy. The origins of the 'challenge of labour' in the 1880s must in part be attributed, therefore, to this growing threat to the dominant ideology and was not unrelated to Britain's increasing economic difficulties. The latter were most obviously manifest in the growing crisis of the large cities, especially London which was also the centre of the state apparatus.[40]

The response of wage-earners to more intensive labour utilisation, unemployment and increasing urban poverty was shaped by the fact that labour is by definition a creative act, identifying man as a social animal. It was thus bound to be affected by the associations, traditions, loyalties and ideologies which were part of labour's relationship with Victorian society as a whole. At the workplace, the industrial strife of the late 1870s, when trade unions were generally unsuccessful in resisting wage reductions, was followed by a period of demoralisation in terms of organisation. Membership of unions affiliated to the TUC declined from a peak of 1,192,000 in 1874 to just 464,000 by 1881, and recovery thereafter was slow, TUC-affiliated membership standing at only 636,000 in 1886. In addition to the impact of unemployment, which sapped workers' ability to subscribe to union membership, the climate of industrial relations did not encourage a policy of aggressive recruitment. The defeat and demoralisation of rank-and-file organisation that had formed the basis for many of labour's successful struggles in the early 1870s left the unions in the tightening grip of official leaders who became increasingly isolated from the problems of the mass of workers. In many cases, union leaders tried merely to keep their organisations intact and preserve their own position, at whatever the cost. Priority was given to avoiding disputes and disciplining the rank and file.[41] In the political sphere, the Parliamentary Committee of the TUC became more unashamedly the lapdog of the Liberal Party, its obsession with 'practical' questions like factory and mines inspection meaning the appointment of 'right' people to responsible positions in the state apparatus.[42] There was little thought given to attacking the fundamental problems of falling wages, worsening conditions, unemployment and the larger question of poverty.

This relative acquiescence of the leadership of organised labour rested on the comparatively privileged position of the diminishing proportion of trade unionists whose ability to retain their employment in a period of depression intensified the process of differentiation within the working class as a whole. Although skilled trade unionists were not unaffected by the impact of more intensive labour utilisation and unemployment, there is little doubt that the major part of this burden was shouldered by the unskilled and unorganised residuum in the large cities. Whilst wage cuts and worsening conditions were the rule in many centres of export industry, the effects of depression were by no means felt uniformly throughout the country.[43] Yet the isolation of the leadership of the organised minority of workers from the experience of the great mass of wage-earners created an opportunity for putting forward alternative policies, which sought to organise the majority of workers most affected by the Great Depression. The basis for this was provided initially by the consequences of changes in the labour process.

At the workplace, more intensive methods of labour utilisation took the form of a greater subdivision of labour, closer supervision and the more widespread use of monetary incentives. This process began to transform the undifferentiated 'labourer' of the mid-Victorian period into the prototype of the modern semi-skilled worker. The latter may lack allround skill and a broadly-based bargaining position, but acquires experience at a particular job within the production process. This development was most evident in the rapidly expanding transport sector of the economy and in the newer sectors of an established industry like engineering that produced the semi-skilled 'machine men'.[44] In the same way that the mid-Victorian labour aristocracy had come to conceive of the wage contract as a cash calculation, yielding as much as the market might bear, the new semi-skilled workers of the 1880s began to 'learn the rules' of the capitalist game in response to the pressures and incentives of more intensive methods of labour utilisation.[45]

Yet unlike the privileged elite of the 1850s and 1860s, working in what was virtually a sellers' market, the semi-skilled groups of the 1880s were less clearly differentiated from the wage-earning class as a whole. They lacked a tradition of organisation as well as the established bargaining position that during the mid-Victorian years had functioned as a point of transmission for the dominant ideology. Isolated from the practices and attitudes of existing unions, with their sectional exclusiveness, the semi-skilled workers' new appreciation of 'playing the market' during the 1880s encouraged a more militant if not 'revolutionary' conception of trade unionism as an all-grades movement cutting across established occupational and even industrial divisions. Trade unionism of this kind had, by definition, to be more militant and lent itself to generalised agitation for the right of workers to organise. It was also more explicitly political since the semi-skilled did not possess the industrial muscle to win *and* secure their demands by means of trade union action alone. Increasingly, therefore, they looked to the state for assistance. The negative posture of the TUC in regards to the desirability of more state intervention was clearly not appropriate in their case. Such are the origins of the so-called 'New Unionism' of 1888–9, which appeared to contemporaries as the most striking manifestation of the challenge of labour to its earlier relationship with Victorian society.

At the same time, the effects of economic change were beginning to undermine the privileged position of a rising number of labour aristocrats that had hitherto vindicated the conciliatory policies of the official trade union leadership. The latter's conscious and deliberate class-collaborationist tactics came to be seen as less justified by the end of the 1880s. In the engineering industry, for example, the demands of more intensive labour utilisation led not only to closer managerial control, with frequent complaints about 'taskwork' and greater employer 'vigilance', but also initiated a new phase of labour-saving investment threatening the position of the fitters and turners who dominated the Amalgamated Society of Engineers.[46] It is noteworthy that the changing industrial experience of the 1880s produced a new generation of militant leaders like John Burns, Tom Mann and George Barnes. Inspired by socialist ideas, they played a prominent role in organising the New Unionism and sought subsequently to transform the Amalgamated Society of Engineers into a genuinely industrial union, recruiting workers from every grade of skill. In addition to engineering, attacks on apprenticeship within a wider context of 'deskilling' were also taking place in such disparate trades as building construction, ironmoulding, bookbinding, printing and shoemaking.[47] The deteriorating position of these groups began to discredit the appeal of accepted policies. Some of their number, like the semi-skilled, began to look to the state to intervene directly and protect their industrial position because trade union action alone seemed no longer adequate. Thus at a Trades' Conference held at Glasgow in 1887, a motion proposed by the joiners that Parliament should compel all employers to bind their apprentices received the general support of the skilled trades represented.[48] It would appear that a shared experience of economic difficulty was drawing the labour movement closer together by the end of the 1880s.

The changing character of labour's relationship with the economic system was amplified by a wider process of social change which tended to intensify class antagonism. It was not only the effects of industrial change that were making labour more homogeneous as a *class*. The continuing growth of the commercial and financial apparatus of British capitalism was creating an expanding army of clerks and other white-collar strata whose relatively secure employment, despite comparatively low wages and long working hours, provided a socially deferential and politically conservative support for capitalist society, but which narrowed the career prospects of the traditional labour aristocracy of manual workers. Greater emphasis on formal educational qualifications and more rigidly institutionalised white collar career ladders were now limiting the opportunities for upward social mobility, which had been more abundant in the relatively fluid and informal conditions of mid-Victorian industry.[49] Access to formal education depended largely on financial capacity, yet the increasing disparity between the large size of most working-class families compared with the declining trend typical of the professions, including the white-collar strata who aspired to their status or otherwise wanted to emulate them, implied that most working-class family budgets could not afford the cost.[50]

The evidence points to an increasingly self-contained working-class culture, sharply distinguished from bourgeois society by its own patterns of housing, consumption and recreation. The effects of demolition, commercial development and suburbanisation led to the consolidation of working-class districts that in the large cities became virtually self-contained communities. Whilst it is unlikely that the falling trend of prices led directly to any corresponding rise in working-class nutritional standards, even by the 1890s, this did stimulate the activities of entrepreneurs in retail trading like John Lewis, who began to produce cheap standardised goods specifically for mass consumption. This provided an external dimension to the increasing homogeneity of working-class life.[51] A similar trend was evident in the recreational sphere. The new popularity of organised professional sport, especially football, offered escape and excitement for the skilled operative seeking diversion from a more alienating work-situation as well as for the unskilled.[52] The 1880s also witnessed the 'rebellion' of the working men's clubs against middle-class patronage, with the result that they became genuinely working-class organisations for the first time.[53] There are also signs that religion was losing its force in mediating labour's relationship with the wider society. The churches tried unsuccessfully, for example, to maintain control over the recreation and leisure activities of the working class, as part of their drive to establish urban order.[54] The nonconformists, in particular, suffered as a result of the diversion of working-class energy and income into football or betting on the horses, which received wide publicity in the new popular press. These developments were thus eroding the forms of *cultural* mediation that had adapted labour to its *economic* situation during the mid-Victorian period.

The Crisis of Liberalism

The difficulties of the British economy after 1873 had an analogue in the increasing polarisation of political life along class lines. Control of the state began to shift to those groups that directly comprised the 'real' class base of late Victorian society—the new plutocracy—in contrast to the relative heterogeneity of the mid-

Victorian power bloc. This sprang from the economic and social assimilation of the wealthiest section of the industrial bourgeoisie into a comparatively homogeneous ruling class of super rich, isolated by its sense of cultural superiority as well as its wealth and power from the majority of the population. The result gave rise to two interrelated developments that werc crucially important in *politicising* labour's discontent.

First, the tradition of Liberalism–Radicalism began to attract the support of a diminishing proportion of the industrial bourgeoisie, whose economic and social position was undergoing such fundamental change. The key instrument of hegemonic control in the 1850s and 1860s thus became blunted. The second development, related to the first, was the transformation of Conservatism from the politics of *land-holding*, with a sprinkling of support from bankers, brewers and other miscellaneous 'respectables', into a broader-based politics of *property-holding* representing industrial, commercial as well as landed interests. This marked a convergence in political terms of the *class* interests of the dominant groups in British society. The closer approximation of political power to its 'real' class base was articulated by the urban gentry of late Victorian intellectuals whose 'organic' links with an increasingly homogeneous ruling class became more complete during the last quarter of the century.[55]

It may appear paradoxical that the growing crisis of Liberalism coincided with the reorganisation of the Liberal Party following the formation of the National Liberal Federation in 1877. This marked an attempt by the Liberal–Radicals, led by Joseph Chamberlain, to rejuvenate their party by establishing a popularly-based electoral machine involving rank-and-file members in the constituencies, and thus end once and for all the power of the Whig magnates. Chamberlain appreciated that the future of Liberalism depended on its ability to mobilise mass electoral support, particularly the rising number of working-class voters enfranchised since 1867. Yet he had also to reckon with the reality of class polarisation, which made traditional Radical demands like church disestablishment and land reform increasingly irrelevant to both wage-earners and employers. At the same time, Chamberlain had to take into account the interests of the Whig magnates and especially the business plutocracy who were afraid that Radical rhetoric might unleash a revolutionary movement against the rights of property. The sharpening division between the Liberal leadership and its Radical wing was accentuated following the party's victory in the 1880 General

Election. This had owed much to the organisation of the National Liberal Federation, but yielded little reward in terms of Radical influence in the new Cabinet.

Chamberlain's hostility to the Whigs led by Hartington ruled out any ambitious Liberal programme for tackling domestic problems, despite the publicity given to issues like unemployment, bad housing and poverty.[56] In the constituencies, power continued to reside with a small number of wealthy benefactors, although the National Liberal Federation tried unsuccessfully to appeal to small subscribers.[57] In Parliament, MPs with industrial or commercial interests constituted the largest single bloc of Liberal members. In short, the class composition of the Liberal Party made it an unlikely agent of social reform. It was the problem of Ireland that was the occasion but not the underlying cause of the conflict of interests which was to split the Liberal Party and signal the restructuring of British politics along class lines. The rising tide of agitation for land reform in Ireland resulting from the effects of the agricultural depression triggered a series of much publicised 'outrages', and became the basis of a campaign for Home Rule that secured the support of 86 Nationalist MPs in the General Election of 1885, following the assimilation of the county franchise to the conditions obtaining in the boroughs since 1867. Home Rule for Ireland seemed to be in the best traditions of mid-Victorian Liberalism, and Gladstone's 'conversion' to it can be represented as a practical application of the Liberal belief in the right of national self-determination. Yet this decision of the Liberal Party's venerable leader, reached as a result of following the strict logic of his principles to their ultimate conclusion, served only to demonstrate his isolation from the process of class polarisation at work around him. Gladstone's action alienated not only the Whigs in his own party, some of whom had estates in Ireland, but also a major part of the plutocracy and almost all the leading intellectual figures of the day who viewed the prospect of land reform in Ireland as part of 'a creeping conspiracy against property'.[58]

It was thus the Conservative leader, Lord Salisbury, and not Gladstone, who caught the mood of property when he warned in 1884:[59]

We are on an inclined plane leading from the position of Lord Hartington to that of Mr. Chamberlain and so on to the depths over which Mr. Henry George rules supreme.

The spectre of Henry George and his proposal for a single tax on land was especially alarming to property-owners because his speaking tours of metropolitan Britain were so immensely popular. It was this alarm that justified opposition to even moderate instalments of reform like the Employers' Liability Act of 1880, which some employers tried to defeat in spirit by coercing workers into 'contracting out'. This example of the efforts made to preserve the prerogatives of property against 'outside' interference was part of the growing and widespread fears among wealth-holders during this period that led to the setting up of associations like the Liberty and Property Defence League.[60] Thus Gladstone merely confirmed a wider process of social transformation when his conversion to Irish Home Rule precipitated a flight of capital from Liberalism to Conservatism.[61] In particular, the consequent split in the Liberal Party doomed Chamberlain and his followers to a future of comparative ineffectiveness in an uneasy alliance with the Conservatives. Yet it was this demise of Liberal–Radicalism that was to create new opportunities for the political mobilisation of working-class consciousness.

The increasing polarisation of British society along class lines gave birth to new forms of working-class politics that sought directly to challenge rather than mediate labour's relationship with the existing distribution of power and wealth in society as a whole. Although even universal manhood suffrage was not realised in Britain until 1918, the provisions of the 1867 Reform Act enfranchised a rising proportion of the working-class electorate, especially after the Franchise and Redistribution Acts of 1885 extended the vote to important groups of workers in rural areas like the miners and created more seats in the expanding urban areas. There appeared to be a widening discrepancy between the new status bestowed upon labour by its access to the ballot box and the day-to-day experience of workshop, factory and mine, where more intensive labour utilisation and rising unemployment were affecting the skilled tradesman as well as the unskilled labourer.

The greater homogeneity or 'solidification' of working-class communities, in the wider cultural sense, encouraged the development of new political ideologies. The mid-Victorian tradition of 'labourism', which was based upon class collaboration in the political sphere, seemed less justified in the economic and social context of the 1880s when it became increasingly difficult to argue that the defence of working-class interests was possible within a society where private property and the free market were held to be sacrosanct. 'Rebellion' against prevailing values and institutions tends to be more likely when a minority subculture exists or is created, functioning as a 'barrier' to the dominant influences in society.[62] The evidence would suggest that by the 1880s the preconditions for a flourishing sub-culture within the working class had been created, although it should be appreciated that it had never disappeared entirely, even in the 1850s and 1860s.[63] What helped to fructify this after 1870 was, first, the extension of popular education which brought about a signi-ficant reduction in illiteracy and produced a growing number of largely self-taught intellectuals within the working class, who were able to articulate an alternative ideology to that purveyed by the established intelligentsia. Voluntary bodies like the University Extension Movement organised lectures that during the winter of 1883–4, for example, were attended by more than 1,000 members of the Durham Miners' Association who risked loss of wages and fines for missed shifts.[64] Other organisations that expanded during this period included the Labour Emancipation League and the Social and Political Education League. The latter were avowedly socialist in their outlook, holding classes specifically for working men, and they were instrumental in winning recruits to new socialist organis-ations like the Social Democratic Federation.[65]

The growth of these self-consciously secularist and often socialist-inspired educational associations played an important role in erod-ing the influence of religion among the more literate elements of the working class. In any case, the effect of sharpening class divisions was such that organised religion was more overtly becoming a creature of the established social order, especially since in the instance of nonconformist congregations the ministers' income depended dir-ectly on the generosity of the richer members among their com-municants. The dismissal of nonconformist ministers who were considered by their congregations to be too 'radical' or 'advanced' became commonplace by the end of the century.[66] This represented a serious weakening of one of the mechanisms of hegemonic control that had been so effective in the mid-Victorian period. The shift to secularism was also a result of the rising barriers to upward social mobility in increasingly homogeneous working-class communities. This implied that the justification for the traditional distinction made between the 'roughs' and the 'respectables' became less and less convincing. It appears that the spread of unbelief was particu-larly widespread among those 'respectable' working-class elements who found their prospects of rising in society blocked.[67] Labour's disillusionment with organised religion was especially marked in large cities where the extent of occupational and spatial segregation had become more extreme than elsewhere. By the end of the century, for example, contemporary surveys showed that in London less than 15% of the population was attending religious worship in solidly working-class districts.[68]

Against the background of deepening depression in the 1880s, the experience of an increasingly numerous body of literate working men produced an explicitly secularist outlook, which took an influential minority along the path to socialist commitment. A new generation of labour leaders was created whose consciousness was distinguished from the Liberal loyalties of the previous generation. The shift in outlook from religiosity to secularism, and eventually to socialism, is clearly evident in the personal histories of working-class leaders of the calibre of Keir Hardie, Will Thorne and Tom Mann.[69] It is interesting that a large number of the most aggressively labour leaders of the late Victorian period were skilled workers, including engineering tradesmen like John Burns and George Barnes as well as Tom Mann, whose traditions of craft autonomy that led them to conceive of human labour as a creative activity contrasted unfavourably with the increasingly alienating conditions in industry during the 1880s, when even skilled men had to cope with speed-up, greater managerial supervision and skilled labour substitution. When John Burns joined the Social Democratic Federation in 1884, for example, he already had three years experience of speaking at Radical Clubs and Secular Societies where his campaigning for trade unionism aimed not only at economic improvement but also the 'civic and political' development of the working man as a total human being.[70]

One of the first of the new political groupings formed in the 1880s was the Social Democratic Federation (SDF). The conversion to Marxism of its founder, H. M. Hyndman, made the SDF the first organisation set up in Britain with the specific purpose of spreading the principles of 'scientific socialism'. Although Hyndman's egocentric and contradictory personality proved a serious obstacle in recruiting (and keeping) members, it did succeed in attracting a small number of working-class militants who became acquainted for the first time with some of the fundamentals of Marxist analysis. Much of what was learned was partial and sometimes erroneous, yet the SDF's singular contribution was that it rejected the basic tenet of labourism which argued that labour should ally itself with 'progressive' bourgeois elements in order to achieve 'moderate' reform.[71] Its objective was always that socialism could only be achieved by the working class acting independently by and for itself. It was for this reason that the SDF included within its ranks some of the most prominent labour leaders of the day, like Tom Mann, John Burns and Will Thorne, although its total membership remained minuscule—claimed membership was less than 2,000 in 1889.[72]

Much of the SDF's failure to strike deeper roots in the working class stemmed from Hyndman's belief in the 'uselessness' of trade unionism and industrial struggle as instruments for class mobilisation. Again, this sprang from theoretical ignorance that construed Marxism in terms of a crude acceptance of the 'iron law' of wages, denying any value to class struggle at the point of production.[73] Hyndman argued that the trade unions had become hopelessly compromised by their association with Liberalism, a view that justified among other things his acceptance of financial help from the Tories in running candidates in local elections. This was unlikely to improve the organisation's credibility with labour militants. Yet its programme of 'palliatives', especially the demand for an eight-hour day guaranteed by legislative enactment, was intended to take the working class step by step along the road to socialism, and had considerable mass appeal. The SDF was also active in agitating for the creation of a genuinely independent working-class presence in Parliament. The irony was that these objectives were particularly well received by the trade unions whose value Hyndman personally held in such low esteem. Thus a conference of trade union delegates meeting in Glasgow in 1887 passed resolutions in favour of both the eight-hours' and independent labour representation in Parliament by large majorities.[74] And leading SDF members like Mann, Burns and Thorne also provided the leadership in the movement to organise the unskilled and semi-skilled in the late 1880s. In fact, the SDF and its successor (and rival) organisations influenced the thinking of an entire generation of working-class leaders who were active in the period between the 1880s and the 1930s. Its existence and influence were thus part of the growing challenge that labour was to pose to its established relationship with British society.

The interaction of economic, political and cultural factors catalysed by the propaganda of new socialist groupings like the SDF combined together to detach an increasing proportion of the working class from its earlier association with Liberalism. Not that this alone was responsible for the Conservative and Liberal Unionist victories of 1886 because the electoral system continued to be biased against the labour vote, despite the Franchise Acts of 1884–5, and favoured the Tories who were well placed to mobilise support from among the increasingly homogeneous class identifying itself as property-holders. Household, residence and registration require- ments still effectively excluded 70% of the adult male population from the electorate in working-class constituencies, and the cost of registering electors in addition to other anomalies like plural voting clearly favoured the existing party machines.[75] The mobility of the large residuum of casual labour excluded them from the franchise because of registration difficulties. This was particularly damaging to the Liberals in big urban centres like London where the shift in the loyalties of property in favour of the Tories was decisive and deprived the Liberal Party of much-needed financial support.[76]

It is important to appreciate the impact of economic depression in making the wealth that had traditionally supported the Liberals reluctant to pay the 'ransom' in the form of higher taxation de- manded by Radical proposals for land reform and 'free education'. The Liberal success in the election of November 1885 had indeed been a pyrrhic victory. This had been a direct consequence of the Franchise Acts of 1884–5, which had extended the franchise to about two million miners and agricultural workers located in the counties. Yet the Liberal Party had done badly in urban areas where Radicalism as Chamberlain himself acknowledged had little appeal, attracting a diminishing proportion of the enfranchised working class.[77] And the Radicals had been unable to persuade the Liberal leadership to swallow even their limited programme of reform. Hartington, the leader of the Liberal Whigs, expressed the reservations of 'property' as follows in response to Radical de- mands:[78]

I will frankly admit to you that I do not believe in the efficiency or advantage of any of those proposals for arbitrarily or forcibly redistributing the land of this country... It may not be at present the popular thing to say anything in defence of the rights of property; but I am of opinion that it is a most grave and serious matter to do anything which may rashly and in any unsound manner, affect those rights. Whatever principles may be applied to land are likely, sooner or later, to be applied to other descrip- tions of property...

Radical measures that implied heavier taxes were thus seen as potentially threatening the wealth of all property-owners, including the wealth of the new plutocracy.

The coalescing of the interests of property in opposition to the Radical wing of the Liberal Party was first mobilised at Westminster early in 1885 on the occasion of the introduction of Mundella's Railway and Canal Traffic Bill. This proposed to set up special courts to hear disputes between consumers and the railway companies arising from 'unequal' freight rates. Mundella's bill antagonised the 'moneyed world' of railway directors and shareholders, including Whig magnates like the Duke of Argyll who also happened to be a director of the Callendar and Oban Railway, and created a 'cave' of opposition within the Liberal Party prior to Gladstone's public announcement of his conversion to Irish Home Rule.[79] In fact, the decision by the Chamberlainites to leave the Liberal Party, at the same time as the Whigs, was caused not so much by their opposition to Home Rule as such but to Gladstone's projected Land Purchase Bill, which proposed to allocate 50 million pounds of credit in order to buy out Irish landlords and create a more broadly-based independent peasantry. Chamberlain feared that this would divert resources away from the Radical programme of reform which would otherwise have to be financed by additional taxation. Gladstone himself was only too well aware that the latter would be unacceptable to the moneyed interests within the Liberal ranks, whatever their objection in principle to Irish Home Rule. Yet his efforts to preserve the unity of the party served only to plunge it into the widening ideological divide. His backstage manoeuvres had failed, in the meantime, to convince his Irish Nationalist supporters led by Parnell who had instructed his followers to vote Tory in the 1885 election. This led directly to the public announcement of Gladstone's conversion to Home Rule, but the result was the desertion of his erstwhile Whig supporters, thus precipitating the General Election of 1886.

Chamberlain and his followers had also joined the opposition to Home Rule in April 1886, but for different reasons. They considered it not only an unpopular 'diversion' that directed attention away from their domestic programme, but expected that Gladstone's anticipated defeat would lead to his retirement and leave the Radicals free to lead a Liberal Party now cleansed of its Whig elements.[80] The Radical and Whig desertions led, as expected, to a major Tory victory in the 1886 election. But Gladstone refused to admit defeat and retire, which left the Chamberlainites isolated and ultimately dependent on the Tories whose new Whig allies implied that the new Conservative government was unlikely to embark on a programme of Radical reform. At the same time, the loss of the Chamberlainites deprived Liberalism of much of the mass appeal it had managed to retain. The Liberal hegemony was thus seriously undermined. The drift of capital away from Liberalism, depriving it not only of votes but also funds, left the Party less capable of organising the reformist 'left' in Parliament and created a political vacuum that was difficult to fill because of lack of resources and the electoral system's bias against the working-class vote. The result was that during the years 1885–1900 the Liberal's share of the vote remained stagnant in the face of rising labour militancy.[81] The problems of unemployment, bad housing and poverty were left largely unresolved during the rule of Tory Unionism. It is not surprising that in this context there was a resurgence in working-class agitation out of doors, led by new socialist organisations like the Social Democratic Federation. The unemployment demonstrations of 1886 and 1887—the latter culminating in the 'Bloody Sunday' confrontation between police and demonstrators—highlighted the failure of Britain's political system to deal with a particularly pressing social problem.[82] This apparent paralysis of *political* will led the most vulnerable sections of the working class to take *industrial* action on their own account.

The 'New Unionism' and the Beginnings of Independent Labour Politics

The end of the 1880s found British trade unionism at a low ebb. Persistently high levels of unemployment, even among skilled workers, had reduced union membership from the peak of the early 1870s. It is estimated that scarcely 5 % of the occupied population was organised in trade unions in 1888, and the bulk of their members was confined largely to the 'labour aristocratic' grades in metals, engineering and shipbuilding; mining and quarrying; textiles; and building construction.[83] The isolation of the comparatively privileged elite from the great majority of workers was confirmed by the relative acquiescence of their official leaders. Yet the class-collaborationist policies of the TUC, which the labour aristocracy continued to dominate, seemed incapable of meeting the challenge *to* labour posed by unemployment, poverty and the degradation of work itself. Militants like John Burns and Tom Mann were critical of the role of existing trade unions and the conciliatory policies of their leaders. They argued for new forms of labour organisation, as well as the reconstruction of established ones, which would be more responsive to the needs of the working class as a whole. In 1886, for example, Tom Mann had founded the Eight-Hours League with the specific intention of bringing together trade unionists and revolutionary socialists.

The so-called 'New Unionism' was thus not so much an institutional development creating new organisations, but signified a broader movement advocating more positively aggressive if not explicitly socialist policies. These sought to appeal in *class* terms to all grades of labour, including workers already organised in existing unions.[84] The campaign for the eight-hour day, for example, was intended to mobilise general working-class support for a demand that it was hoped would reduce unemployment, offer some relief from the effects of more intensive labour utilisation, and create a focus for independent labour politics. It directly inspired the establishment of the National Labour Federation on Tyneside in November 1886, seeking specifically to unionise unskilled workers. The success of the eight-hours' agitation was such that by 1889 two-thirds of the unions affiliated to the TUC that had balloted their members on the issue voted in favour of the demand.[85] The New Unionism was thus anticipated by the setting up of several new labour organisations in the late 1880s, including the British Steel Smelters' Association, the National Amalgamated Union of Seamen and Firemen, and the Miners' Federation of Great Britain, which were formed prior to the upturn in the economy that triggered the famous London dock strike of 1889.

It is not surprising that the new spirit of aggression abroad among the working class in the late 1880s should have achieved its perhaps most important victory in the London docks. The latter attracted the reservoir of unskilled and casual labour that was the most striking manifestation of the extent of urban degeneration in the capital.[86] London illustrated in most extreme form the intensifying contradictions of capitalist development in Britain after 1870. Whilst its position as an expanding centre of finance, commerce and distribution continued to sustain an increasingly affluent plutocracy, reflected in the intense competition for scarce urban land and the consequently enormous rise in rents, its traditional trades that had remained relatively unaffected by industrialisation began to suffer severely from factory-based competition in the provinces where production costs were lower. The resulting growth in London of the 'reserve army' of labour, which was enlarged further by the influx of workers from depressed agricultural districts, implied that sweated labour was commonplace in the capital, and this was not only driven hard and irregularly employed but also received very low wages. It was ignored by the exclusive character of London's trade unions which managed to organise only 3.25 % of the city's occupied population even at the height of the boom in trade during 1889–91.[87]

This superabundant supply of labour competed desperately for any work that was available, including labouring in the docks where the growth in employment had been relatively rapid since the 1870s. It is true that within the docks there were a number of specialist grades like the watermen, lightermen and stevedores who were comparatively well paid and possessed an effective trade union organisation, but they were outnumbered by a vast army of casual labourers, and there were normally 30 % more of the latter than could be absorbed by the work available.[88] Skilled stevedoring, for example, made up less than 12 % of London's dock labour force, leaving the large majority in casual employment literally on an hour-to-hour basis with rates of pay as low as 5d or 4d per hour. This was scarcely sufficient to guarantee a minimum level of subsistence, providing there was regular work available, and the extent of rack-renting in the metropolis meant that as much as one-third of what was no more than a subsistence wage could be absorbed by the cost of accommodation. Moreover, the effects of depression during the 1880s had created surplus capacity at docks and warehouses, which led to fierce competition as firms reduced their charges in an attempt to maximise their share of a contracting market. In 1888, the East and West India Dock Company went bankrupt, and others were only saved from the same fate by cutting the prices paid to subcontractors who were responsible for hiring, supervising and paying the wages of dock labourers. This forced the subcontractors, in their turn, to economise on their use of labour by employing fewer men and driving them longer and harder.[89] This made worse the problem of the surplus of workers in the docks, while more intensive labour utilisation bore heavily on those operatives who did manage to find employment. Most of them received such low wages that their resistance to physical deterioration, arising from the almost totally unmechanised character of their labour, was seriously reduced.

The steady improvement in trading conditions during 1887–9 was the occasion for the setting up of new forms of trade unionism in the docks, like the Tea Operatives and General Labourers' Association established in 1887. Membership of this organisation, as its title suggests, reflected the casual nature of waterside employment and included gas stokers like Will Thorne of the SDF who sought work in the docks during the slack summer months. In fact, after two years' agitation, which did not yield more than 800 members for the new union, it was the intervention of Thorne and his fellow SDF members, Burns and Mann, that led eventually to strike action in August 1888.[90] The dockers' demands were for 6d an hour, overtime rates, and a minimum period of engagement of four hours, together with the abolition of subcontracting. The strike quickly became a mass movement of all dock workers, spreading to the relatively privileged grades like the stevedores and lightermen who withdrew their labour in sympathy, refusing to work with the strike-breakers introduced by the employers. The adhesion of groups like the stevedores with prior experience of organisation, and the leadership provided by SDF members like Tom Mann, were decisive in the effective co-ordination of the strike and were vital to its final success. There was subsequently a considerable expansion of trade unionism among the various grades of waterside labour. The Tea Operatives' Association transformed itself into the Dock, Wharf, Riverside and General Labourers' Union of Great Britain and Ireland—or the Dockers' Union—having a membership of 25,531 along the Thames by July 1890 and electing Tom Mann as President. The success of the strike also stimulated the growth of other waterside unions, the next largest being the South Side Labour Protection League with 5,000 members, which had another SDF member, Harry Quelch, as its General Secretary.

Yet the success of the London dock strike in mobilising workers as a class on an industrial basis must be qualified. The centralised organisation adopted by the Dockers' Union was in a sense not appropriate to the occupational structure of the waterside, which remained divided by fine distinctions reflecting differences in jobs and status, and Tom Mann's often overbearing leadership antago-nised the rank and file.[91] Sectional associations recruiting the more privileged grades like the stevedores retained their separate identity, moreover, while the unions' successful attack on casualisation failed to resolve the problem of the surplus of labour that inevitably reappeared once the boom in trade had run its course. Their determination that the docks were not to become an 'agency for outdoor relief' implied that the improvement in the conditions of regular dock workers was achieved at the expense of fewer opportunities for employment. Many bourgeois observers had, in fact, been largely sympathetic to the London dock strike because they believed that the effect of a victorious outcome would be to enforce more rigidly the separation of the 'respectable' working class in regular employment from the unemployable residuum.[92] In this respect, the very success of the strike served the aims of social policy in transforming what was regarded as the revolutionary threat posed by the capital's casual poor into a 'social problem', which could be responsibly handled by the co-operation of trade unions, employers and state agencies. There was also the increasingly conciliatory and moderate tone of the New Unionism, especially of its leaders once they had established their position, and this created a problem for those socialists who tried to use industrial action for political ends.[93]

In the gas industry, for example, the workers' experience of more intensive labour-utilisation had, like conditions in the docks, provided a favourable environment for trade unionism. Will Thorne's decisive intervention in the London docks was an indication of his previous record of success in organising workers at Beckton gasworks in West Ham, who had been able to win their demand for the eight-hour day without a strike. Yet the employers' subsequent decision late in 1889 to introduce a productivity scheme in order to offset the anticipated rise in labour costs precipitated a three-month strike, ending in defeat for the strikers and the emasculation of the Gas Workers' Union.[94] The strategy of George Livesey, the manager of the South Metropolitan Gas Company, in promising job security linked to a profit–bonus arrangement, led to an agreement with the Beckton workers that succeeded in outmanoeuvring the union despite Thorne's leadership. On the railways, too, the appearance of New Unionism in the form of the General Railway Workers' Union during 1889 succeeded only in breaking the hold of the established and more exclusive Amalgamated Society of Railway Servants in London, and to a lesser extent in Lancashire.[95] The latter body continued to dominate the rest of the country and its decision in 1890 to retain permanent employment as a precondition for membership, although dues were reduced, confirmed the privileged position of the 'respectables' in guaranteed employment.

In fact, rising militancy became as much a characteristic of workers already possessing some experience of trade union organisation, in comparison with the so-called New Unionism of dockers and gas workers. In coal-mining, the revival of trade during 1888 initiated a wage advance movement in the inland coalfields that had secured a general rise of 40% by 1890.[96] A conference of district delegates meeting at Newport in November 1889 agreed to establish the Miners' Federation of Great Britain (MFGB), distinct from the existing Miners' National Union with its conciliatory policies that was confined to Northumberland and Durham. Coal-mining was subsequently transformed into one of the most densely unionised industries, and the federation's demands for a 'minimum' wage and the eight-hour day reflected the influence of socialist agitation as well as the harsh conditions in the coalfields. The federation was later to become one of the most militant sections of organised labour. Similarly, the London, West Riding and Scottish branches of the Amalgamated Society of Engineers voted heavily in favour of legislation to secure the eight-hour day, and it is no coincidence that these were also centres of socialist propaganda.[97] Even in cotton textiles, which had a reputation for relatively quiescent industrial relations, a combination of speed-up, wage cuts and diminishing prospects for promotion to the better-paid grades in the late 1880s led to rising dissatisfaction among the rank and file. Thus the United Textile Factory Workers' Association, representing all the unions in the industry, voted in favour of the eight-hour day despite the hostility of their officials, and in September 1890 a separate union recruiting piecer assistants was formed in cotton-spinning because the existing Spinners' Association seemed unable or unwilling to protect their interests.[98]

The success of socialists in posing industrial conflict in class terms thus varied from industry to industry, and was not confined to the dramatic 'explosions' of unrest associated with the New Unionism. In fact, the latter found it impossible to secure the gains made in the late 1880s once the upturn in trade had passed its peak. Socialist groups like the SDF emphasised that industrial action alone could not solve the problems of unemployment, wage reductions and poverty, which could be resolved by one section of workers only at the expense of another. The hopes of the TUC leadership that the existing alliance with the Liberal Party would yield a steady rate of economic and social progress reckoned without Liberalism's growing impotence. At the 1886 TUC, it was not only SDF members but also union leaders as moderate as James Mawdsley of the Cotton Spinners' Amalgamation who recognised that there was no chance of improvement in labour conditions whilst 'the present state of society continued to exist', and it is significant that this was the occasion for the setting up of a standing 'Electoral Association', which many delegates hoped would be the agent for creating a completely independent labour presence in Parliament.[99]

The growing pressure for an independent labour party derived in particular from some coal-mining constituencies, enfranchised in 1885, but whose traditional allegiance to Liberalism was steadily undermined by a combination of socialist agitation and the party's ineffectiveness following the 1886 General Election. It is not surprising that this mining background produced a leading proponent of independent labour representation in the figure of Keir Hardie, whose conversion to socialism was a direct outcome of the crisis in the Scottish coal industry during 1886–7.[100] The employers' blatant manipulation of the forces of law and order in breaking the Lanarkshire strike of 1887, which was received with silent approval by the Liberal press, convinced Hardie that the working class could no longer look hopefully to the Liberal Party for the amelioration of its condition. His subsequent founding of the Scottish Labour Party in 1888 represented a milestone in the history of the British labour movement. This had been preceded in 1887 by Hardie's publication in the *Miner* of a skeleton programme for the new party, including the demands for the eight-hour day in the mines (and elsewhere), state insurance against unemployment and the nationalisation of the coal industry.[101] This was the product not only of Hardie's personal experience as a working man, it was also the outcome of wider contacts with socialists, including meetings in London with figures like Tom Mann.

The crisis in the Scottish coal industry during 1886–7 was not an isolated instance but was part of a wider movement that was to detach an increasing proportion of the working-class electorate from its earlier alliance with Liberalism. In the West Riding of Yorkshire, for example, the effects of depression were felt especially severely in the 1880s by the woollen textile workers.[102] The growth of foreign competition, aggravated by rising tariffs that virtually closed the American and German markets, led to a falling rate of profit following the boom years of 1870–4 when capacity had been greatly extended and mill valuations inflated. The burden of adjustment employers sought subsequently to make was borne by the operatives as price lists were cut and labour utilisation intensified. Yet it was the publicity given to the movements among unskilled workers elsewhere, especially in London, and the agitation of local socialists like Tom Maguire and Joseph Burgess who was editor of the *Yorkshire Factory Times*, which transformed these sectional grievances into class-based militancy.

During 1889–90, there was an outbreak of almost spontaneous strike activity among such disparate groups as the textile operatives, gasworks labourers and tailoring workers in the Leeds and Bradford area. Local socialists were quick to mobilise this unrest for a political purpose. By March 1890, it had coalesced around a new organisation—the Yorkshire Labour Council—and in the following year it found a political voice in the Bradford Labour Union. This was to be the lever for setting up the Independent Labour Party (ILP) in 1892. It is true that the resulting influx of disillusioned or opportunist ex-Liberals and Tories into its ranks prevented the ILP from adopting a root-and-branch socialist programme. Yet it did provide a focus for socialist propaganda that struck deep roots into the labour movement within a remarkably short period of time. The existing Trades Councils in the West Riding, for example, which had initially remained aloof from the unrest of 1889–90, had shifted decidedly to the left by February 1894 when the Yorkshire Federation of Trades Councils passed a resolution in favour of 'the nationalisation of the land, minerals, railways, and all the means of production and distribution, as a means of helping to solve the unemployed question'.[103]

The movement for independent labour politics extended also to London where the realignment of political life along class lines had become especially clear cut. The magnitude of the capital's social problems had forced Parliament to pass the Local Government Act of 1888, which transferred its administration from justices of the peace to elected county councils, in an attempt to resolve the chaos of divided jurisdictions including four different counties and six separate governing bodies. The establishment of the London County Council, popularly elected after 1894, had overall authority for the administration of the metropolis. It was hailed by one of its most bitter opponents as 'a political and social revolution', while one of its most fervent supporters described it as 'the machinery of social democracy'.[104] This reform gave rise to the Progressive Alliance of ex-Liberals, Radicals and socialists that became a dynamic force in London politics, setting up educational, health, housing, recreational and transport facilities, as well as attacking unemployment and regulating wages, hours and working conditions of municipal employees. Although the continuing weakness of trade unionism in the capital delayed the formation of the London Labour Party until 1914, socialist groups like the SDF and politically active Trades Councils campaigned successfully for independent labour councillors in working-class constituencies like Battersea and Woolwich.[105]

The agitation of socialists produced a growing awareness of the advantages of independent labour representation even in areas of the country like the Lancashire textile districts, where traditional loyalties to either the Tories (cotton-spinning) or the Liberals (weaving) were well entrenched. Thus the agent of the Northern Counties Weavers' Amalgamation called for the setting up of 'a gigantic labour organization' to force from capital its 'ill-gotten gains'.[106] During the great lock-out of 1892–3, the employers' leader John Brown Tattersall claimed that the dispute reflected the growing danger of socialism in the cotton districts.[107] It was in this way that the interdependence of industrial and political unrest during the late 1880s was perceived as a generalised threat to property. This is the background to the counter-attack organised against labour unrest in the 1890s, which had both an industrial and political dimension.

This response was to owe much of its vitality to new currents in the thinking of an articulate body of ruling opinion. Crude applications of Darwinian theories of evolution by natural selection, which argued that 'the survival of the fittest' applied to human society as well as to animal organisms, created a new climate of opinion that assumed a more positive role for the state than was allowed by mid-Victorian Liberalism. Imperialism attracted the support of an impressive body of business opinion as well as a large number of intellectuals who had deserted Liberalism because of Irish Home Rule.[108] A subsequently influential group of imperialist politicians, including former Radicals like Chamberlain, argued that colonial expansion was necessary in order to create the wealth that would make possible social reform at home.[109] This policy promised to avoid any massive attack on the wealth of property-owners, in the form of heavier taxation. It also held out the prospect of unifying the British nation, including 'Britain overseas', and resolving the threat to property associated with industrial unrest and the growth of socialism.

Notes

1. S. B. Saul, *The Myth of the Great Depression* (London: Macmillan, 1969), p. 54.

2. W. P. Kennedy, 'Foreign Investment, Trade and Growth in the United Kingdom, 1870–1913', *Explorations in Economic History*, 2nd series, 11 (1973–4), no. 4, pp. 425–6.

3. W. W. Rostow, 'Investment and the Great Depression', *Economic History Review*, VIII (1938), p. 144.

4. The rise of the Oldham limited-liability companies in cotton-spinning during the 1870s is a classic example of this response: see Roland Smith, 'An Oldham limited liability company 1875–1896', *Business History*, IV (1961–2); for contemporary evidence with reference to shipping see Parl. Papers, *Royal Commission on the Depression of Trade and Industry*, 1886 (XXIII), Third Report, Minutes of Evidence, p. 133.

5. E. H. Phelps Brown and Margaret H. Browne, *A Century of Pay* (London: Macmillan, 1968), Appendix 2, p. 412.

6. *Royal Commission on the Depression of Trade and Industry*, 1886 (XXI), First Report, Appendix A, p. 83.

7. Ibid., for replies to questionnaire.

8. Brown and Browne, *Century of Pay*, Appendix 2, p. 417.

9. Saul, *Great Depression*, Table IV, p. 36.

10. David S. Landes, *The Unbound Prometheus* (Cambridge: University Press, 1969), Ch. 5, contains a discussion of international comparisons.

11. W. L. Arnstein, 'The Survival of the Victorian Aristocracy' in F. C. Jaher (ed.), *The Rich, the Well Born and the Powerful: Elites and Upper Classes in History* (Chicago: University of Illinois Press, 1973), p. 229.

12. Harold Perkin, *The Origins of Modern English Society* (London: Routledge & Kegan Paul, 1969), Table 5, p. 415.

13. Ibid., pp. 433 ff.

14. See, for example, C. Erickson, *British Industrialists. Steel and Hosiery, 1850–1950* (Cambridge: University Press, 1959), especially the section on the steel industry.

15. Kennedy, 'Foreign Investment', p. 428.

16. W. D. Rubinstein, 'The Victorian Middle Classes: Wealth, Occupation, and Geography', *Economic History Review*, 2nd series, XXX (1977), no. 4, Tables 1–3, pp. 605–7.

17. Erickson, *British Industrialists*, Table 15, p. 45; see also David Ward, 'The Public Schools and Industry in Britain after 1870', *Journal of Contemporary History*, 2 (1967), no. 3.

18. W. L. Guttsman, *The British Political Elite* (London: Macgibbon & Kee, 1965), pp. 173–80.

19. This is explored more fully in D. C. Coleman, 'Gentlemen and Players', *Economic History Review*, 2nd series, XXVI (1973), no. 1.

20. Brown and Browne, *Century of Pay*, Appendix 3.

21. Keith Burgess, *The Origins of British Industrial Relations* (London: Croom Helm, 1975), especially pp. 44–5, 126–7, 191–200, 266–7.

22. *Capital and Labour*, 31 July 1878, p. 470.

23. Brown and Browne, *Century of Pay*, Appendix 3, where it is estimated that the cost of living had fallen by 20% during the 1880s.

24. S. Pollard, 'Trade Unions and the Labour Market, 1870–1914', *Yorkshire Bulletin of Economic and Social Research*, 17 (1965), no. 1, Table 1, p. 102.

25. Jürgen Kuczynski, *A Short History of Labour Conditions Under Industrial Capitalism* (London: Frederick Muller, 1972), pp. 82–3.

26. This has been recognised from different theoretical perspectives: see, for example, E. J. Hobsbawm, 'Custom, Wages and Work-load in Nineteenth-century

Industry', in the same author's, *Labouring Men. Studies in the History of Labour* (London: Weidenfeld & Nicolson, 1968); Rostow, *Investment*, p. 147.

27. B. C. M. Weekes, 'The Amalgamated Society of Engineers, 1880–1914. A Study of Trade Union Government, Politics and Industrial Policy', unpublished PhD thesis, University of Warwick, 1970, pp. 71–2.

28. D. W. Crowley, 'The Origins of the Revolt of the British Labour Movement from Liberalism, 1875–1906', unpublished PhD thesis, University of London, 1952, p. 12.

29. *Royal Commission on the Depression of Trade and Industry*, 1886 (XXIII), Third Report, Minutes of Evidence, p. 193.

30. Ibid., 1886 (XXII), Appendix D, pt II, p. 44.

31. Perkin, *Origins*, p. 423.

32. José Harris, *Unemployment and Politics* (Oxford: Clarendon Press, 1972), pp. 52–4.

33. Michael E. Rose, *The Relief of Poverty, 1834–1914* (London: Macmillan, 1972), p. 53.

34. D. J. Oddy, 'Working-Class Diets in Late Nineteenth Century Britain', *Economic History Review*, 2nd series, XXIII (1970), no. 2, pp. 317–20.

35. Anthony S. Wohl, 'The Bitter Cry of Outcast London', *International Review of Social History*, XIII (1968), pp. 235–6.

36. Helen Merrell Lynd, *England in the Eighteen-Eighties* (London: Frank Cass, 1968), p. 145.

37. Harris, *Unemployment*, p. 36.

38. Cited in O. R. McGregor, 'Social Research and Social Policy in the Nineteenth Century', *British Journal of Sociology*, 8 (1957), p. 153.

39. Calvin Woodard, 'Reality and Social Reform: the Transition from Laissez-Faire to the Welfare State', *Yale Law Review*, 72 (1962), no. 2, pp. 320–3.

40. A seminal discussion of this crisis is contained in Gareth Stedman Jones, *Outcast London. A Study of the Relationship Between Classes in Victorian Society* (Oxford: University Press, 1971).

41. Burgess, *Industrial Relations*.

42. V. L. Allen, 'The Trades Union Congress before Socialism, 1875–1886' in the same author's *The Sociology of Industrial Relations. Studies in Method* (London: Longmans, 1971).

43. *Royal Commission on the Depression of Trade and Industry*, 1886 (XXII), Appendix D, pt II, pp. 9, 17–18.

44. Hobsbawm, *Labouring Men*, pp. 323–4; Burgess, *Industrial Relations*, pp. 49 ff.

45. Hobsbawm, *Labouring Men*, pp. 385–63.

46. Burgess, *Industrial Relations*.

47. For a local study of this phenomenon see Robert Q. Gray, *The Labour Aristocracy in Victorian Edinburgh* (Oxford: University Press, 1976), pp. 57 ff.

48. Webb Collection E (Trade Unions), London School of Economics and Political Science, *Report of Trades' Conference*, Glasgow, January–March 1887, section B, v. XVII, pt 7.

49. Gray, *Labour Aristocracy*, pp. 118–20, 134.

50. E. H. Phelps Brown, *The Growth of British Industrial Relations* (London: Macmillan, 1959), pp. 4–5.

51. A stimulating treatment of the growing 'social apartness' of working-class life is contained in David Kynaston, *King Labour. The British Working Class, 1850–1914* (London: Allen & Unwin, 1976), pp. 100–2.

52. Gray, *Labour Aristocracy*, pp. 116–17.

53. Richard Price, 'The Working Men's Club Movement and Victorian Social Reform Ideology', *Victorian Studies*, XV (1971), pp. 132–9.

54. J. H. S. Kent, 'The Role of Religion in the Cultural Structure of the Late Victorian City', *Transactions of the Royal Historical Society*, 5th series, 23 (1973).

55. Noel. G. Annan, 'The Intellectual Aristocracy' in J. H. Plumb (ed.), *Studies in Social History* (London: Longmans, 1955), pp. 253 ff.

56. See, for example, Wohl, 'Outcast London'.

57. H. J. Hanham, *Elections and Party Management. Politics in the Time of Disraeli and Gladstone* (London: Longmans, 1959), pp. 125, 132–3.

58. H. J. Perkin, 'Land Reform and Class Conflict in Victorian Britain' in J. Butt and I. F. Clarke (eds.), *The Victorians and Social Protest* (Newton Abbot: David & Charles, 1973), pp. 206–11.

59. Cited in Lynd, *Eighteen-Eighties*, p. 142.

60. N. Soldon, 'Laissez-Faire as Dogma: The Liberty and Property Defence League, 1882–1914' in Kenneth D. Brown (ed.), *Essays in Anti-Labour History* (London: Macmillan, 1974).

61. John Cornford, 'The Transformation of Late Nineteenth Century Conservatism', *Victorian Studies*, VII (1963).

62. F. Parkin, 'Working Class Conservatism: A Theory of Political Deviance', *British Journal of Sociology*, 18 (1967), no. 3; for supporting evidence in late Victorian Edinburgh see Gray, *Labour Aristocracy*, pp. 176–80.

63. Stan Shipley, *Club Life and Socialism in Mid-Victorian London* (Oxford: Ruskin College History Workshop Pamphlet No. 5, 1971).

64. E. Welbourne, *The Miners' Unions of Northumberland and Durham* (Cambridge: University Press, 1923), pp. 204–5.

65. Brian Simon, *Education and the Labour Movement 1870–1920* (London: Lawrence & Wishart, 1974), pp. 204–5.

66. K. S. Inglis, 'English Nonconformity and Social Reform, 1880–1900', *Past and Present*, 13 (1958), pp. 79–82.

67. Susan Budd, 'The Loss of Faith in England 1850–1950', *Past and Present*, 36 (1967), pp. 124–5.

68. Paul Thompson, *Socialists, Liberals and Labour. The Struggle for London, 1885–1914* (London: Routledge & Kegan Paul, 1967), pp. 17–18.

69. See, for example, Tom Mann, *Memoirs* (London: Labour Publishing Co., 1923), pp. 30–1.

70. Simon, *Education*, p. 23.

71. Hobsbawm, *Labouring Men*, p. 236.

72. C. Tsuzuki, *H. M. Hyndman and British Socialism* (Oxford: University Press, 1961), p. 284.

73. Henry Collins, 'The Marxism of the Social Democratic Federation' in Asa Briggs and John Saville (eds.), *Essays in Labour History 1886–1923* (London: Macmillan, 1971), pp. 52–5.

74. Webb Collection E (Trade Unions), *Report of Trades' Conference*, Section B, v. XVII, pt 7.

75. N. Blewett, 'The Franchise in the U.K. 1885–1918', *Past and Present*, 32 (1965).

76. Thompson, *Struggle for London*, pp. 70–1.

77. M. K. Barker, 'The Formation of Liberal Party Policy, 1885–92', unpublished PhD thesis, University of Wales, 1972, p. 63.

78. *Annual Register*, 1885, pp. 145–6.

79. W. H. G. Armytage, 'The Railway Rates Question and the Fall of the Third Gladstone Ministry', *English Historical Review*, LXV (1950), no. 254.

80. Gordon L. Goodman, 'Liberal Unionism: The Revolt of the Whigs', *Victorian Studies*, III (1959), no. 2.

81. J. P. D. Dunbabin, 'Parliamentary Elections in Great Britain, 1886–1900. A Psephological Note', *English Historical Review*, LXXXI (1966), no. 81, is a detailed analysis of election results.

82. Harris, *Unemployment*, contains a thorough discussion of these events.

83. H. A. Clegg, Alan Fox, A. F. Thompson, *A History of British Trade Unions since 1889* (Oxford: University Press, 1964), vol. I, p. 1.

84. A. E. P. Duffy, 'New Unionism in Britain, 1889–1890: A Reappraisal', *Economic History Review*, 2nd series, XIV (1961–2), no. 2, is an effective critique of the commonly held distinction between 'Old' and 'New' Unionism.

85. Crowley, 'Origins of Revolt', pp. 321–2.

86. Stedman Jones, *Outcast London*.

87. Thompson, *Struggle for London*, pp. 39 ff.

88. Ibid., p. 49,

89. Hobsbawm, *Labouring Men*, p. 213; John Lovell, *Stevedores and Dockers. A Study of Trade Unionism in the Port of London, 1870–1914* (London: Macmillan, 1969), pp. 93–4.

90. Lovell, *Stevedores and Dockers*, pp. 99–101, for the confused beginnings of the strike.

91. Ibid., pp. 114–15.

92. Stedman Jones, *Outcast London*, pp. 317–18.

93. See, for example, E. L. Taplin, *Liverpool Dockers and Seamen 1870–1890* (University of Hull: Occasional Papers in Economic & Social History, no. 6, 1974); Crowley, 'Origins of Revolt', pp. 383–4.

94. Joseph Melling, 'Industrial Strife and Business Welfare Philosophy: The Case of the South Metropolitan Gas Company from the 1880's to the War', *Business History*, XXI (1979), no. 2, pp. 167–70.

95. P. S. Gupta, 'Railway Trade Unionism in Britain, c. 1880–1900', *Economic History Review*, 2nd series, XIX (1966), no. 1.

96. Burgess, *Industrial Relations*, pp. 200–3, has more details.

97. Ibid., pp. 54–5.

98. Roland Smith, 'A History of the Lancashire Cotton Industry between the years 1873 and 1896', unpublished PhD thesis, University of Birmingham, 1954, vol. II, pp. 684–5; see also Burgess, *Industrial Relations*, p. 271.

99. Crowley, 'Origins of Revolt', pp. 241–2.

100. Fred Reid, 'Keir Hardie's Conversion to Socialism' in Briggs and Saville.

101. Ibid., p. 44.

102. E. P. Thompson, 'Homage to Tom Maguire' in Briggs and Saville, is the source for the following discussion.

103. Ibid., cited p. 312 (footnote).

104. Lynd, *Eighteen-Eighties*, cited pp. 171–2.

105. Thompson, 'Tom Maguire', p. 251; Chris Wrigley, 'Liberals and the Desire for Working-class Representatives in Battersea, 1886–1922' in Kenneth D. Brown (ed.), *Essays in Anti-Labour History* (London: Macmillan, 1974).

106. Smith, 'Cotton Industry', vol. II, pp. 324, 344; *The Textile Mercury*, 7 December, 1889, p. 595.

107. Smith, 'Cotton Industry', vol. II, p. 494.

108. *Royal Commission on the Depression of Trade and Industry*, 1886 (XXI), First and Second Reports, Minutes of Evidence & Appendices A & B, pp. 90, 269, 380, 444, 625, 631 & 639; Arnstein, 'Survival of Aristocracy', p. 252.

109. A pioneering study of this group's importance is contained in Elie Halévy, *Imperialism and the Rise of Labour, 1895–1905* (New York: Barnes & Noble, 1961); for a more recent treatment see Bernard Semmel, *Imperialism and Social Reform* (London: Allen & Unwin, 1968).

CHAPTER 3

The Struggle for Control, 1890–1906

Labour and Economy: Unresolved Problems

The phase in the development of British capitalism between the 1880s and the First World War was one of intensifying contradictions. The growth of per capita incomes during the 1880s, despite persistently high levels of unemployment and evidence of widespread poverty, was sustained during the 1890s by the 'Home Boom' that marked the end of the 'Great Depression'. Yet there seems to have been a check to economic growth at the turn of the century and, thereafter, per capita incomes stagnated or even declined in real terms during the period down to 1914.[1] An explanation of this check to economic growth can be found in the failure of industrial profits and investment to recover from the depression of the 1880s, and thus increase incomes via the multiplier effect. It is true that the returns to capital, including profits overseas, were generally rising as a percentage of national income between the 1890s and 1914, but the rate of yield on capital in the industrial sector continued the downward trend that it had registered since the early 1870s, despite some recovery during the 1890s.[2] The impact of the Home Boom in the 1890s seems to have been transitory and heavily dependent on the expansion of building construction.[3] The rate of growth of industrial production was at its lowest point for the entire epoch 1847–1913 between the years 1900–7 and 1908–13, and in per capita terms there was an absolute decline in industrial production during the latter period.[4] This was related to the low rate of return on capital in the industrial sector, which did not encourage the expansion of physical capital invested in industry.[5]

What appears to have occurred is that the scope for maintaining the rate of profit in industry by using existing capitals more intensively, which had been widespread in the 1870s and 1880s, began to yield diminishing returns as the limits were reached for improving efficiency with established techniques. It is noteworthy, in this respect, that industry's unit wage costs that had fallen steadily since the 1870s rose almost continuously between 1896–7 and 1913, and more so, ominously, than in a rival economy like Germany.[6] Yet this was a period when there was little increase in money wages, and in real terms they actually declined.[7] The rise in Britain's overseas investment portfolio by 38 % during the years 1907–13 alone had the effect of stimulating demand for the products of the well-established export trades like cotton textiles, which suffered especially from technological stagnation, declining productivity and diminishing returns.[8] It is also clear that in the great overseas investment boom just prior to the First World War the outflow of funds was so great that it was unable to draw enough British goods in its wake to offset the drain on the gold reserves, thus forcing the Bank of England to apply restrictive policies in the form of a higher bank rate, particularly after 1905.[9] In this way, the prospects for increasing investment and employment at home were depressed.

While the overseas operations of Britain's finance houses reaped ever-increasing profits, and consequently strengthened the interdependence of Britain and the world economy, an analysis of the trends in the flow of imports and exports shows that the position of the economy in relation to world trade began steadily to deteriorate after 1890. By 1913, Britain was dependent on overseas supplies for seven-eighths of its raw materials (excluding coal), and more than one-half of its food supplies.[10] Yet the impact of rising tariffs, increasing self-sufficiency and growing competition in neutral markets combined to force the staple export trades to concentrate on the manufacture of specialised commodities, like steam coal and cotton textiles, which were especially dependent upon the economy's pre-eminence as the financier of world trade. The effect of overseas investment, in particular, was to strengthen Britain's dependence on exports that, relatively speaking, were shrinking as a proportion of the aggregate total of commodities entering world trade. The result was that industry became increasingly reliant on exporting products where overseas demand was rising less rapidly, while there was little diversification into the newer sectors of industries like chemicals and electricals that were a far more expansive sector of world trade, and which potentially could be expected to yield the highest rate of return.[11]

It is not surprising, therefore, that the period 1900–14 failed to yield any sustained growth in employment incomes. In real terms, the check to wages after 1900 was reinforced by the movement in the terms of trade against the industrialised countries in general, including Britain.[12] Britain's concentration on manufactured exports where demand was less resilient, compared with its almost insatiable appetite for imports, implied that import prices tended to move higher than export prices. Whereas in the case of the American and German economies, which were anyway less dependent upon imports than Britain, the effect on incomes of the unfavourable movement in the terms of trade was largely offset by their continued ability to increase productivity and keep down costs, in Britain the stagnation and then absolute decline in productivity meant that rising import prices were passed on directly to consumers in the form of higher prices, leading subsequently to falling real wages.[13] This was to become a major cause of labour unrest during the years immediately prior to the First World War.

An analysis of labour's relationship with British society must, therefore, take into account the comparative failure of the economic system to increase employment incomes, especially wages. The continued growth in the incomes of wealth-holders, on the other hand, consolidated the historically high degree of inequality between capital and labour that itself has been cited as an important cause of relatively low industrial investment during this period, especially in the expanding areas of standardised consumer goods production.[14] The share of wages in the national income fell steadily from the peak registered in 1893, until by 1913 wages constituted a smaller share of the national income than in 1870.[15] The rise in profits during these years appears to have had virtually no effect on wage levels.[16] A comparison of the relative shares of wages and capital in industrial per capita production shows that the trend continued to be clearly unfavourable to labour.[17] In both money and real terms, wages were rising more slowly in Britain than in other advanced economies after 1890 (with the possible exception of France), and it is significant that in contrast to the experience of Germany, Sweden and the USA, real wages in Britain actually fell during the period 1895–1913.[18]

Declining real wages were a result not only of comparatively low industrial investment and stagnant or falling productivity, which failed to offset the impact of price increases as the terms of trade moved against Britain, but were also a consequence of the persistently high rate of growth in the labour supply. The proportion of the resident population between the ages of 15 and 64 continued to grow by at least 10% each decade after 1870 until 1910, and the

abundance of the labour market even in skilled occupations discouraged the introduction of more capital-intensive and labour-
saving techniques.[19] While this contributed to the slowing down in
the economy's rate of growth, including the growth in employment
incomes, it did have a stabilising effect on the demand for labour
since the reduced pace of technological change and the persistence
of established production methods had a labour-using rather than
labour-saving effect. The loss of jobs attributable directly to technological displacement was generally limited although it was far
from negligible in certain trades. At the same time, the recovery in
commodity prices from the late 1890s increased demand for many of
Britain's traditional exports among primary producers abroad, and
this was directly beneficial in maintaining employment. The latter
was sustained subsequently by the boom in overseas investment that
drew exports in its wake. The result was that unemployment was
lower after 1895, compared with the late 1870s and 1880s, and this
helped stabilise money wages and especially earnings although these
were eventually to be overtaken by the rising trend of prices in the
years just prior to 1914.[20] The relatively tighter labour market
during the period 1895–1913, in conjunction with stagnant or
declining *real* wages and increasing inequality in the *distribution* of
income, led to a new phase of labour unrest, particularly after 1910.

The persistence of glaring inequalities during the first decade of
the century emphasises that the most basic problem of the economy
was not so much the generation of wealth but its 'equitable' distribution. While there are no really 'objective' criteria for determining
equity in income distribution in capitalist societies, perceptions of
what is equitable do change and these are related to how well-off
individuals see themselves in relation to others. For many working
people, the rising trend of prices was probably more important in its
effect on their perception of what was equitable than it was in
strictly objective terms since the fall in real wages before 1914 was
quite marginal, even if this did occur after decades of almost
continuous advance. It was this change that in itself may have had a
far more profound impact than the objective changes in living
standards might suggest. What contributed to a greater awareness
of inequality in the years before the First World War was that
despite the fact that the great majority of the population remained
wage-earners, occupations yielding significantly higher incomes
were expanding more rapidly, especially in the professions.[21] And
the traditionally high social status ascribed to these occupations

intensified the sense of low esteem or 'inferiority' of most categories of manual labour. Finally, the concentration of wealth-holding in London represented an agglomeration of wealth, power and privilege remote from the experience of most working people, although the spread of mass communications, particularly the popular press, made them increasingly aware of its existence.

Contemporary estimates of the concentration of wealth-holding in Britain, which have never been convincingly refuted, show that 13% of the population owned 92% of the national capital in 1911–13.[22] While property-owners were guaranteed rising incomes by the relative security of returns to fixed-interest bearing investments and capital appreciation, including assets overseas, wage-earners were exposed directly to the consequences of low industrial investment and falling productivity, which led to declining real wages as the terms of trade moved against Britain. In economic terms, the homogeneity of capital and labour in their respective class positions was probably never as great as in the period immediately before the First World War. In particular, home investment was not sufficiently high to resolve the problem of the residuum of under-employed casual labour living at or below subsistence level in the large cities, despite the comparative prosperity and lack of un-employment in the staple export trades. The number of vagrants and paupers in receipt of Poor Relief rose steadily after 1900 until 1911–12.[23] A comparison of the size of estates of rich and poor who died in an average year during this period emphasises the extremes of poverty in the midst of increasing wealth. Thus while the number of millionaires more than doubled in the London area alone between 1880–99 and 1900–14, and the estates of 27,500 of the richest individuals who died in the latter period were worth £257 million, the 'estates' of 686,000 of the poorest individuals deceased in the same period left only £29 million.[24] In addition to labour's growing sense of relative deprivation, therefore, there remained the problem of absolute want that was to become a particularly explosive social issue in the political context of 1906–14.

Confrontation in the Workplace

The benefits of a relatively tighter labour market during the period 1890–1914 are reflected in the changing distribution of trade union members in these years, and affected profoundly the course of

labour unrest. The distribution of trade unionists in Britain remained almost unchanged until just prior to the First World War,
notwithstanding the attention that has been focused on the New
Unionism. Trade union members tended to be those workers who
had established a tradition of organisation prior to the late 1880s,
employed mostly in the staple industries, while the superabundance
of the labour market continued to impede the unionisation of the
unskilled and semi-skilled in the large cities. Thus most of the
estimated 25 % rise in trade union membership between 1892 and
1906 was concentrated in metals, engineering and shipbuilding;
mining and quarrying; textiles; and building construction. In several
of these industries, trade unionism achieved a significant degree of
penetration. In shipbuilding, for example, union density rose from
36 % in 1888 to 60 % by 1901; in mining and quarrying, from 19 %
to 56 %; and, in cotton textiles, from 16 % to 35 % during the same
period.[25]

This extension of union membership was unable to prevent the
decline in the wages share of the national income after 1893 because
industries where the increase in union membership was heavily
concentrated were able to pass on to consumers in the form of
higher prices any wage rises they were forced to concede.[26] This was
in contrast to the situation obtaining in the 1870s and 1880s, which
was a period of falling prices and profits. The average pit-head price
of coal, for example, rose by about 20 % between 1892–3 and 1909,
and led to a spectacular increase in colliery profits after 1897–8.[27]
Cotton prices also recovered from the period of declining prices
between 1873 and 1896 at the turn of the century, and spinning
margins (defined as the difference between the price of raw cotton
and the price of yarn) staged a rapid rise after 1900.[28] The growing
profitability of the non-industrial commercial and financial sectors
of the economy, which tended not to be highly labour-intensive,
contributed further to the rise in the share of profits in the national
income. On the other hand, the difficulty in organising the unskilled
and semi-skilled neutralised a potentially important agent for raising the wages share of the national income during a period when
union density in a sector of the economy like transport was considerably less than 20 %.

Thus the character of British trade unionism in the early 1900s
remained typically 'Victorian' in terms of its composition, membership being confined largely to the staple industries that still enjoyed
a position of comparative prosperity in world markets. Yet even for

these relatively privileged grades of workers, the process of adjustment to changing market conditions led to the implementation by
employers of new strategies for more effectively controlling their
labour force. These included more organised forms of industrial
combination; attempts to limit the incidence of disputes by resort to
legal prosecution; the centralisation of conciliation and arbitration
procedures; the introduction of welfare schemes; and the implementation of an entire range of controls that later became known as
'scientific management'. The outcome was often to intensify and
widen the scope of labour unrest, which was to become increasingly
menacing in the years just prior to the First World War.

The creation of wider and more effective means of combination
among employers dates from the late 1880s when the upsurge in
labour militancy associated with the New Unionism led to the
formation of industrywide groupings like the Shipping Federation
and the Mining Association of Great Britain. Similar bodies were
also established in the cotton and engineering trades. The new
machinery for collective bargaining subsequently adopted confirmed the prevailing view that voluntaryism should be the guiding
principle for settling disputes between labour and capital, with the
minimum of state intervention and direction. This was given official
approval by the majority report of the Royal Commission on
Labour published in 1894 and was the basis for the Conciliation Act
of 1896. The latter authorised the Board of Trade to investigate
disputes, try to bring the parties together and provide a
government-appointed conciliator, but only on condition that this
was acceptable to the parties in dispute.[29] The conciliator could
make recommendations but his decision was not legally binding on
either employers or workers. It is doubtful whether the guiding
principle of voluntaryism in industrial relations would have continued to be so generally accepted if employers had been less
successful in containing the labour unrest of the 1890s and early
1900s by their own efforts.

The need for more effective means of dealing with labour unrest
after 1890 arose directly from workers' changing experience of the
labour process itself. The efforts to make existing capitals more
productive took new and more sophisticated forms, as the earlier
strategy of using labour more intensively in combination with
established forms of work organisation began to yield diminishing
returns. Job routines were increasingly subdivided into specialised
operations in an attempt to achieve the maximum managerial

control over the speed of work. Examples of this included the phasing out of subcontractors in industries like coal-mining and engineering, and replacing them with forms of piecework or payment by results negotiated directly between the individual worker and management. This greatly increased the authority of foremen and supervisors.[30] It was often associated with the introduction of scientific management or 'Taylorism' (after its American protagonist), which involved the 'measurement' of the time and effort required at each stage of production in order that 'optimal' levels of performance might be laid down and the expected output predetermined with more precision.[31] The general aim of scientific management was to raise labour productivity to its optimum level permitted by existing techniques of manufacture. This frequently led to the breaking down of customary lines of demarcation between skills, in the pursuit of more 'flexible' manning arrangements, and the circumvention of apprenticeship regulations reserving certain work for skilled operatives, especially in engineering and building construction.[32] The spread of payment by results methods of wage determination, like the premium bonus system, gave employers greater control over the production process by the exercise of rate-fixing, enabling managers to reduce progressively 'the rate for the job' until the worker achieved the optimal level of output. But this provoked bitterness and resentment among many skilled workers who considered scientific management to be as much a threat to their social status as injurious in strictly economic terms.[33]

A survey of industrial disputes during the period 1900–13 shows that conflict over 'managerial prerogatives' arising from changes in working arrangements or rules became increasingly common.[34] In the metals, engineering and shipbuilding trades, disputes of this kind involved more than 20% of the workers affected by all stoppages. And it is significant that the employers' efforts to raise labour productivity by strengthening managerial control failed to yield any sustained increase in real wages after 1900, in contrast to the substantial growth in real wages taking place in previous decades. The precise causal relation that this had with labour unrest is problematical, although it has been suggested that when the individual worker's involvement, responsibility and creativity in the labour process declines, he is more likely to concentrate on maximising his income so as to enjoy to the full his private life outside the work situation.[35] It may also lead to greater solidarity as the opportunities for individual self-fulfilment at work diminish.[36] Thus conflict over managerial prerogatives can readily 'spill over' into other areas of disputes, like wages and hours of work. It was this that helped persuade employers to agree to increasingly elaborate forms of collective bargaining and explains in part the growing popularity of welfare schemes.[37]

While these developments were concentrated in industries where workers had an established tradition of trade union organisation, the bargaining strength of the so-called 'New Unions' proved more transitory. The persistence of a large residuum of casual under-employed, which dwindled only during periods of exceptionally good trade, limited the opportunities for regular employment that is the key prerequisite for the development of group solidarity and permanent trade union organisation. Membership of the Dockers' Union, for example, numbered 56,000 in 1890 but had fallen to 22,913 by 1892, and in 1900 it was as low as 13,829.[38] Similarly, the Gasworkers' Union with 60,000 members in 1890 failed to retain its membership that fell to 36,108 in 1892, and it was 47,979 in 1900.[39] Trade unions in the transport sector as a whole recruited 12 % of its labour force in 1901, compared with 5 % prior to the upturn in trade in 1888, but this was still considerably below the degree of union organisation in most of the staple industries. The significance of the New Unionism in the short-term was in the reaction it provoked from employers. The success of new employers' combinations like the Shipping Federation was to have a 'demonstration effect' on other industries where the stronger bargaining position of workers could be expected to offer much stiffer resistance. What gave the employers' counter-attack its rationale were the tactics of the un-skilled and semi-skilled unions that sought to establish control over hiring and firing, thus threatening the basic prerogatives of all employers as property-owners. It was also argued, with some justifi-cation, that productivity fell markedly where union monopoly over job control had been secured.[40]

The systematic introduction of non-union labour in a conscious attempt to destroy the New Unionism followed the setting up of the Shipping Federation in September 1890, which was an alliance of the major shipping companies. In November, the federation terminated the agreement settling the London dock strike of 1889 and refused to deal any further with union representatives. A series of disputes ensued and the employers successfully exploited sectional anti-pathies between the Stevedores' and Dockers' Unions, with the result that the latter was virtually extinct in London by 1906.[41] The unions were also defeated elsewhere as in Liverpool, for example, and this led to the creation of an alliance between the Liverpool employers and the London-based Shipping Federation.[42] Union membership held up better among the gas workers in municipally-owned provincial works like Birmingham where the 48-hour week was secured, although less so in privately-owned companies like the South Metropolitan.[43] On the railways, too, an 'all-grades' movement seeking union recognition from employers was defeated during 1896–7 when the companies broke the railwaymen's united front by granting concessions to particular groups like the goods guards.[44] The relative failure of New Unionism to secure the gains made in 1888–90 is indicative of the effectiveness of *organised* employers in manipulating the market for unskilled and semi-skilled labour to their advantage during the 1890s. This was part of the general intensification of class conflict after 1890 involving an increasingly aggressive response from organisations representing both capital and labour. It was most obviously manifest in the legal offensive against trade unionism that was to culminate in the Taff Vale decision, but led also to a succession of major disputes in the staple industries.

Again, it was the difficulty of the New Unions in conducting industrial disputes that was the occasion for the legal offensive against trade unionism as a whole. The fact that no more than the most militant or strategically placed of the unskilled and semi-skilled were unionised, leaving the majority unorganised even during the membership peak of 1889–90, made the task of picketing an especially difficult one given the abundant supply of potential strike-breakers. Accusations of union 'coercion' and 'tyranny' in the tactics adopted to deter non-unionists from applying for work during disputes reflected the prevailing assumptions about 'freedom of contract'.[45] Yet however much employers and their apologists might appeal in abstract terms to the inviolability of individual 'freedom' and 'liberty', it was acknowledged that the realities of the situation demanded more *collective* organisation and not less. In the process, employers too came to appreciate the value of 'coercion'. The pressure applied by the Shipping Federation, for example, on the leading shipping company in Hull, which had previously bargained amicably with the Dockers' Union, was eventually successful in forcing the firm to rejoin the federation. This united front of employers was able subsequently to transform what had been the best-organised port in the country into 'a stronghold of Free

Labour' by the summer of 1893.[46] This mobilisation of the employers' power involved the systematic importation of non-unionists via the federation's 'free' British Labour Exchange, in close co-operation with the local authorities who provided police and military protection and openly recruited able-bodied labourers seeking Poor Relief for employment in the docks.[47] The Shipping Federation's special Labour Department had the particular responsibility for organising strike-breaking on a national scale, and by the early 1900s had taken control of 50 fictitious working-class bodies as recruiting agencies for free labour.

The employers' efforts to set up alternatives to trade unionism gave rise directly to the establishment of widely-based groupings like the Free Labour Protection Association, which received support from coal-owners like Sir William Lewis and the Tyneside engineering employer, Sir Benjamin Browne. The more thoroughly studied National Free Labour Association, formed in 1893, was not simply a puppet of the employers but was run by a miscellaneous group of renegade trade unionists who may have registered as many as 850,000 workmen as free labourers between 1893 and 1913.[48] The association's sources of financial support remain obscure although it is almost certain that it received donations from employers, in addition to the fees it charged for supplying strike-breakers in particular disputes. The association seems to have been most successful in breaking small-scale strikes, mostly involving unskilled and semi-skilled labour in the docks, and intervened decisively in the Taff Vale dispute by providing workers who had signed a contract committing themselves to employment, which led subsequently to the famous legal case against the Amalgamated Society of Railway Servants for inducing breach of contract.[49] The National Free Labour Association was also active in other industries like the building trade where a special conference convened in June 1894 led to the establishment of the 'Independent Carpenters' and Joiners' Protection Society', a client of the association that tried to break the hold of the recently formed Building Trades' Federation over London's building workers.[50] After 1890, the Liberty and Property Defence League that had been active in the previous decade in defending the rights of property began to function increasingly as an umbrella organisation in mobilising the employers' counter-attack against labour unrest.[51]

In their attempts to deal with rising labour militancy, employers received the support of the legal system that viewed with alarm the efforts by the unions to obtain a degree of monopoly control over the labour market, by resorting to tactics like the mass picket. The historic roots of the law, giving priority to the protection of property, led the courts to take an increasingly hostile line in their attitude towards the recognised immunity of trade unions from legal action, involving the pursuit of damages incurred as a result of an industrial dispute. The basis for this legal attack on the status of trade unions, as established by the Trade Union Act of 1871 and the Conspiracy and Protection of Property Act of 1875, was an ambiguity in the law concerning what in practice constituted 'intimidation' and 'malicious' behaviour in trade disputes, which could be proceeded against in the courts.[52] The sensitivity of judge-made law to the changing mood of ruling opinion, alarmed by the aggressive tactics and 'socialistic' inclinations of the New Unionism, led to a succession of legal decisions that were steadily to undermine the unions' immunities and culminated finally in the famous Taff Vale decision of 1901.

The most important of these were *Temperton v. Russell* (1893), *Trollope & Sons v. London Building Trades Federation* (1896) and *Lyons v. Wilkins* (1899). These together effectively denied the unions the right to organise a mass picket that might cause potential loss for an employer concerned, without incurring the risk of civil action in pursuit of damages. The important point about these cases was their implication that the unions could now be regarded as corporate bodies, which could be sued for tortious acts committed on their behalf, although this had been expressly denied by previous legislation. The accumulation of precedents was sufficient, however, to justify the successful action taken in 1901 by the Taff Vale Railway Company against the Amalgamated Society of Railway Servants following a strike in August 1900. This ended with the union being ordered to pay £23,000 in settlement of damages to the company as a result of its attempts to persuade strike-breakers to leave their employment, thus causing the employer loss of revenue. A further decision in respect of *Quinn v. Leathem*, concluded shortly afterwards, confirmed the right of an employer to sue a trade union in its corporate identity for damages resulting from the threat to strike a customer of the employer, unless he stopped trading with him, as a means of forcing the employer to dismiss his non-union labour. The outcome was that even a threat to strike, or impose a boycott, would make a trade union liable to civil action for damages, either real or potential. These legal decisions set a precedent not only for the widespread introduction of free labour, which threatened especially the unions of unskilled and semi-skilled workers, but trade unions as a body could now be taken to the courts by employers for damages incurred as a result of industrial disputes. The implications of this state of affairs in terms of the political stance of the unions were to be far reaching.

Despite the publicity attracted by the New Unions, and the more profound threat to trade unionism as a whole posed by the changing climate of legal opinion, it was in the staple export industries where the biggest disputes were fought during the 1890s. Workers in these trades continued to be subject to more intensive labour utilisation, as firms sought to raise profit margins from the low levels of the 1880s, yet unemployment had fallen dramatically in the late 1880s, and although it rose again during 1892–3, the rest of the 1890s saw the downward trend of unemployment renewed. Besides this relatively favourable market situation of workers in industries where the bulk of trade unionists were still concentrated, the labour unrest of the late 1880s had witnessed the dissemination of socialist ideas as well as a new spirit of militancy, which could not fail to influence workers with an established tradition of organisation. Employers were also aware of the crucial problem of falling productivity, which made them particularly sensitive to the level of their wage costs. What was required was an aggressive reassertion of managerial authority as a means of persuading labour to accept wages and working conditions that were compatible with industry's market situation. The conflict this provoked gave rise to new forms of resolution, especially the development of more centralised procedures for collective bargaining. These aimed to limit labour unrest, maintain managerial authority in the workplace, and generally keep wage costs under control.

The resolve of employers faced its first and perhaps stiffest test in the coal industry.[53] The trend of falling prices and wage reductions that had undermined collective bargaining in the coal industry after 1873–4 reached its nadir during the years 1886–7. An overall revival of trade was required to ease competitive pressures and sustain efforts to increase trade union membership, and this was especially necessary in the inland coalfields in contrast to the coastal districts where export demand had been more resilient during the long years of depression. The old-established Miners' National Union, dominated by the colliers' associations in Northumberland and Durham, enjoyed a comparatively privileged position and remained loyal to the 'class harmony' approach to industrial relations embodied in the sliding scale.[54] In the inland coalfields, however, schemes to restrict output gradually gave way to the demand for a legally enacted eight-hour day as a means of reducing unemployment, preventing 'overproduction' and maintaining coal prices; and a militant wages policy came increasingly to reflect a desire for a 'minimum standard' of life, irrespective of the fluctuations in coal prices. Both demands were indicative of the spread of socialist ideas, but they posed a fundamental challenge to the prerogatives of employers in managing the industry according to their estimation of how it might be expected to yield the maximum profit. The official leadership of the Miners' National Union also found demands for the eight-hour day and a minimum standard of life unacceptable.

The foundations for a new union organising miners in the inland districts had been laid during the years 1888–90 when an increase in coal prices formed the basis for a succession of wage movements that raised rates by some 40%. The result of this remarkable success was a series of delegate conferences during 1889, giving birth to the Miners' Federation of Great Britain (MFGB). This initially represented colliers in Yorkshire, Nottinghamshire, Derbyshire, Lancashire, North Wales, Staffordshire, Warwickshire and Leicestershire. The potential threat of this new organisation with its successful background of proven militancy was not lost on the coalowners who agreed subsequently to federate, and this body represented each of the regional owners' associations except the sliding scale districts of South Wales, Northumberland and Durham remaining outside the MFGB. Employers in the coal industry had clearly to resort to different tactics from those used to combat New Unionism because large-scale strike breaking was generally not practicable in relatively isolated and homogeneous mining communities. It appeared more sensible to head off militancy by conciliation rather than confrontation. A suitable instrument was to hand in the form of the Conciliation Board, which had served the industry so well in the sliding-scale districts of Northumberland and Durham, not least because it conceded the basic trade union demand for recognition. Conciliation Boards were subsequently established in each of the county constituents of the MFGB during 1888 to formalise wage standards and make adjustments to them. These consisted of equal number of owners and miners' representatives, together with a permanent independent chairman who had a casting vote in case of disagreement.

The apparent willingness of employers in the coal industry to opt for conciliation rather than confrontation as a means of resolving disputes should not imply that labour unrest was negligible or absent. In fact, one of the biggest disputes to take place during the 1890s was the lock-out of 1893 affecting 300,000 miners in the inland coalfields.[55] Its underlying cause was the fall in coal prices after 1890, estimated by the owners to have been in the order of 35% by 1893, and led to the demand for an overall reduction in wages of 25% in the districts covered by the Miners' Federation. The latter's refusal to agree resulted in a general lock-out, beginning in the last week of July 1893 and lasting until the following November. The settlement of this dispute created a Conciliation Board for the entire federated area, similar to those already extant in each of the districts. This concession of collective bargaining did not involve the coal-owners in any significant embarrassment. The Conciliation Board was authorised to make percentage adjustments to basic rates negotiated in the various districts, but the miners' claim for a minimum wage was rejected outright. The movement of coal prices continued to determine miners' wages, thus protecting the owners' profit margins when prices fell, while the Conciliation Board could do nothing to prevent the owners from cutting labour costs by resorting to other expedients like short-time working that could substantially reduce the miners' actual earnings.[56] Many miners became convinced that the working of conciliation boards meant 'collective bargaining' on the employers' terms since they were prevented from making the most of years of rising prices but were unable to check loss of earnings caused by short-time working. Rank-and-file discontent and unofficial strikes were widespread during the boom of 1899–1901, for example, when the Conciliation Board imposed limits on wage increases, and it is no surprise to discover that profits rose substantially after 1895.[57]

In addition to the wages question, meanwhile, the Miners' Federation had even less success with its other main objective, to obtain the eight-hour day by legal enactment. The coal-owners' representatives in Parliament claimed that any reduction in hours would aggravate the already serious problems of declining productivity and rising labour costs, and they cited as well the hoary argument against legislative interference with the working conditions of adult males. As late as 1905, only two of the major coalfields that were outside the Miners' Federation—Northumberland and Durham—worked their miners fewer than eight hours per

shift, and these districts had enjoyed this privilege prior to 1890.[58]
The 1890s had thus witnessed the development of collective bargaining in the coal industry, which especially in the inland districts
had been quite successful in resolving labour unrest, without requiring the employers to sacrifice any of their prerogatives as property-
owners.

Cotton-spinning and the engineering trade were two other of
Britain's staple industries where the outcome of major disputes
produced a settlement that was not unfavourable to the interests of
employers. In cotton spinning, the newly formed Federation of
Master Cotton Spinners notified their operatives that a decline in
yarn prices, following the revival of 1889–91, justified a 5% reduction in basic rates. It is not clear whether the employers actually
believed this would appreciably ease their difficulties or whether
they anticipated that it would lead to a large-scale stoppage and
thus fulfil their real intention of clearing 'surplus' stocks in order to
push up prices.[59] The Oldham limited companies, in particular,
wanted a showdown and many firms looked forward to it as a
means of checking the rising discontent of their operatives and
generally reasserting managerial prerogatives.[60] The operatives,
meanwhile, were becoming dissatisfied with their role of sacrificial
lamb to the 'natural laws' of political economy, and influenced by a
growing socialist presence in the cotton districts, were opposed to
any reduction in wages. John Brown Tattersall, the Secretary of the
Masters' Federation, spoke of the increasing danger of socialism and
referred to 'men of small intelligence and large pockets' who were
described as 'a public nuisance which requires to be suppressed'.[61]

The lock-out that ensued during 1892–3 was settled by the
Brooklands Agreement establishing new machinery for collective
bargaining in cotton-spinning. This gave the Amalgamated
Association of Operative Cotton Spinners, representing about
20,000 senior minders, effective control over the operatives' participation in the agreement, which also affected the large majority of
subordinate piecer assistants and other ancillary grades who had no
share in drawing up the settlement and little say in its practical
working. Although the Brooklands Agreement was of immediate
benefit to all workers in the spinning section since it cut the wage
reduction demanded by employers from 5% to 2.9%, its procedure
for settling disputes confirmed the privileged position of the senior
minders in relation to the large majority of operatives in the trade.
Any mill grievance, for example, had to pass through a three-stage

disputes machinery, culminating in a joint committee of workers and employers' representatives sitting in Manchester. The delays arising as grievances were dealt with allowed firms to reduce costs by increasing workloads or using inferior raw cotton, for example, without fear of official strike action, although most operatives did not share at all in the additional allowances, often amounting to 15s weekly, extracted by the senior minders from employers in compensation for worsening conditions and loss of earnings. This left employers and senior minders a free hand in operating a system of 'coexploitation', affecting the large majority of operatives who had little or no control over their wages or working conditions. The employers could only gain from this state of affairs. After the lock-out of 1892–3, the number of disputes was less than half the average prevailing in the late 1880s.[62] Firms were able to maximise their share of the industry's reviving prosperity after 1896, whilst wages were held down by the ceiling on increases imposed by the Brooklands Agreement.

The engineering industry was also marked by rising tensions between capital and labour, leading to the lock-out of 1897–8.[63] A more competitive market environment, especially overseas, justified new forms of labour-saving investment and working arrangements, which had the effect of undermining the relatively privileged position of the fitters and turners who dominated the Amalgamated Society of Engineers (ASE), by far the largest and most powerful union in the industry. Skilled labour substitution eroded apprenticeship and led to an influx of unskilled workers into the industry. Firms also claimed that their 'almost automatic' machines made piecework the best method of increasing efficiency, and payment by results spread rapidly during the 1890s. Yet workers claimed that this encouraged skilled-labour substitution and systematic overtime. Moreover, a semi-skilled machinist paid by results could produce more and often earn as much as a time-served fitter and turner paid on an hourly basis. There was also the complaint that piecework enabled employers to adjust rates at will, without regard to collective agreements. The industrial basis of rising labour militancy in the engineering industry was mobilised by committed socialists like John Burns and Tom Mann who wished to see the ASE transformed into a genuinely industrial union, recruiting workers from every grade of skill, in order to challenge more effectively the employers' prerogatives to do as they liked with their 'property'. In 1896, the socialists achieved a notable victory when George Barnes, a member of the Independent Labour Party, was elected as ASE General Secretary.

As the militants took control of the ASE in certain areas, they concentrated on the eight-hours issue, although this often linked to other questions. One reason for this was that systematic overtime, commonly associated with the introduction of capital-intensive technology, was widespread in the 1890s and acted as a drag on efforts to raise basic wage rates. It was also urged that the eight-hours limit would reduce unemployment that was aggravated further by skilled-labour substitution. But the employers regarded the demand as an unacceptable invasion of their 'power to manage', and they recognised that it was related to other issues like the manning of new machinery, which posed an even more fundamental threat to their authority. It was in response to a growing number of local disputes over questions like piecework, apprenticeship ratios and manning arrangements that led the employers' associations to combine in 1896 to form the Engineering Employers' Federation. They were intent on forcing a showdown with the ASE, resulting in the nationwide lock-out of 1897–8.

The lock-out that began at the end of July 1897 lasted until January of the following year and ended in humiliation for the ASE. The eight-hours demand was lost outright. The defeat was indicative of the ASE's failure to obtain wider support from the majority of workers in the industry who were not 'skilled' according to its own criteria, and thus not eligible for membership, and its position was undermined further by the refusal of related unions like the Boilermakers' Society to strike in support. The isolation of the ASE was underlined by the fact that although its members' absence from work slowed down production this was not sufficient to stop it altogether, and the National Free Labour Association claimed to have kept going 20 of the largest firms in London alone with supplies of non-union labour. Yet this mobilisation of the employers' strength was not intent on destroying trade unionism in the industry since most firms realised that in the long term the co-operation of skilled ASE members remained essential. What they sought was to define clearly the 'proper' functions of trade unionism, insisting on 'no interference with the management of business', which implied acceptance of the employers' right to hire non-unionists and introduce piecework. This was substantially achieved in the settlement that ended the lock-out.[64] There was also a 'Provisions for Avoiding Disputes' clause designed to prevent local militants from taking unofficial action without approval of the ASE Executive. This settlement was the basis for resolving disputes in the engineering industry, which as later amended survived until the end of the 1960s. The decade 1898–1908 was one of relative industrial peace when employers usually got disputes settled on terms favourable to themselves. In the 1902 Carlisle Agreement, for example, the employers were able to persuade the ASE Executive to recognise their right to introduce the premium bonus system—a productivity-linked method of wage payment—despite rank-and-file opposition leading to unofficial strikes.[65] Thus the forms of collective bargaining introduced in the engineering industry had the effect of safeguarding rather than undermining employers' prerogatives.

Political Outcomes: Class Conflict and its Resolution

The mobilisation of the employers' counter-attack to the challenge of labour in the industrial sphere, which had achieved a remarkable degree of success by the end of the 1890s, created new forms of *class* organisation representing the wider interests of capital and labour. This had significant political implications. Additional impetus was given to the process of class polarisation that had been restructuring Britain's political system since the 1880s, and was increasingly commented upon by contemporary observers. The *Spectator*, for example, noted in 1894:[66]

> The upper section of society is becoming dangerously unanimous...The squires are as single-minded as the peers, and so in the main are the new millionaires, the great merchants, the whole class down to a much lower stratum than is usually believed, of what may be called 'solid men.'

This 'unanimity' was now manifest in direct intervention into the political arena by organisations like the Liberty and Property Defence League, which in 1891 was responsible for setting up the London Ratepayers Defence League to lead opposition to the Progressives on the London County Council, and its Press Correspondence Department was active after 1895 in circulating propaganda.[67] The National Free Labour Association was also active politically, claiming responsibility for the defeat of four parliamentary candidates whose views it suspected in the 1895 General Election.[68]

Labour's limited gains from the industrial confrontations of the 1890s, on the other hand, emphasised that its aspirations could not be realised by resort to struggle at the workplace alone. Yet Britain's political institutions continued to exclude much of the working class from effective participation in parliamentary decision-making. It has been estimated that even after the electoral reforms of 1884–5, only 28% of all adults had the right to vote and about 44% of males over 21 years of age were still disenfranchised.[69] As late as 1912, the number of disenfranchised males may have been as high as 4.8 millions and, moreover, the working-class vote was concentrated largely in industrial towns with comparatively few representatives.[70] A study of Lancashire politics during this period has stressed the importance of financial support obtained from membership in one or other of the major parties in enabling lodgers to get their claim to the vote recognised by the barristers and JPs who ran the revision courts.[71] Elected political office itself did not bear a regular income except at the highest levels of government, which was a further constraint on the ability of wage-earners to pursue political careers. It is thus no surprise to find that in the 1900 Parliament only 21 out of a total of 670 MPs were clearly identified as working class, in comparison with 227 who had been pupils at public schools and 255 who had attended either Oxford or Cambridge.[72]

At the same time, the Liberal Party's massive defeat in the 1895 General Election highlighted the predicament of Liberalism in its efforts to present itself as the party of the 'people', rather than one representing a particular class. Deepening class divisions since the 1880s were making this ideal difficult to sustain, and was reflected in problems of finance, organisation and policy. After 1895, the Tory domination of south and central England was complete, thriving on the support it obtained from the growing wealth of the commercial and financial plutocracy centred on London and the home counties.[73] The Liberal Party suffered as a result and saw its strength recede to the Celtic fringes and its traditional strongholds in the industrial north where it was heavily dependent on local industrial families like the Peases and the Brunner-Mond connection. Even in these areas, the cost of contesting elections was becoming enormous and brought J. A. Pease, in particular, to the brink of bankruptcy in 1903. The funds required for electioneering in large conurbations like London placed an almost impossible burden on the party's resources.

Liberalism's reliance on its old-established connections also made the task of developing new policies more difficult. The caucus system based on alliances of local notables was increasingly incapable of maintaining the party's presence between elections, which required large numbers of full-time agents whom it could ill afford. The Liberal strategy of concentrating on issues appealing to the 'good sense' of the electorate, whilst eschewing details of everyday organisation, failed to appreciate that questions like Home Rule and church disestablishment had little to offer most voters, and even less potential in terms of the working-class non-electors who had commonly been the raw material for Liberal-sponsored agitation out of doors. The much publicised Newcastle Programme of 1891 was an indication of Liberalism's fear that it was losing working-class support, yet this differed little from Gladstone's 'umbrella' of the 1880s and evaded issues like the eight-hour day and unemployment, while it rejected the need for more working-class representation in Parliament on the grounds that the interests of 'community' came before that of 'class'. Labour leaders who were keen to co-operate with the Liberals were steadily disillusioned by the attitude of the constituency caucuses who continued to opt for 'solid' candidates of local standing and pass over men with experience of working-class leadership.[74] In the 1890s, the limits of Liberal 'Social Radicalism' hastened the growth of independent labour politics, notwithstanding the constraints of the electoral system, as the interests of capital and property consolidated their class position.

Although there is substantial evidence to support the argument for increasing working-class 'solidification' since the late 1870s, both at the workplace and in the community, it was by no means inevitable that this should have produced an independent labour party, let alone a specifically 'socialist' one. Among the unskilled and semi-skilled, for example, trade unionism was confined to the fortunate minority who were regularly employed, and they were distinguished from the majority of casual 'unemployables' most of whom were non-electors. The emergence of new forms of differentiation that continued to divide the working class applied also to the staple industries where the development of collective bargaining served to confirm the comparatively privileged position of workers like the senior minders in cotton-spinning. The latter retained much of their traditional authority at the point of production as well as their wage differentials, even if it was the employers who benefited most from the new arrangements designed to resolve industrial conflict. At the same time, the power and prestige associated with the labour aristocracy's control of labour's self-help institutions in the working-class community remained remarkably resistant to economic and social change. The working class in general was also subjected to a propaganda offensive from organisations like the National Free Labour Association. This had particular impact among many unskilled and semi-skilled workers like the 'machine men' in the engineering industry who were portrayed as the victims of the craft exclusiveness of the Amalgamated Society of Engineers, and aimed to discredit trade union militancy in general. Then there was the wider appeal of imperialism appealing to workers in cotton textiles, for example, where colonial trade was important, and this received support from working-class newspapers as well as the new popular press.[75] The presentation of imperialism as a 'bread-and-butter' issue yielded significant electoral advantages for the Tories who were most closely identified with an aggressive policy of colonial expansion.

The advocates of independent labour politics thus faced an uphill struggle given the anomalies of the electoral system, the continued fragmentation of the working class making it vulnerable to dominant ideologies, and the inertia resulting from accepted practices and loyalties. And much of the socialists' failure to widen the scope of their popular appeal stemmed from their theoretical and tactical perspectives. The Social Democratic Federation, for example, had to say the least a very ambivalent attitude towards working in co-operation with labour organisations like the trades unions because they were 'non-socialist', despite the fact that many of its members worked actively in their unions, and the separation made subsequently by the SDF between party and union confined it to relative isolation and ineffectiveness.[76] The other organisation regarding itself as identifiably socialist in the 1890s was the Fabian Society. Yet its tactic of 'permeating' existing political groupings, justified by its rejection of the theory of surplus value and the necessity of class conflict, led it into an alliance with the Liberal Party since it refused to admit that labour acting independently could achieve socialism.[77]

The relative isolation of committed socialists during the 1890s and early 1900s was especially important since this period coincided with the formative years in the development of the Independent Labour Party (ILP). The problem for socialists like Blatchford who chose to work within the ILP was to secure its commitment to socialism based upon a generalised class-consciousness. To this end,

Blatchford wanted to see established a United Socialist Party, formed by a fusion of groups including the ILP and the SDF. Yet the ILP leadership, particularly Keir Hardie, rejected the SDF's campaign of 'class war' and its implications of violent revolution.[78] Hardie's expressly ethical if not explicitly religious conception of social relations, reflecting his Congregationalist background, struck a responsive chord in working-class experience and has led to the observation that the ILP was nothing more than 'a new religion—a heresy'.[79] A recent study of the ILP in Yorkshire has located its early activists like Philip Snowden in 'the mainstream of radical dissent' who rejected a class analysis of labour politics.[80] Snowden's conception of socialism, for example, was 'but the application of moral and Christian principles to commercial relationships'.

Yet if the prospects for socialism appeared dim, the very success of the employers' counter-attack during the 1890s lent weight to the opinions of those who argued that political power was increasingly necessary to protect and improve labour's industrial position. On the railways, the failure of the Amalgamated Society of Railway Servants' rank-and-file movement to obtain union recognition during 1897–8 led its General Secretary, the non-ILP Richard Bell, to table a motion at the 1899 TUC instructing its Parliamentary Committee to co-operate with other 'working-class organisations' in convening a special conference, with a view to increasing the number of 'labour' members in the next Parliament. This proposal was duly accepted and led to a conference in February 1900 of delegates representing about 500,000 trade unionists, as well as political organisations like the ILP and SDF. The outcome was the setting up of the Labour Representation Committee (LRC), composed of seven trade union members, two each from the ILP and SDF, and one Fabian, with Ramsay MacDonald of the ILP as Secretary. Hardie was the chief tactician behind the scenes who managed to get the committee to agree to work for the establishment of 'a distinct Labour group' in Parliament. But this was left to pursue policies of its own choosing, with recognition of its right to co-operate with any other party, in contrast to an SDF resolution that was rejected calling for 'a distinct party' prepared to wage 'class war'. Opposition to the latter was led by the ILP delegates. The union officials comprising the majority of delegates were especially concerned to preserve the independence of their own organisations, and not allow socialist groups like the SDF to get control of the committee.[81]

During 1900–1, 41 unions representing 353,070 workers affiliated to the LRC—equivalent to 29 % of TUC membership. Yet it was the impact of the Taff Vale decision, marking the climax to the legal offensive of the previous decade, that transformed the LRC into a genuinely representative body. When the actual figure for damages was announced in January 1903—amounting to £30,000 including costs—the precedent established posed a serious threat to the very existence of trade unionism. This did more than anything else to increase affiliation to the LRC to 956,025 by 1903–4, including now the major unions like the Amalgamated Society of Engineers and the United Textile Workers' Association.[82] The ILP-led Labour Representation Committee had thus acquired almost fortuitously rather than by design a substantial measure of control over labour's political voice. Although three LRC-sponsored candidates were elected to Parliament, its political fund that was based on a levy of a penny each year from every affiliated union member remained insufficient to run Labour candidates on a large scale. The record of labour members during the years 1900–5 shows that they usually voted with the Liberals on issues like fiscal policy, education and opposition to the annexation of the Boer Republics, which is hardly surprising given the nonconformist background of most of them.[83]

The links between the LRC and the Liberals were formalised as a result of secret negotiations during 1903 between Herbert Gladstone, the Liberal Chief Whip, and Ramsay MacDonald.[84] This led to an agreement whereby Liberal headquarters promised to use its influence on local caucuses to dissuade them from nominating their own candidates in about 30 seats where the LRC hoped to run its own men. The moderating effect this had on LRC policy was profound. In a memorandum from Herbert Gladstone dated 13 March 1903, for example, the Liberals expressed their willingness to 'ascertain from *qualified* and *responsible* Labour leaders how far Labour candidates can be given an open field against a *common enemy*', with the result that 'it would increase progressive forces generally and the Liberal Party as the best available instrument of progress'.[85] The agreement explicitly stated that Labour candidates who would be given 'an open field' would be those supporting 'the general objects of the Liberal party', and MacDonald was forced subsequently to ignore local feeling when it did not coincide with Liberal calculations.[86] While this agreement could be justified on grounds of expediency, the evidence of the zeal with which the LRC implemented it suggests that it was what leaders like MacDonald had actually wanted from the beginning. In practice, the role of LRC-sponsored MPs as a support to the Radical wing of the Liberal Party served to emphasise the isolation of committed socialists from effective political influence among the ranks of organised labour.

Support for this new focus of 'Social Radicalism' was strongest in areas like the West Riding of Yorkshire where the Liberal non-conformist traditions of organised labour proved an impenetrable barrier to the propaganda of overtly secular and identifiably social-ist organisations like the SDF. It was this as much as any dramatic rise in ILP membership that gave credibility to the policies implied by the 1903 pact between the LRC and the Liberal Party. As late as 1907, the paying membership of the ILP was only 15,340, compared with 6,000 for the SDF.[87] The ILP was especially weak in London, for example, where the crisis of Liberalism had become particularly acute and nonconformity had degenerated into a middle-class sect.[88] It might be expected that the miners would be receptive to a movement for independent labour representation since they were concentrated in relatively homogeneous working-class constituen-cies, and had their established traditions of union organisation with recent experience of bitter industrial disputes. Yet the fact remains that before 1906 only the Lancashire and Cheshire affiliate of the Miners' Federation had thrown in its lot with the LRC. The most important reason for this was the continuing strength of the Lib–Lab tradition among the officials of the miners' unions, espe-cially Ben Pickard, the Yorkshire miners' leader who was President of the MFGB. They felt that adhesion to the LRC would allow other unions to use the financial support provided by the federation to get candidates elected who would not represent miners' interests, com-pared with the existing miners' MPs sitting as Liberals who could claim that they already represented them in Parliament.[89] In ad-dition, while many leading lights of the SDF doubted the value of trade unionism, miners' officials like Pickard could point to their established reputations as organisers and courageous leaders during industrial disputes, and this the socialists found difficult to counter.[90]

Committed socialists found the vagueness of what the LRC actually stood for increasingly exasperating. The antagonism be-tween themselves and the official union leaders, who were the main supporters of MacDonald's conciliatory tactics on the LRC, was to grow after 1906 as the expectations of the rank and file began to outrun the achievements of their leaders. Robert Blatchford had anticipated this development as early as 1898 when he complained bitterly about the failure of the TUC Parliamentary Committee to convene a special conference in response to the engineering lock-out:[91]

> The plain truth about the thing is that a well paid trade union official, after a few years service, almost invariably, becomes useless to those who pay his wages. He puts on size, he apes the parliamentary air, he gets corrupted by the deference and high wages paid him. He likes to be a personage, and he grows comfortably used to the pleasant security and easily gained importance of his situation. The result is a strong temptation to advertise himself, to secure his own position, and to oppose overtly or openly any change in the tactics or methods of the workers which might endanger his pre-eminence, importance, power or pay.

Yet there were signs of a genuinely revolutionary socialist movement emerging in Britain during the early 1900s, which sought to distinguish itself from the sectarian aridity of the SDF. During 1902–3, a group known within the SDF as the 'impossibilists' launched a concerted attack on Hyndman and the organisation's leadership, disgusted at its obsession with electoral manoeuvrings and its quasi-imperialist fervour.[92] The impossibilists drew most of their support from Scotland where contact had been made with the writings of Daniel De Leon and the publications of the American Socialist Labour Party, as a result of propaganda tours by speakers of the calibre of James Connolly. They wished to apply the trans-atlantic experience of class struggle waged in the workplace to the British situation. Their hostility to Hyndman and his supporters led to their expulsion from the SDF in 1903, with the result that a new organisation called the Socialist Labour Party after its American model was established. Much more was to be heard from its tiny but dedicated cadre of members who were to bring to British socialism a new theoretical rigour as well as an appreciation of the revolutionary potential of industrial unionism, especially in the context of growing industrial unrest after 1906.

In explaining the continued willingness of the official labour leadership to work with the Liberal Party, and reject the root-and-branch socialism of organisations like the SDF, attention should also be directed to Liberalism's capacity to develop new perspectives and strategies aimed at tackling the causes of social unrest, without disturbing in any fundamental way the existing distribution of wealth and power in British society. This implied abandoning in some degree accepted orthodoxy in the sphere of economic and social policy, and assumed a more positive and purposive role for the state in alleviating the most chronic ills of industrial-capitalist society. Socialist demands like the eight-hour day appeared to run along similar lines, but in important respects these differed from the perspectives and strategies of the 'New Liberalism'. Socialist agitation on issues like the eight-hours was regarded as essentially a tactical device for mobilising the working class into *self-activity*, as a step towards the complete transformation of society, whereas Liberal reform involved the granting of concessions *from above*, in a way that sought deliberately to prevent the mobilisation of the working class in favour of fundamental change. The New Liberalism advocated state-sponsored initiatives only when existing institutions had most palpably failed, and it tried wherever possible to formulate policies that would complement and support, but not replace or undermine, labour's proven capacity for self-help and self-improvement. It had no desire to do away with private property or the free market mechanism but sought to preserve both by an *ad hoc* programme of palliatives designed to encourage workers to acquire property and make provision for their own welfare, within the overall framework of a capitalist economy.

It could be argued, in fact, that the underlying aim of the New Liberalism was to use state initiatives to improve labour's 'market-ability', as a means of increasing the efficiency of the existing economic system. Such a programme of *ad hoc* reform, which promised to yield immediate and specific benefits, could be expected to appeal especially to the pragmatic orientation of the official leadership of organised labour who had remained so closely as-sociated with Liberalism. Moreover, working-class individuals who were the direct beneficiaries of reform could be persuaded that an amelioration of their own and their families' condition was possible, without fundamental change, and that this was attainable by the individual acting directly and responsibly in pursuit of his own self-interest, with the assistance that the state was willing to provide. This was a powerful antidote to the distant vision of a collectivist utopia offered by revolutionary socialists, which seemed not only unattainable in the foreseeable future but, in practice, impossible to plan for on an everyday basis.

The new directions in which Liberalism might move were recognised by Gladstone himself in the twilight of his political career. During the debate on the Small Holdings Bill in 1892, for example, he remarked that the Liberal Party had,[93]

> come generally to the conclusion...that it is hard even for the industrious and sober man, under very ordinary conditions, to secure a provision for his old age. Very large propositions...have been submitted to the public, for the purpose of securing such a provision independent of the labourer himself. I am not going to criticise these proposals, and I am only referring to them as signs that there is much to be done...It is eminently our duty to develop in the *first instance*, every means we may possibly devise whereby, *if possible*, the labourer may be able to make this provision for himself.

This statement is of interest for two reasons. First, it admits that the accepted orthodoxy of self-help may no longer provide sufficient basis for social policy—'that there is much to be done'. Secondly, Gladstone anticipates the subsequent development of the New Liberalism when he emphasises that any measure of 'collective' or state action must be prefaced on the assumption that it should endeavour to encourage and support 'every means' whereby individuals could provide for themselves. This was a tacit approval of the traditional doctrine that the individual should ultimately be free to do what he likes with his own 'property', in the context of a free capitalist market, and unfettered by any collectivist 'coercion'.

There is little indication that the Liberal Party as a whole worked through the full implications of Gladstone's rather criptic observations during the 1890s, and until the early 1900s its domestic policy continued to rely on the 'staple diet' of Home Rule, disestablishment, retrenchment, and educátional, licensing and electoral reform.[94] Yet a younger generation of Liberal thinkers like R. B. Haldane spoke increasingly in terms of 'the language of the social good', reflecting the influence of T. H. Green at Balliol over an entire generation of intellectuals. In this respect, the almost caste-like quality of British intellectual life, with its intimate 'organic' relationship with the ruling class, was of positive assistance in disseminating new ideas among the governing elite. Informal groups of self-conscious intellectuals like 'The Souls' mixed freely in high society, and it is noteworthy that both Haldane and Asquith had access to them. The acceptance of a more positive role for the state in resolving social problems was part of a wider change in the intellectual climate, which rejected the atomistic conceptions of social relations prevailing earlier in the nineteenth century and stressed instead the solidaristic and moralistic quality of society that the state was ideally placed to promote.[95] This also reflected the current fashion of applying biological conceptions of human evolution to the development of society. The latter was seen as evolving from 'lower' to 'higher' forms, with the implication that man's capacity for rational conduct should be deliberately cultivated by the state acting as agent for the social good.

Yet the ideal hankered after by the 'New Liberals' was not a collectivist utopia, without private property or a free market, but rather a kind of 'moralised' capitalism compatible with their own social and economic background. Their utopia was expressed succinctly by T. H. Green who described how,[96]

> in the well-paid industries of England, the better sort of labourers do become capitalists to the extent of owning their own houses and a great deal of furniture, of having an interest in stores and of belonging to the benefit societies through which they make provision for the future.

The extent to which this idealised view fitted the experience of even 'well-paid' workers in the late nineteenth century is debatable, but this is beside the point. The fact was that intellectuals like Arnold Toynbee were convinced that 'equality of rights' and 'equality of culture' were possible, and his claim that 'We are all now, workers as well as employers... no longer members of a single class, but fellow citizens of one great people,' implied that the state was bound to intervene and promote the growth of 'the citizen stage' in society's development. This notion of 'citizenship' was essentially Liberal and individualistic in the sense that it lacked a class analysis and rejected implicitly the Marxist theory of value. Yet it promised labour concrete improvement that could not be ignored. It was left to economists like Marshall and 'social engineers' like the Webbs to give the New Liberalism its practical content. Thus Marshall argued before the Royal Commission on the Aged Poor in 1893 that payments to the poor need not depress wages because these would tend to raise efficiency and consumption levels.[97]

In an important respect, the debates over poverty in the 1880s

gave birth to new control strategies in terms of social policy that
were subsequently to influence the New Liberalism. T. H. Green's
idealisation of the better-paid worker as the model citizen of tomorrow, secure in his own property and self-respect, was given practical
form by a growing body of opinion within the Charity Organisation
Society, which considered that the existing administration of the
Poor Law was failing to distinguish the 'true' working class *deserving* assistance from the unemployable residuum *demanding* quite
different treatment.[98] If it was from the ranks of the 'true' working
class that the model citizens of tomorrow were to be recruited, it
followed that government policy should do its utmost to prevent
them from descending into the residuum for no fault of their own,
with the attendant danger of spreading social discontent. Thus
reformers like Arnold Toynbee and Canon Barnett hoped to devise
a scheme of 'scientific charity' for the deserving poor, in co-
operation with labour's own self-help institutions, while the residuum would be consigned to farm settlements or labour colonies
abroad where they were to be 'rehabilitated' under strict supervision
by the Poor Law authorities. Barnett, for example, advocated non-
contributory pensions paid for by the state to those who had
managed to keep themselves *outside* the workhouse. The argument
for granting concessions like pensions to the 'respectable' working
class was strengthened in the 1890s as the increasing moderation of
the New Unionism testified to the existence of a regularly employed
stratum among the unskilled and semi-skilled that was in every
sense 'deserving', although unable to afford the subscriptions required in return for the benefits offered by the craft unions and
friendly societies. The growing appeal of imperialism as a panacea
for Britain's ills gave additional impetus to the development of
social policy, with proposals for state-assisted emigration of the
casual unemployed to settlements in the Empire. There was also the
example of welfare schemes implemented by an increasing number
of employers, which might be taken up and extended further by the
state. According to one authority:[99]

It became profitable from the point of view of productivity... to
develop and maintain the capacity and willingness to work.
Social insurance became one of the means of investing in human
capital.

These policy proposals were not translated immediately into

legislative activity, but they did help create a climate of opinion that was to influence the future character of Liberal welfare reform. It was thus a combination of factors that led to the formulation of a new role for the state in relation to the working class, which was attracting a rising number of influential supporters in the 1890s and early 1900s. A greater awareness of the extent of poverty, resulting from contemporary investigations, was connected in the public mind with labour unrest and the spread of 'socialism' that appeared to threaten the stability of British society. New strategies were seen to be required to head off this menace. These were developed in light of the changing climate of ideas, which redefined the relationship between the individual and society in terms of the rights *and* duties of citizenship, expressing an organic conception of the role of the state in society. This implied that government was directly responsible for actively promoting the 'common good'. The slowing down in the economy's rate of growth and a hardening of the lines of class cleavage also exposed the growing inability of both working-class self-help and the Poor Law either to resolve the problem of poverty or maintain social discipline. The prospect of the deserving poor descending into the abyss of the residuum was an alarming spectre haunting the ruling-class mind in the late Victorian and Edwardian periods. How the state might act to assist the 'true' working class in attaining full citizenship was posed very much in terms of the need to preserve social order and ensure the nation's 'hygiene' and 'efficiency'.

The Liberal welfare reformers were to differ fundamentally therefore from those socialists who regarded state initiatives as a means of mobilising working-class support for revolutionary change. Some degree of *collectivism* or state intervention was not to be confused with *socialism*. As Hubert Bland, the Fabian essayist, perciplently observed:[100]

> It is not so much to the thing the State does as to the end for which it does it that we must look before we decide whether it is a Socialist State or not.

Most of the proposals for state-sponsored welfare provision enacted by the Liberal government after 1906 demonstrate that socialism was not the aim of government but rather a form of 'moralised' capitalism created by an *ad hoc* package of ameliorative measures that would legitimate private property and a free market economy.

This entailed some modification of prevailing assumptions, first, by seeking to provide individuals and families with an undefined level of 'minimum' subsistence, which was guaranteed irrespective of the market value of their work or property; and secondly, by enabling individuals and families to meet certain specific 'social contingencies', like old age, which they were unable to provide for entirely on their own account.[101] The overall objective was to encourage the working class to help itself, to generalise T. H. Green's ideal of the 'better sort' of labourers who became 'capitalists'. This was far removed from the socialist utopia of equality in standards of income and services, available to everybody as of right. As one historian has written, 'The New Liberalism can be seen as an attempt to define true socialism as a special case of Liberalism.'[102]

The New Liberalism thus sought to generate support for a programme of evolutionary change that cut across class divisions and appealed particularly to *organised* labour, which had proved its 'rationality' by its willingness to work with rather than against the Liberal Party. The casual and peripatetic residuum having recourse to the Poor Law, for example, were excluded *both* from the right to vote *and* the benefits of Liberal welfare legislation like Old Age Pensions and later National Insurance. In practice, the New Liberalism's ideal of citizenship was clearly restricted to the organised and respectable working class in regular employment. This was the very same stratum to which the Labour Representation Committee appealed for support. And, moreover, there seemed little to distinguish the 'ethical' socialism of the Independent Labour Party from the politics of the New Liberalism. The latter's appeal to wage-earners who did have the vote explains the newly found strength of the Liberal Party in a traditionally Conservative area like Lancashire and in a working-class London borough like Battersea.[103] Liberalism's recognition of the causes and process of class polarisation thus led it to evolve new strategies that promised to contain the 'Challenge of Labour'.

Notes

1. E. H. Phelps Brown and Margaret H. Browne, *A Century of Pay* (London: Macmillan, 1968), Appendix 3; Derek H. Aldcroft and Harry W. Richardson, *The British Economy, 1870–1939* (London: Macmillan, 1969), Table 1, p. 105.

2. E. H. Phelps Brown and B. Weber, 'Accumulation, Productivity and Distribution in the British Economy, 1870–1938', *Economic Journal*, LXIII (1953), Fig. 5.

3. E. M. Sigsworth and J. Blackman, 'The Home Boom of the 1890's', *Yorkshire Bulletin of Economic and Social Research*, 17 (1965), no. 1.

4. S. B. Saul, *The Myth of the Great Depression, 1873–96* (London: Macmillan, 1969), Table IV, p. 36.

5. Sidney Pollard and David W. Crossley, *The Wealth of Britain, 1085–1966* (London: Batsford, 1968), p. 228.

6. Brown and Browne, *Century of Pay*, pp. 189–90, Fig. 18.

7. S. Pollard, 'Trade Unions and the Labour Market, 1870–1914', *Yorkshire Bulletin of Economic and Social Research*, 17 (1965), no. 1, Diagram 1, p. 101.

8. Aldcroft and Richardson, *British Economy*, p. 128; W. P. Kennedy, 'Foreign Investment, Trade and Growth in the United Kingdom, 1870–1913', *Explorations in Economic History*, 2nd series, 11 (1973–4), no. 4, pp. 425–6.

9. A. J. Brown, 'Britain and the World Economy, 1870–1914', *Yorkshire Bulletin of Economic and Social Research*, 17 (1965), no. 1, pp. 54–5.

10. S. B. Saul, 'The Export Economy, 1870–1914', *Yorkshire Bulletin of Economic and Social Research*, 17 (1965), no. 1, p. 9.

11. Ibid., p. 13.

12. Brown and Browne, *Century of Pay*, Fig. 27.

13. Ibid., Table 13, p. 170.

14. J. Saville, 'Some Retarding Factors in the British Economy Before 1914', *Yorkshire Bulletin of Economic and Social Research*, 13 (1961), no. 1, pp. 56–7; Kennedy, 'Foreign Investment', pp. 434–5.

15. Pollard, 'Trade Unions', p. 101.

16. R. G. Lipsey and M. D. Steuer, 'The Relation between Profits and Wage Rates', *Economica*, new series, XXVIII (1961), no. 110, pp. 147–8.

17. Jürgen Kuczynski, *A Short History of Labour Conditions Under Industrial Capitalism* (London: Frederick Muller, 1972), p. 119.

18. Brown and Browne, *Century of Pay*, Fig. 2, p. 67; Table 13, p. 170.

19. Ibid., Table 8, pp. 91–2; C. K. Harley, 'Skilled Labour and the Choice of Technique in Edwardian Industry', *Explorations in Economic History*, 2nd series, 11 (1973–4), no. 4.

20. Brown and Browne, *Century of Pay*, Figs. 6 and 7.

21. F. Musgrove, 'Middle Class Education and Employment in the Nineteenth Century', *Economic History Review*, 2nd series, XII (1959–60), no. 2, Table 3, p. 328; H. J. Perkin, 'Middle Class Education and Employment in the Nineteenth Century: A Critical Note', *Economic History Review*, 2nd series, XIV (1961–2), no. 1, Table 3, p. 129; Paul Thompson, *The Edwardians* (London: Weidenfeld & Nicolson, 1975), Table 3, p. 14.

22. Thompson, *Edwardians*, Table 2, p. 12.

23. I owe this information to Dr M. A. Crowther who kindly showed me material to be published in her forthcoming book, *The Workhouse System 1834–1939* (London: Batsford).

24. W. D. Rubinstein, 'Wealth, Elites and the Class Structure of Modern Britain', *Past and Present*, 76 (1977), p. 105; Thompson, *Edwardians*, Table 1, p. 12.

25. H. A. Clegg, A. Fox and A. F. Thompson, *A History of British Trade Unions since 1889* (Oxford: Clarendon Press, 1964), vol. 1, Table 6, p. 468.

26. E. H. Phelps Brown and P. E. Hart, 'The Share of Wages in the National Income', *Economic Journal*, LXII (1952), especially Fig. 5.

27. J. C. Stamp, 'The Effect of Trade Fluctuations upon Profits', *Journal of the Royal Statistical Society*, LXXXI (1918), Fig. 2, p. 572.

28. John Jewkes and E. M. Gray, *Wages and Labour in the Lancashire Cotton Spinning Industry* (Manchester: University Press, 1935), Appendix IV, Table II, p. 211; R. E. Tyson, 'The Cotton Industry' in Derek H. Aldcroft (ed.), *The Development of British Industry and Foreign Competition, 1875–1914* (London: Allen & Unwin, 1968), pp. 102–3.

29. E. H. Phelps Brown, *The Growth of British Industrial Relations* (London: Macmillan, 1959), pp. 181 ff.

30. Ibid., pp. 110–13.

31. Harry Braverman, *Labor and Monopoly Capital* (New York: Monthly Review Press, 1974), Ch. 4, contains a general discussion on the basic principles of 'scientific management'.

32. Keith Burgess, *The Origins of British Industrial Relations* (London: Croom Helm, 1975), especially pp. 60–4, 95–6.

33. Alfred Williams, *Life in a Railway Factory* (Newton Abbot: David & Charles, reprint, 1969), is a classic contemporary account.

34. A. L. Levine, *Industrial Retardation in Britain, 1880–1914* (London: Weidenfeld & Nicolson, 1967), Table 8, p. 105.

35. A. Touraine *et al.*, *Workers' Attitudes to Technical Change* (Paris: OECD, 1965), especially p. 30.

36. Ibid., p. 22.

37. This is examined in more detail in the forthcoming PhD thesis by Joseph L. Melling, 'Employers and the Development of Industrial Welfare Schemes in Britain: a Regional and Industrial Comparison, c. 1880–1920', Department of Economic History, University of Glasgow.

38. Clegg *et al.*, *History of Unions*, p. 83.

39. Ibid.

40. John Lovell, *Stevedores and Dockers. A Study of Trade Unionism in the Port of London, 1870–1914* (London: Macmillan, 1969), p. 125.

41. Ibid., p. 146.

42. R. Bean, 'Employers' Associations in the Port of Liverpool, 1890–1914', *International Review of Social History*, XXI (1976), pt 3.

43. E. J. Hobsbawn, 'British Gas-workers, 1873–1914' in the same author's *Labouring Men. Studies in the History of Labour* (London: Weidenfeld & Nicolson, 1968), p. 171.

44. P. S. Gupta, 'Railway Trade Unionism in Britain, c. 1880–1900', *Economic History Review*, 2nd series, XIX (1966), no. 1, pp. 145–8, 152.

45. John Saville, 'Trade Unions and Free Labour: the Background to the Taff Vale Decision' in Asa Briggs and John Saville (eds.), *Essays in Labour History* (London: Macmillan, 1967), p. 320.

46. Ibid., pp. 328–9.

47. Ibid., pp. 329–30.

48. Geoffrey Alderman, 'The National Free Labour Association. A Case-study of Organized Strike-breaking in the Late Nineteenth and Early Twentieth Centuries', *International Review of Social History*, XXI (1976), pt 3.

49. Ibid., pp. 324–5.

50. Webb Collection E (Trade Unions), London School of Economics and Political Science, *Verbatim Report*, Section B, vol. CXVII, pt 13; the background to the establishment of the Building Trades' Federation is discussed in Burgess, *Industrial Relations*, pp. 134–8.

51. N. Soldon, 'Laissez-Faire as Dogma: The Liberty and Property Defence League, 1882–1914' in Kenneth D. Brown (ed.), *Essays in Anti-Labour History* (London: Macmillan, 1974), p. 216.

52. The following discussion is based upon Saville 'Trade Unions' in Briggs and Saville.

53. See Burgess, *Industrial Relations*, pp. 200 ff.

54. Ibid., p. 210.

55. Ibid., pp. 205–8, where the significance of the dispute is discussed in some detail.

56. Ibid., pp. 207–8.

57. Stamp, 'Trade Fluctuations', Fig. 2, p. 572; Table I, p. 576.

58. B. McCormick and J. E. Williams, 'The Miners and the Eight-hour Day, 1863–1910', *Economic History Review*, 2nd series, XII (1959–60), Table 3, p. 283.

59. Burgess, *Industrial Relations*, pp. 282–3.

60. J. H. Porter, 'Industrial Peace in the Cotton Trade, 1875–1913', *Yorkshire Bulletin of Economic and Social Research*, 19 (1967), p. 52.

61. Roland Smith, 'A History of the Lancashire Cotton Industry between 1873 and 1896', unpublished PhD thesis, University of Birmingham, 1954, vol. II, cited p. 494.

62. Burgess, *Industrial Relations*, pp. 284–90, for a detailed discussion of the significance of the Brooklands Agreement.

63. Ibid., pp. 49 ff., is the basis of the following discussion.

64. Ibid., pp. 68–71.

65. B. C. M. Weekes, 'The Amalgamated Society of Engineers, 1880–1914. A Study of Trade Union Government, Politics, and Industrial Policy', unpublished PhD thesis, University of Warwick, 1970, pp. 179 ff.

66. Cited in Gordon L. Goodman, 'Liberal Unionism: The Revolt of the Whigs', *Victorian Studies*, III (1959), no. 2, p. 189.

67. Soldon, 'Laissez-Faire', pp. 217–18.

68. Alderman, 'National Free Labour', p. 320.

69. C. Chamberlain, 'The Growth of Support for the Labour Party in Britain', *British Journal of Sociology*, 24 (1973), p. 476.

70. H. C. G. Matthew, R. I. McKibbin and J. A. Kay, 'The Franchise Factor in the Rise of the Labour Party', *English Historical Review*, XCI (1976), p. 727.

71. P. F. Clarke, *Lancashire and the New Liberalism* (Cambridge: University Press, 1971), pp. 104–9.

72. H. R. G. Greaves, 'Personal Origins and Interrelations of the Houses of Parliament (since 1832)', *Economica*, IX (1929), no. 26, Tables III and IV.

73. The geographic location of party electoral support is discussed in H. V. Emy, *Liberals, Radicals and Social Politics, 1892–1914* (Cambridge: University Press, 1973), pp. 94–8.

74. B. David Rubinstein, 'The Decline of the Liberal Party, 1880–1900', unpublished PhD thesis, University of London, 1956, p. 347.

75. A policy of imperial expansion had been advocated in the *Cotton Factory Times*, for example, since the 1880s.

76. Henry Collins, 'The Marxism of the Social Democratic Federation' in Briggs and Saville, pp. 65–7.

77. E. J. Hobsbawm, 'The Fabians Reconsidered' in *Labouring Men*.

78. Frank Bealey and Henry Pelling, *Labour and Politics 1900–1906* (London: Macmillan, 1958), pp. 178–9.

79. David Kynaston, *King Labour, The British Working Class, 1850–1914* (London: Allen & Unwin, 1976), p. 133.

80. Bernard Barker, 'Anatomy of Reformism: The Social and Political Ideas of the Labour Leadership in Yorkshire', *International Review of Social History*, XVIII (1973), especially p. 4.

81. Bealey and Pelling, *Labour 1900–1906*, p. 26.

82. Clegg *et al.*, *History of Unions*, p. 375.

83. Bealey and Pelling, *Labour 1900–1906*, pp. 197–203.

84. Frank Bealey, 'Negotiations between the Liberal Party and the Labour Representation Committee before the General Election of 1906', *Bulletin of the Institute of Historical Research*, XXIX (1956).

85. Ibid., cited p. 269; my italics.

86. Ibid., p. 271, where in the instance of West Salford the local Labour candidate was withdrawn.

87. R. Dowse, *Left in the Centre. The Independent Labour Party, 1893–1940* (London: Longmans Green, 1966), pp. 9, 12; C. Tsuzuki, *H. M. Hyndman and British Socialism* (Oxford: University Press, 1961), p. 284.

88. Paul Thompson, *Socialists, Liberals and Labour. The Struggle for London, 1885–1914* (London: Routledge & Kegan Paul, 1967), especially pp. 161–83, for the weakness of the ILP in London during the 1890s.

89. Roy Gregory, *The Miners and British Politics, 1906–1914* (Oxford: University Press, 1968), pp. 23–5.

90. John Saville, 'Notes on Ideology and the Miners before the World War I', *Bulletin of the Society for the Study of Labour History*, 23 (1971), p. 26.

91. Weekes, 'Engineers', cited pp. 127–8, from *Clarion*, 8 June, 1898.

92. The most recent account of the early development of revolutionary socialism in Britain is contained in Raymond Challinor's *The Origins of British Bolshevism* (London: Croom Helm, 1978).

93. Cited in M. K. Barker, 'The Formation of Liberal Party Policy, 1885–92', unpublished PhD thesis, University of Wales, 1972, p. 402.

94. Emy, *Liberals*, pp. 68–71.

95. See Gareth Stedman Jones, *Outcast London. A Study in the Relationship Between Classes in Victorian Society* (Oxford: University Press, 1971), pp. 6–10, for a stimulating discussion of this development.

96. Ibid., cited p. 9.

97. J. R. Hay, *The Origins of the Liberal Welfare Reforms 1906–1914* (London: Macmillan, 1975), p. 47 (footnote).

98. Stedman Jones, *Outcast London*, pp. 301 ff.

99. G. V. Rimlinger, *Welfare Policy and Industrialization in Europe, America and Russia* (New York: Wiley, 1971), pp. 9–10; see also Roy Hay, 'Employers and Social Policy in Britain: The Evolution of Welfare Legislation, 1905–1914', *Social History*, no. 4 (1977).

100. Asa Briggs, 'The Welfare State in Historical Perspective', *Archives Européenes de Sociologie*, II (1961), no. 2, cited p. 233.

101. Ibid., p. 228.

102. P. F. Clarke, 'The Progressive Movement in England', *Transactions of the Royal Historical Society*, 5th series, 24 (1974), pp. 161–5.

103. Clarke, *Lancashire and the New Liberalism*; Chris Wrigley, 'Liberals and the Desire for Working-class Representatives in Battersea, 1886–1922' in Kenneth D. Brown (ed.), *Essays in Anti-Labour History* (London: Macmillan, 1974).

CHAPTER 4

The Edwardian 'Crisis', 1906–14

The Economy and Labour

The period 1906–14 in Britain's economic and social development posed difficulties for the New Liberalism's capacity to re-establish the hegemony of capital and property in relation to the working class. Whether these difficulties amounted to a 'crisis' or general breakdown in the legitimacy of the existing social order is far from clear, although after 1910 the signs of a deep-seated social malaise impressed contemporaries and have been widely discussed by subsequent generations of historians.[1] It can be argued that this period was one of crisis in the strict sense of marking a decisive juncture or pass, the outcome of which served as a turning-point in the making of modern Britain. Yet the changing direction of Britain's development was not clearly identifiable by 1914; it was the First World War together with its consequences that were to decide the final outcome. What remains irrefutable is that the years 1906–14 were not a period of crisis in the classical Marxist sense of a collapse in British capitalism's profitability. An estimate of the rate of profit in the United Kingdom shows a sharp recovery after 1905–6, following the downward trend since the late 1870s, and it was higher than in either Germany or the USA.[2] The rising volume of capital exports sustained the overall rate of accumulation in the economy as a whole until 1914 when Britain's investments overseas comprised almost one-half the world's total. More than 40% of the world's trade passed through Britain in these years, earning spectacular returns for its financiers and traders.

Yet the enormous benefit enjoyed by Britain as the centre of world trade and finance began to yield diminishing returns. The deterioration in the international political climate, manifest in a succession of diplomatic confrontations, undermined confidence abroad in the sterling bill of exchange and led to an incessant demand for gold that the Bank of England found increasingly difficult to meet. Despite the rise in the discount rate to 7% in 1907—the highest level since the crisis of 1873—this managed to attract only short-term deposits at the expense of precipitating an industrial slump.[3] The international rush into liquidity just prior to the First World War emphasised the fragility of Britain's financial position. The small size of its gold reserves was related to the levelling-off in world gold production after 1906, whilst the Bank of England's foreign currency holdings were steadily whittled away as the worldwide demand for gold intensified.[4] At the same time, the low yields on capital invested in industry, compared with the higher returns obtained from overseas investment and other commercial or financial ventures, discouraged the banks and financial institutions from investing in industry, thus maintaining the historic separateness in Britain of finance and industry. In 1906, only 16 of Britain's top 50 industrial enterprises were connected by shared directorships with either banking or insurance firms, in marked contrast to the situation obtaining in either Germany or the USA.[5] This was an important reason why the combination movement, making possible standardisation, rationalisation and economies of scale, affected only a small part of British industry prior to 1914.[6] It is noteworthy that the industrial firms having interlocking directorships with banking companies in 1906 also figured among the 52 largest industrial enterprises in 1905.[7]

The slowing down in the economy's rate of growth during the Edwardian period exposed the high levels of inequality in British society. In the decade 1900–10, while national income per capita rose by 5%, compared with 11% in the 1890s and 39% during the 1880s, real wages *fell* by 6%, compared with a rise of 11% in the 1890s and 21% during the 1880s.[8] And the downward trend of real wages was not reversed in the years before 1914.[9] The continued prosperity of British finance and trade benefited only a small proportion of the occupied population because these sectors were relatively capital-intensive rather than labour-intensive, which concentrated the national wealth in comparatively few hands. By 1911–13, the richest 1% of the population aged 25 and over owned 69% of the national capital. The rising cost of living highlighted the problem of diminishing returns in the staple export trades. Thus in 1913 the index of real wages included in the Oldham spinning list measured 127 (1880 = 100), compared with the peak of 145 registered in 1908.[10] Rising import prices and stagnant productivity failed to yield any growth in real wages, and this bore especially hard on the unskilled and semi-skilled whose incomes were spent mostly on basic necessities. Studies of poverty made in Northampton, Warrington, Stanley and Reading during 1912–13 show that the earnings of the unskilled were at all times too low to keep a family of three children above the poverty line, and in 1914 nearly 25% of all adult wage-earners had incomes below the poverty line.[11]

It was not only the semi-skilled and unskilled who suffered from the persistence of inequalities in the context of rising prices. The advent of 'scientific management' and the steady introduction of 'deskilling' machinery in the engineering industry, for example, posed a serious threat to one of the most 'labour aristocratic' of skilled trades. Sir Andrew Noble, Chairman of Armstrong Whitworth, testified before the Royal Commission on Trades Disputes in 1906 that he had 'hundreds' of milling machines at which no time-served turner or 'high-class' machinist was employed since 'it was not at all necessary'.[12] The wages of semi-skilled milling machinists were estimated at 25–8s weekly—little above subsistence level for a family man—compared with 36–8s weekly earned by the fully-skilled apprenticed operatives whose multifunctional expertise was steadily confined to the toolroom and phased out of general production.[13] The erosion of craft privileges and autonomy accompanying the spread of piecework and productivity-linked methods of wage payment, like the premium bonus system, produced higher earnings for only a minority of skilled workers who were able to offset the rising cost of living at the expense of surrendering some degree of job control.[14]

The effect of rising prices and marked inequalities during the years just prior to the First World War created new forms of class differentiation as well as confirmed existing ones. The benefits of cheaper food made possible by increased imports since the 1870s, for example, ceased to apply as the price of basic foodstuffs moved ahead of money wages after 1900. The relatively high cost of fresh milk in urban centres encouraged the consumption of canned condensed milk as a cheap substitute, but it contained little of vitamins A and D with the result that the incidence of rickets among working-class children was common.[15] Class differences in general standards of health were reflected in differentials for death-rates. Thus in England and Wales during 1900–2, the death-rate among general labourers was more than four times higher than for the clergy.[16] The impact of rising prices and especially high interest rates after 1906 caused the provision of working-class housing to fall behind the needs of a growing population. In 29 districts of outer London, for example, the number of rooms provided fell from 38,473 in 1902 to 7,452 in 1913, although the increase in population in these districts was described as 'very striking'.[17] In Wandsworth, which had the highest rate of population growth of the inner districts, the number of rooms provided fell from 8,906 in 1903 to 709 in 1913.[18] A worsening shortage of working-class housing also existed in other large cities like Glasgow.[19] Moreover, the comparatively low levels of unemployment among trade unionists during this period, with the exception of the slump of 1907–9, did not extend to the underemployed residuum whose dire condition led to the publication in 1909 of William Beveridge's *Unemployment: A Problem of Industry.* What made class inequalities such a potent source of social instability in the period immediately prior to the First World War was not just their existence but society's awareness of their existence, especially among the working class. In this respect, the virtual elimination of illiteracy in Britain during the first two decades of the twentieth century was of decisive importance.[20] As Ernest Bevin remarked when justifying his decision to stand for Parliament in 1918: 'You cannot have the schoolmaster abroad for fifty years and still keep the working class at only a living wage.'[21]

The economic pressures affecting the working class during the period 1906–14 produced a greater awareness of common interests among wage-earners who had previously been much more comprehensively divided by differences in skill, earnings, status and patterns of residence and association. In the sphere of wage-earnings, for example, the apparent persistence of nineteenth-century differentials until 1914 fails to take into account the effects of changes in the labour process narrowing the scope for multifunctional expertise, which became the prerogative of a diminishing proportion of even skilled workers. The potential for working-class activity was realised further by the intense public debates on proposals for greater government intervention and regulation, which were themselves the outcome of an increasing awareness of Britain's economic and social problems. This created opportunities for *politicising* what had been strictly economic or sectional grievances, making labour more conscious of its *class* position. Of course, it has to be acknowledged that before 1914 only a very small minority of wage-earners had moved beyond the corporate-type class-consciousness based on shared economic interest to formulate a 'hegemonic' outlook of their own, which generalised at a political level the collectivist norms of their own experience. Yet the expanding circulation of socialist journals like *Labour Leader*, *Justice* and *Clarion*, and the educational activities of groups like the SDF, the Workers' Educational Association and the University Extension movement, had the effect of building further on the rising expectations nourished by the advent of mass literacy.[22] A tiny but committed socialist cadre was formed who discovered new opportunities for extending their influence.

The revision of the law governing industrial disputes created an environment that was favourable to the mobilisation of the class interests of wage-earners. The resignation of the Balfour ministry in 1905, reflecting a Conservative Party hopelessly split over the issue of tariff reform, led to a Liberal administration under Campbell-Bannerman who recognised that his party's electoral pact with the Labour Representation Committee required 'sops' for Labour.[23] This implied some amendment of the legal position of the trade unions, following the series of legal decisions culminating in the Taff Vale case. It was thus political expediency that persuaded the Liberal government to ignore the recommendations of the Royal Commission on Trade Disputes published in February 1906 shortly after the General Election, which had returned the Liberals to power with a huge majority. The Royal Commission was opposed to the reversal of Taff Vale on the grounds that legal immunity for trade union funds in respect of labour disputes would endow a privileged class above the law.[24] The large majority of employers submitting evidence, including representatives of the Employers' Parliamentary Council and the Liberty and Property Defence League, were in favour of the legal incorporation of trade unions, thus making them liable for damages, and they were especially insistent in advocating restrictions on picketing that was likely to involve 'intimidation'.[25] The Royal Commission for its part was prepared to accept the unions' liability for damages when actions had been committed with the prior sanction of their executives, but it was favourable to 'peaceful' picketing although 'intimidation' was to be outlawed.

The 29 Labour MPs elected in January 1906 were opposed to a Liberal bill based on the Royal Commission's recommendations. The proposal for liability in cases where an action had been approved by the union executive would have placed the latter in an invidious position in relation to its own rank and file because the authority of union leaders would have been seriously jeopardised. The Royal Commission seemed unaware that many labour disputes were 'unofficial', at least in origins, and would thus remain outside the law. The Liberal government could clearly not proceed with legislation that would antagonise the union leaders who effectively controlled the LRC. The government's legal advisers also pointed out that if trade unions were recognised as fully incorporated bodies, which appeared the only way of making them 'responsible', they could then proceed *against* workers who refused to obey strike calls, as well as employers who tried to dissuade their employees from striking, since this would constitute a breach of contract between a union and its members.[26] The result would have been to strengthen the trade union 'tyranny' that both government and employers were seeking to avoid. Complete legal immunity for the unions in respect of trade disputes appeared the best guarantee of 'orderly' collective bargaining as well as success for the Lib–Lab pact. This was subsequently established by the Trades Disputes Act of 1906. It also liberalised the right to picket by allowing persons involved in a dispute to attend at or near a house or place of business, in order to persuade other persons not to work, in addition merely to get or give information, although any form of violence in a trade dispute was still illegal.

The liberalisation of the law on picketing was to be of special benefit to the unions in the large-scale confrontations affecting the coal and transport industries after 1906. Yet few could have anticipated these developments in the climate of industrial relations prevailing during 1905–6, which was relatively quiescent.[27] The provisions of the 1906 Trade Disputes Act reflected a widespread acceptance of the voluntaryist basis of collective bargaining in Britain that eschewed government regulation, particularly legal compulsion. Even a leading employer like Sir Benjamin Browne in his evidence to the Royal Commission had admitted that trade unions obtained benefits for their members 'in a more far-seeing way and much more smoothly than non-union men would do', and he had no hesitation in adding 'that all over the kingdom they have made for peace'.[28] But these complacent observations did not take into account the adverse economic trends affecting the working class after 1906, which not only placed increasing strain on existing procedures of collective bargaining but threatened to spill over into political activity aimed at overturning the dominant social order.

The appreciation by leading employers like Sir Benjamin Browne of the value of trade unions in contributing to industrial peace rested on their awareness of the advantages they had discovered from negotiating with the officials of the craft unions. Yet in the engineering industry, for example, the proportion of engineering workers enjoying the accepted privileges and prerogatives of the skilled craftsman was steadily dwindling. Consequently, the rank and file was becoming increasingly dissatisfied with the machinery for collective bargaining established by the settlement to the 1897–8 lock-out, especially the avoidance-of-disputes clause requiring that grievances had to pass through the entire procedure up to national level whilst the men remained at work. Skilled labour substitution, the spread of piecework, and the introduction of new forms of wage payment like the premium bonus system made national and even district bargaining over time rates, involving only ASE officials under the 1898 agreement, less relevant to workers at the plant level, whether or not they were 'skilled' as defined by the ASE. The growth of plant bargaining by shop stewards or working representatives in a particular establishment negotiating on behalf of all employees, including non-unionists, began to create a parallel if not rival structure of bargaining to the procedures set up in 1898, which had been relatively favourable to the interests of employers.[29] Centralised collective bargaining imposed delays in settling grievances that were especially resented because the rapidly changing conditions at the workplace, including the fixing of job prices, strengthened managerial prerogatives and encouraged 'unofficial' strikes.[30] Rank-and-file discontent began to mount over the employers' implementation of the premium bonus system that in conjunction with new processes like high-speed steel was used to reduce time allowances and generally intensified the pace of work, which bore particularly hard on older workers. Moreover, in 1909 the decision of the ASE Executive to enter into an agreement with the Employers' Federation stipulating that wage rates were to be unchanged for five years was unfortunate for the union's leadership since this period was to be one of rising prices.[31] 'Orderly' collective bargaining was thus discredited in the eyes of many workers and created an industrial climate that was fertile ground for the propagation of syndicalist ideas.[32]

Cotton textiles was another industry where elaborate machinery for collective bargaining established during the 1890s came under increasing strain after 1906. In particular, the disputes procedure introduced by the Brooklands Agreement caused long delays in settling operatives' grievances, at the same time that strikes were officially forbidden. These delays were felt especially hard by the operatives since the initiative for making alterations in working arrangements, including machinery speed-up, lay with the employers; while the 5 % ceiling imposed by the Brooklands settlement on wage advances limited the bargaining strength of the operatives' unions during periods of rising prices and comparative prosperity, like the years 1912–13.[33] The number of disputes submitted to the industry's dispute procedure was particularly high during the years 1911–12, and matters came to a head in January 1913 when both the card room and spinners' unions decided to withdraw from the 1893 agreement.[34] The breakdown of collective bargaining in one of the most highly organised industries was an indication of the workers' frustration in what has been recognised as a relatively quiescent and politically conservative labour force.[35]

The creation of industrywide collective bargaining in the inland coalfields during the 1890s, extended subsequently to Scotland, South Wales and, after 1900, Northumberland and Durham, was also unable to achieve any permanent resolution of conflict between miners and owners. In 1906, the two principal demands of the miners—the eight-hour day and the 'minimum' wage—had yet to be realised. Coal prices were maintained at a generally high level after 1896 by buoyant demand, especially overseas, but in long-established pits the excavation of less-accessible seams that increased the distance between the surface bank and the coalface aggravated the problem of diminishing returns. This led to rising production costs since most owners remained reluctant to install cutting or haulage machinery. Labour productivity both above and below ground fell steadily during the years 1899–1913, and the proportion of relatively low-paid oncost daywagemen in relation to the face-workers rose as a result.[36] Moreover, the limits imposed upon wage movements by conciliation agreements meant that miners' wages did not share in the massive increase in coal prices, which yielded large profits for the owners during the years 1898–1900, 1906–7 and 1912–13, whilst wage-earnings remained vulnerable to reductions caused by short-time working when trade was slack.[37] In the federated districts as a whole, real wage rates reached a peak in 1901, after which they fell back to the levels prevailing during the early 1890s.[38] The failure of collective bargaining to protect miners' living standards led to more local stoppages and 'irregular' working, often in opposition to the instructions of the union officials.[39]

The miners' attainment of the eight-hour day by Act of

Parliament in 1908 did not allay the troubles of the coal industry. What the miners had achieved was the eight-hours, defined as 'bank to bank', including the 'winding' or travelling time between the surface bank and the coalface, which in some pits could be as much as 90 minutes each way per shift.[40] The limitations consequently imposed upon the hewers' ability to maintain their piecework earnings led to serious labour unrest in South Wales over the extra payments negotiated for working in 'abnormal' places or inaccessible or unproductive seams. The miners now sought to secure these payments as a fixed and guaranteed entitlement. The unrest over the question of abnormal places became a catalyst for the demand for a minimum wage, which miners came to regard as even more of a necessity following the Eight-Hours Act.[41] Yet this was bitterly resisted by the owners who considered it an intolerable invasion of their prerogatives. A series of disputes that included the Cambrian Combine strike in South Wales and a national coal strike in 1912 eventually forced the government to push through a Minimum Wage Act. The latter did little, however, to relieve the atmosphere of bitterness and tension in the industry as the downward trend in real wages continued until the First World War. Moreover, the increasing involvement of the state in regulating conditions in the coal industry had the important effect of politicising the discontent of the miners.

The deteriorating state of industrial relations in the engineering, cotton and coal industries after 1905–6 was part of a general rise in labour militancy that lifted trade union membership from about two millions in 1905 to more than four millions by 1913, with the density of union membership rising from 11.9% to 23.1% in the same period.[42] During these years, the number of industrial disputes recorded by the Board of Trade increased almost continuously from 349 in 1905 to 1,459 in 1913.[43] The scale and rapidity of the growth in union membership, and the upsurge in militancy associated with it, moved ahead of the established practices of sectionalised leadership and collective bargaining, which seemed incapable of satisfying rank-and-file expectations that their grievances would be resolved. The distinction between the 'old' and 'new' trade unionism became blurred as the workers' efforts to settle their strictly economic demands raised basic issues of job control and began to question the prerogatives of capital and property, in a way that was perceived as almost 'revolutionary' by many contemporaries.

On the railways, for example, the concession of conciliation boards obtained as a direct result of government pressure on the employers in 1907 fell short of what the workers wanted—union recognition. This, the companies feared, would if granted unleash a wave of demands and undermine further their already parlous financial condition.[44] In the docks, the upturn in trade after 1909 led to the setting up of the National Transport Workers' Federation that revived the dockers' claim for the compulsory union ticket as the condition for employment, which had been so violently opposed by the employers in the 1890s.[45] What is significant about the labour unrest of the period 1910–14 was the conjuncture of developments in different industries, casting doubt on previously accepted practices of collective bargaining and shifting the focus of conflict from well-defined questions like wage rates to the issue of control of work itself. This created opportunities for generalising the class interests of wage-earners across different trades and industries, in the face of the institutional obstacles to collective action that had appeared insuperable in 1900. Finally, and perhaps most important of all, the growing intervention of government in attempting to deal with the consequences of such a fundamental shift in the focus of industrial conflict, which employers were clearly not able to resolve entirely on their own, raised the basic question of the *political* relationship of labour with British society that had traditionally been masked by the burden of accepted practices, loyalties, ideologies and institutions.

The Prospects for the 'New Liberalism'

The extent to which there was an articulation between the growth and changing character of industrial unrest during the period 1906–14 and its mobilisation in political terms is one of the most problematic aspects of labour's relationship with British society in the years just prior to the First World War. The number of trade unionists affiliated to the Parliamentary Labour Party did rise from 975,000 in 1906 to 1,858,000 in 1912.[46] It is far from clear, however, what this massive increase represented as an indication of the changing consciousness of the rank-and-file trade unionist. Moreover, the ability of Labour MPs to pursue identifiable policies of their own was limited by the secret electoral pact negotiated with the Liberal Party in 1903, which allowed them to be subsumed under the umbrella of the New Liberalism. Yet it is arguable that despite the landslide victory of the Liberals in the 1906 General Election, which also swept 29 LRC-sponsored candidates into Parliament, the authority of the subsequent administration rested on fragile foundations. This was the background to the increasingly extraparliamentary character of labour unrest during the period 1910–14.

The magnitude of the Liberal success in 1906 has been explained as a result of 'incidental unity', following the divisions in the Conservative Party over tariff reform. This produced a loose alliance of free traders, MPs who had committed themselves to a revision of the law governing trade unions, and disgruntled nonconformists displeased with the 1902 Education Act.[47] It is noteworthy that although 24 of the 29 successful LRC candidates had been unopposed by Liberals, in accordance with the 1903 agreement, the remaining five successes had been gained in 18 contests *against* the Liberals.[48] Any commitment on behalf of the Liberal government to radical policies, with working-class voters in mind, ran the risk of alienating traditional sources of support among northern businessmen and made it vulnerable to disaffection given the franchise's bias in favour of wealth. By 1910, for example, the Lancashire cotton magnates had moved into the Conservative camp, abandoning their doctrinaire belief in free trade that had identified them with Liberalism.[49] At the same time, even the self-conscious radicalism of a leading New Liberal like Lloyd George contained an important element of equivocation when it came to the claims of organised labour. He was always happier attacking the 'abuses' of landownership rather than the prerogatives of capital, and his support for greater labour representation was based on his calculation of the benefits that it would yield for the Liberal Party: he remained consistently opposed to 'socialism'.[50]

Lloyd George's special blend of 'Social Radicalism' struck a positive response from the LRC-sponsored MPs whose largely nonconformist background he shared. Few of them appear to have had much interest in or knowledge of socialism.[51] The same might also be said of the rank-and-file trade unionist, but it was he who had directly to carry the burden of falling living standards and worsening conditions after 1906. Thus while Ramsay MacDonald spoke in glowing terms of the principles of democratic government, which on no account should agitation over issues like unemployment be allowed to undermine, workers took to the streets during the slump of 1907–8 and joined in 'right-to-work' demonstrations that owed much to the propaganda of the Social Democratic Federation.[52] Agitation over unemployment fell away after 1909 as trade revived, but the Liberal government's evident inability to resolve the question was indicative of the limits of social radicalism as a parliamentary force. It also emphasised the seriousness of the dilemma facing those Labour MPs who sought to represent the interests of the working *class*, and not just the minority of working-class *voters*. The complete exclusion of women from the franchise, for example, was an ideal issue for mobilising the economic and social grievances of women on a political basis, and the growth in female employment outside the notoriously 'deferential' category of domestic service during this period created a new focus for collective action that emerged in the campaign for women's suffrage.[53] By 1914, a narrowly conceived agitation for this demand, as an end in itself, had been widened by the activities of organisations like Sylvia Pankhurst's East London Federation, which sought to relate the suffrage question to broader economic and social issues along socialist lines. The viability of Labour's alliance with Liberalism was thus subject to diminishing returns in terms of its 'pay-off' for labour, as the growth of the extraparliamentary challenge to government after 1910 was to demonstrate.

The exasperation of many socialists with the conciliatory tactics of the LRC-sponsored MPs led to major sensation in 1907 with the election of Victor Grayson as an Independent Socialist for Colne Valley. Grayson followed up this success with a campaign for the formation of a new and identifiably 'socialist' party, representing a broad spectrum of left opinion, but he antagonised the leadership of the Labour group in Parliament who retained control of both the ILP and the resources of the trade unions on a crucial vote of confidence in 1909.[54] This helped redirect working-class militancy into the industrial sphere and gave birth to new forms of 'direct action'. The upshot was that growing labour unrest increasingly bypassed established organisations and procedures. What many leading Liberals did not fully anticipate was the effect of their social welfare programme in raising expectations that could not be satisfied by the necessarily limited character of 'reform'. Once it had been admitted that the state did have a direct responsibility for tackling some of the most chronic economic and social ills of the working class, this posed fundamental questions concerning not only how far the scope of this responsibility should extend, but the character of state power itself and the source of its ultimate authority. Was labour prepared simply to be acted upon, however beneficial the results might be, or did the New Liberalism's redefinition of the relationship between the individual and society not imply that government be directly responsible to the working class, in order to ensure that what was meant by the pursuit of the 'social good' reflected the needs and aspirations of the majority of the population?

The support given by Labour MPs to the Liberal government's social welfare legislation appears astonishing given its limited and generally selective character, which denied the principle of equality of provision.[55] This seems even more remarkable when it is appreciated that much of the contents of the welfare proposals, including the details for administering them, were worked out by a small group of permanent civil servants who retained a considerable degree of autonomy in relation to Parliament. This embryonic welfarist bureaucracy was intent on using 'reform' as a means of preserving the established social order, and it had virtually a free hand in doing so because it remained largely insulated from direct working-class pressure and was generally hostile to the more extreme of labour's aspirations.[56] Furthermore, the experience of employers who had introduced welfare schemes for their workers played an important role in determining the subsequent course of state social policy.[57] Senior civil servants were aware of the large body of evidence submitted by chambers of commerce, for example, to the Royal Commission on the Poor Laws during 1905–9, which looked with favour on proposals for the state to complement the private welfare schemes of employers with more comprehensive ones of its own, as a means of increasing industrial efficiency and preserving social order. Thus the chambers of commerce of Hull and Sheffield were convinced of the need for 'comprehensive schemes' instituted by government that would provide adequately for the 'deserving poor', perhaps through contributory insurance, while maintaining control over 'idle and worthless' people.[58] It would seem that the welfarist inclinations of 'progressive' businessmen and the New Liberalism's belief in 'social harmony' were about to converge and produce a new consensus on how to deal with Britain's economic and social problems. Yet the more the *practical implementation* of social policy moved in this direction, the more selective and limited in scope it necessarily became, until the New Liberalism's ideals of 'equality of rights' and 'equality of culture' were steadily lost sight of as the Liberal government strove to reconcile the rising expectations of the working class, which its promises had encouraged, with the vested interests of wealth and power in society as a whole.

After 1906, the Liberal government's welfare legislation illustrates the limits as well as extent of its zeal for reform. The Liberal-sponsored Workmen's Compensation Act of 1906 was the point of departure that anticipated wide-ranging efforts by government to improve workers' conditions. This extended the principle of employers' liability by insisting on compensation for accidents at work in respect of practically all employees receiving less than £250 per annum. But its escape clause excepting liability in case of 'serious and wilful misconduct' indicated the government's concern to use the compensation principle as a means of maintaining labour discipline. The problem of physical deterioration in trades where workers lacked the bargaining strength to protect their conditions of employment was the background to the Trade Boards Act of 1909. This sought to alleviate 'sweating' caused by the superabundance of the labour market, which discouraged employers from modernising antiquated production methods and led them to rely heavily on 'driving' their workers. Three trade boards were set up—in chain-making, paper-box making, and in ready-made and wholesale bespoke male garments—each comprising an independent chairman and an equal number of employers and workers' representatives. These were empowered to set minimum wages and maximum hours of work. Although this measure of state encroachment on the market mechanism could be justified on the traditional assumption that it was mostly women workers who were affected, thus maintaining the hoary distinction between themselves and adult males who were 'free agents', its implications in the context of growing social unrest after 1906 raised the question of a general minimum wage guaranteed by legal enactment.[59]

The 'sweated' labour issue, in particular, gave an extra dimension to the 'Women's Question' that thrust itself into the centre of political debate during these years. Could the New Liberalism's conception of universal citizenship continue to be denied to women in both the industrial and political spheres? The problem for the government was the hostility of vested interests among the more vulnerable factions of British capital who were in no position to meet any generalised demand for a national 'minimum', as the opportunities for accumulation in industry narrowed. Yet a national minimum was exactly what a new generation of working people was coming to expect. In this connection, legislation like the Education (Provision of Meals) Act of 1906 and the authorisation of medical inspection for schoolchildren contained in the Education Act of 1907, which had followed directly from the concern about the physical health of the working population created by the Boer War, represented an extension of services to what was soon to become the young generation of adult workers.[60] If it was accepted, for example, that schoolchildren were entitled to meals provided by the state, how long would it be before these same children as they grew to adulthood begin to demand an equivalent or even greater measure of assistance, in a society where low-paid, casual and dead-end jobs remained the lot of a major section of the labour force?

At the opposite end of the spectrum to the physical health of children was the condition of the aged poor whose plight had given cause for concern since the 1880s. Even before 1906, a number of factors including the growing financial crisis of the friendly societies, the revelations of statistical investigations showing the extent of poverty associated with old age, and the increasing pressure on the resources of the Poor Law authorities, had convinced an influential section of ruling opinion of the need for some form of non-contributory pension scheme financed by the national exchequer.[61] The Liberal government's recognition of its need to secure the compliant co-operation of Labour MPs required that something had to be done, and this was strengthened by the conversion of important sections of organised labour like the cotton operatives in favour of state pensions, who were now inclined to vote Liberal.[62] Yet what was actually achieved serves to emphasise the limited scope of reform in terms of working-class needs and expectations. This is to be explained in part by the attachment of the Liberals to the principles of 'prudent finance', but this was not the only consideration determining the provision of the 1908 Old Age Pensions Act. An influential thinker like William Beveridge, for example, was opposed to the granting of pensions solely on the claim of need and wanted legislation framed in such a way that payments would be made as a reward for a hard-working and 'responsible' life.[63] In this respect, his attitude was shared by the existing self-help institutions of organised labour, representing the working-class electorate, which regarded state pensions as a means of supporting but not replacing their own schemes.[64]

The Act of 1908 provided a state pension of 5s per week to those who had reached the age of 70 and had an income of less than £26 yearly, although this sum was estimated by Rowntree to be 2s below the weekly minimum required for subsistence by a single adult.[65] The government's intention not to discourage 'laudable efforts at thrift' by the working class was reflected in the disqualifications for the receipt of a pension. These excluded any person who had been guilty of 'habitual failure to work according to his ability, opportunity, or need, for his own maintenance or that of his legal relatives'; or who had been in receipt of poor relief after 1 January 1908; or who had been imprisoned for any offence, including drunkenness, during the ten years preceding the claim.[66] The latter disqualification caused considerable hardship for those who had served sentences of only a few days but who were consequently deprived of a pension.[67] The test of being in receipt of poor relief immediately disqualified 284,500 potential claimants in England and Wales.[68] Yet the fact was that almost 500,000 men and women or about 27% of those over 70 in the United Kingdom did meet the stringent test of qualification, and 92% of these were entitled to the maximum pension.[69] This was indicative of the problem of poverty associated with old age. Yet the 1908 Act failed completely to ameliorate the misery of many working people who died, were 'worn out' or otherwise unable to find employment before the age of 70. It thus did not take into account what in practice constituted 'old age' in different trades and industries. The working life of a clerk or shop assistant, for example, could be expected to be considerably longer than that of a cotton-spinner worn out after 20 years at his machine. Moreover, the amount of the pension granted was inadequate even in terms of 1908 prices, and this became increasingly incapable of meeting subsistence needs because of the continuing upward trend in the cost of basic necessities. In establishing the principle of a non-contributory entitlement, however, which unlike the Poor Law did not deprive the recipient of the privileges of citizenship, the concession of state pensions set a precedent for the provision of assistance that working people could demand as a right, and this could be readily generalised to other spheres of welfare policy, especially by socialists in connection with issues like unemployment.

The limitations of the 1908 Old Age Pensions Act in alleviating poverty among those who failed to secure regular employment up to the age of 70 raised the question of the entire structure of the Poor Law, which had been undergoing investigation by a Royal Commission since 1905. The severe slump of 1907–8 highlighted the problem of unemployment among workers who either lacked the support of membership in a friendly society or trade union, or had exhausted their benefit and were unable to find employment again in their old trades.[70] The cost of providing for the unemployed in the workhouse was rapidly becoming prohibitive: by 1913, the Local Government Board calculated that since 1900 it had cost four times as much to maintain each indoor pauper as one on outdoor relief.[71] It was also discovered that even 'respectable men' were to be found having recourse to indoor relief, which formed part of the criticisms of the Poor Law made by the 1909 Minority Report of the Royal Commission.[72] The latter argued that the 'indiscriminate' mixing of the different classes of poor in the workhouse was defeating the whole purpose of the Poor Law in separating out the 'deserving' from the 'residuum'. What was required were more specialised institutions in place of the workhouse like labour colonies, retraining centres or detention camps, depending on the character and aptitude of the individual unemployed.[73] Yet this approach was bound to lead to higher taxation, with the risk of antagonising vested interests of wealth-holders, and the Liberal government chose consequently to pursue the safer course of legislation for the unemployed that would leave the Poor Law intact. It was also led to take this course of action because of the problem of the relationship between imperial and local taxation, especially how the financial burden of replacing the workhouse with more specialised institutions might be shared among rich and poor authorities.[74]

It was the ingenuity and political adroitness of Lloyd George's budget of 1909 that sustained the momentum of Liberal welfare reform. The provision of a far from prohibitive duty of 20% on the 'unearned increment' of the value of land, to be paid when it was sold, in addition to a $\frac{1}{2}$d in the pound tax on the capital value of land when left undeveloped, was in the best traditions of nineteenth-century Liberalism. This promised to raise an extra £3,700,000 whilst not offending too severely the government's solid core of support from among provincial industrialists.[75] An additional £2,250,000 was also expected from Lloyd George's increase in licensing duties, which appealed strongly to the nonconformists. With respect to capital itself, the imposition of a supertax of 6d in the pound on incomes of over £5,000 seemed a small price to pay in return for a limited instalment of social reform, without incurring the dreaded 'stomach tax' implied by tariff reform. The reaction of the House of Lords in throwing out the budget presented the

Liberals with an ideal opportunity for fighting a broad-based election campaign that focused on the power and 'unearned' wealth of
landowners as the scapegoat for the country's economic and social
problems. This was linked to an attack on land 'monopoly' and
emphasised the benefits that would accrue to both labour and
capital if the 'old inexorable laws of supply and demand' could be
made to work efficiently, thereby releasing more land for commercial and industrial use and relieving the superabundance of the
labour market in urban areas, with the result that wages would rise
and strikes become unnecessary.[76] The 'Social Radicalism' of this
line of argument proved attractive to the working-class electorate,
whilst it was formulated in such a way as to not offend overtly the
interests of most of Liberalism's wealthy supporters. The Liberal
government's subsequent victory in the 1910 General Election thus
guaranteed the survival of its welfare programme since the 'People's
Budget' was expected to yield a further £13,600,000 in tax
revenues.[77]

One of the major welfare proposals contained in the 1909 budget
was a scheme for labour exchanges. This sprang from the fertile
mind of William Beveridge whose main concern was to deal specifically with the casual underemployed or 'residuum', whose alacrity in
availing themselves of outdoor relief had so alarmed the Royal
Commission on the Poor Laws.[78] His conception of labour exchanges as a 'department of industrial intelligence', designed to test
and organise the labour market as a means of relieving the surplus
of permanent unemployed, reflected his obsession with 'efficiency'
and the avoidance of 'waste'; but it also contained a moral element
in that labour exchanges would distinguish the 'unfit' from the
genuinely unemployed, and once so identified the former could be
dispatched to 'an institution of disciplinary detention'.[79] This was
part of his overall objective of 'bringing together under public or
semi-public control...the whole process of industrial engagement'.[80] In fact, the 1909 Act setting up labour exchanges was
voluntary rather than compulsory, although this was an indication
of the government's awareness that it would be difficult to enforce
compulsion on skilled and organised workers, together with its fear
that to attempt to eliminate casual labour immediately would be
impossible because of the lack of preparation for dealing with the
'surplus'.[81] The effect of a compulsory scheme would also have been
to encourage an expectation among working people that they had 'a
right to work', which was dangerously close to the socialist argu-

ment. It appeared safer to rely on the market mechanism in persuading the residuum to 'sign on' in their own interest. In this way, the working class could be 'moralised' in the image of what employers considered a 'respectable' and 'competent' workman.[82] It was for this reason that labour exchanges were bitterly attacked at the 1910 TUC, where it was claimed that they assisted in strike-breaking, and it was also argued that women and children were being recruited from workhouses as a means of undermining wage rates and working conditions negotiated by collective bargaining.[83] The fact was that most skilled workers felt there was a stigma attached to using them, and during the years 1910–14 there were three applicants turned away for each one who found a job.[84] It seemed to many working people that labour exchanges were yet another agency, used by the state to act upon the working class in the interests of capital, rather than in accordance with their own needs and aspirations.

The strong element of selectivity embodied in the scheme for labour exchanges was also contained in proposals for unemployment insurance. The Liberal government and its civil servants were determined on a contributory scheme confined to a limited category of occupations that were especially vulnerable to cyclical slumps, and the traditional principle of 'less eligibility' was incorporated in the proviso that any payments to the unemployed should be below the prevailing rate of 'ordinary wages'.[85] The government's intention was clearly not to create a permanent class of able-bodied unemployed maintained by some indiscriminate form of dole. In fact, it was argued that the contributory character of unemployment insurance would have the effect of 'regularising' the labour market by reducing the number of casual workers who did not stand to benefit, with the result that the 'least efficient' would be removed from the labour force.[86] In defence of the cost of the contributions to be borne partly by the employer, the government's view was that this need not be transferred to the consumer or deducted indirectly from wages because the effect of compulsory insurance in removing the 'least efficient' from the labour force would reduce the unit costs of production.[87] Employers were also favourably inclined to a clause in the proposed legislation depriving workers of benefit for six weeks if dismissed for 'misconduct', or if they left work voluntarily 'without due cause', and this disallowed over 50,000 claims during the first two years of the scheme's operation.[88] The responsibility of the labour exchanges in managing the distribution of benefits indicates that government was intent on keeping the service firmly under state control, although this example of state 'coercion' was condemned by the TUC which wanted any provision to be managed by organised labour.[89]

The National Insurance Act of 1911 made unemployment insurance compulsory for an estimated 2,250,000 workers—located primarily in building construction, engineering and shipbuilding—who were entitled to a uniform benefit of 7s a week for up to 15 weeks. This level of compensation, like the sum specified in the 1908 Old Age Pensions Act, was scarcely sufficient to maintain a workers' subsistence without additional assistance from personal savings or benefits provided by a trade union or friendly society. Relief in case of unemployment, contained in Part II of the 1911 Act, was preceded by a section on health insurance. This transferred the control of medical treatment from the friendly societies to specifically appointed Insurance Committees that included representatives of the medical profession, and provision was made for government grants to sanatoria, medical research, and nursing and clinical services run by the local authorities.[90] Even more than in the case of unemployment insurance, health provision indicated a general concern to improve 'national efficiency', which lay behind much of the Liberal government's social welfare legislation. Opposition from the industrial insurance lobby, for example, led to the abandonment of proposals for widows' and orphans' pensions, and it could be argued that the transfer of control of medical treatment from the friendly societies benefited the medical practitioner more than it did the working-class patient. In at least one case, there is evidence of an employer who used the new Insurance Committees as a means of discriminating against a scheme of medical treatment offered by a trade union, in favour of one that was managed by the firm, in order to isolate workers from contact with trade unionism.[91]. The provision of health insurance, like compulsory unemployment insurance, seemed to confirm the worst fears of those critics of the Liberal welfare reforms who saw in them the embodiment of the 'Servile State', which has been defined as[92]

That arrangement of society in which so considerable a number of families and individuals are constrained by positive law to labour for the advantages of other families and individuals as to stamp the whole community with the mark of such labour we call THE SERVILE STATE.

The Liberal government's reluctance to get to grips with the root causes of unemployment is reflected in the failure of what was potentially the most ambitious of all its measures of welfare reform—the Development Act of 1909. This made available £12 million guaranteed for a period of five years to assist local authorities in phasing their public works during the downswing of the trade cycle, as a means of reducing unemployment. Although the absence of suitable administrative machinery and the unwillingness of the local authorities to embark on projects, given the limited life of the scheme, have been emphasised in explaining why less than 5% of the Development Fund was drawn upon during the years 1910–15, it can also be argued that the Act's intention of countering the effects of cyclical depression misconceived the problem of unemployment in the context of the pre-1914 economy. The extent of poverty caused by the lack of opportunities for regular employment, indicated by the high levels of vagrancy and pauperism, was a structural problem arising from striking inequalities in the distribution of wealth and income, which held back the growth of effective demand. This was something that a mild instalment of counter-cyclical expenditure could not be expected to overcome. The perspectives of the New Liberalism lacked an analysis and the political will to attack the structural causes of poverty, which would have required a fundamental shift of power and resources in favour of the working class. But this was far removed from the government's intentions. As Winston Churchill declared when arguing for unemployment insurance in 1909:[93]

> The idea is to increase the stability of our institutions by giving the mass of industrial workers a direct interest in maintaining them. With a 'stake in the country' in the form of insurance against evil days these workers will pay no attention to the vague promises of revolutionary socialism.

It remained to be seen whether Churchill's conceptualisation of the New Liberalism in giving workers a 'stake in the country' would ultimately be acceptable to them.

The Dimensions to the 'Labour Unrest', 1910–14

The limitations of the Liberal welfare reforms in mitigating the causes of working-class discontent, which reflected the essentially 'conservative' assumptions underlying them, implied that new forms of labour unrest were allowed to flourish almost unchecked in the years just prior to the First World War. As trade revived after 1909, the resulting fall in unemployment and upsurge in union membership led to a marked shift in the direction of labour control from the traditional stratagem of 'control through the market' to 'control through organisation'.[94] The advent of increasingly centralised collective bargaining in the industrial sphere was generally favourable to the interests of employers in the context of this period of rising prices. This was complemented in political terms by the growth of a state welfarist bureaucracy. In both spheres, there was a tendency for union leaders and officials to become institutionally isolated from the workers they ostensibly represented. Nationwide machinery for collective bargaining sought to check local militancy, whilst the recruitment of union officials to help run labour exchanges and insurance committees did not always endear them with their rank and file. The outcome was often to create new centres of militancy in particular localities where a younger generation of leaders emerged to challenge the more conciliatory policies of the existing labour leadership.

In the engineering industry, for example, the aftermath of a bitter unofficial strike on the north-east coast of England in 1908, which had involved 10,000 workers in a seven-month stoppage over a proposed wage reduction, led the employers to enforce long-term contracts on local joint negotiating committees as a means of avoiding future disputes. Although workers benefited immediately to the extent that their agreement was secured as a *quid pro quo*, following the employers' withdrawal of their demand for wage reductions, the revival in trade after 1909 made this concession appear an increasingly empty one, and it is generally acknowledged that as a consequence profits rose more than wages.[95] Unofficial strikes continued, nevertheless, and so numerous did these become that in 1912 a special levy was imposed on member firms of the Employers' Federation in order to compensate those who were affected.[96] The character of the labour unrest during these years emphasises that issues more deep seated than concern about wage rates and hours of work lay behind it. The hostility to long-term wage contracts, for example, was part of a much more profound sense of frustration felt by time-served craftsmen as new processes and methods of 'scientific management' continued to erode craft autonomy in the workshop.[97]

A similar sense of social injustice was also felt by workers in the coal industry where wage rates continued to lag behind the rise in prices and profits after 1906. Basic rates negotiated by the Miners' Federation, which subsequently assimilated the export districts to an industrywide pattern of collective bargaining, were still little above their 1900 level in 1913, despite the rise in the cost of living and the record profits of the coal-owners.[98] The continuing growth of coal exports led to large-scale influx of labour into Northumberland, Durham and South Wales where the effect of declining productivity meant that the proportion of comparatively low-paid oncost daywagemen was increasing relative to the face-workers, and where rising costs were pushed even higher as a result of additional burdens imposed by welfare legislation like workmen's compensation and the eight-hour day.[99] The pressures on the face-workers who had traditionally supplied the industry with moderate labour leaders were intensified by the formation of giant amalgamations like the Joicey and Horden companies in Durham and the Cambrian Combine in South Wales, and their aggressive attitude to labour management made the conciliatory policies of the Miners' Federation increasingly unacceptable to the rank and file.[100] On the north-east coast of England and in South Wales, moreover, the influx of migrant labour began to undermine nonconformity and the chapel as the agent of cultural mediation between owners and miners, at the same time that escalating production costs led managers to reduce or abolish completely the allowances paid to face-workers in compensation for 'dead work' or hewing in 'abnormal' places.[101] Unofficial disputes in reaction to the introduction of the eight-hour day, for example, involved 115,000 miners in Durham and Northumberland alone in 1910, a traditionally 'non-militant' area, while the issue of abnormal places led to a similar unofficial strike affecting 30,000 men in South Wales during 1910–11, centred on the collieries of the Cambrian Combine in the Rhondda valley. The widespread use of police to escort strike-breakers created a heightened sense of class antagonism, and instances of violence against property emphasised how far strike activity had extended beyond the accepted norms of collective bargaining.[102]

The failure of the Welsh miners to resolve the question of abnormal places to their satisfaction during 1910–11 laid the basis for an industrywide movement culminating in a national strike for a minimum wage, which paralysed the coal industry in the winter of 1911–12. Even more than the eight-hours issue, this demand marked a fundamental challenge to the owners' prerogatives as property-owners. The latter had been reconciled to accepting collective bargaining during the 1890s on condition that miners' wages should still reflect fluctuations in coal prices. The owners' agreement to a general minimum, on the other hand, would imply that the requirements of the miners' standard of living should become a 'standing charge' on the industry, irrespective of market conditions, and the burden of adjustment to the industry's changing fortunes shifted consequently from labour to capital. A new generation of militant leaders was clearly prepared to use the miners' bargaining muscle to coerce the state, if necessary, in pursuit of the minimum wage demand, and the means discussed often demonstrated an impatience with the established union leadership and a cynicism towards the 'goodwill' of government.[103]

The national strike in the coal industry was settled in April 1912 not on the basis of a specified minimum daily wage of 5s for adult miners and 2s for boys, which had constituted the crux of the miners' demands, but in response to a government promise of an unspecified Minimum Wage Bill for the coal industry. The worst fears of the majority of miners in one or two districts, who had voted against a resumption of work on this basis, appeared confirmed when subsequent legislation recognised only the principle of a minimum wage, leaving the fixing of actual rates to the existing District Boards chaired by 'independent' arbitrators. Throughout 1912, there were not only complaints that the District Boards were in practice ignoring the principle of the minimum wage, as laid down by statute, but that where it was recognised the owners tried to avoid paying it altogether, or sought compensation by introducing new working arrangements that withheld payment unless higher levels of output were achieved.[104] Thus the South Wales affiliate of the Miners' Federation withdrew from its District Board in May 1912. The patent inability of either the existing procedures for collective bargaining or state regulation in resolving labour unrest in the coal industry was part of the widening scope of strike activity during 1912–13, which seemed to justify a growing fear that a 'general strike' was imminent.

The limited character of the Liberal government's welfare reforms was most obvious in the case of casual unskilled and semi-skilled labour that was heavily concentrated in the transport sector, especially dock employment. It was these groups whose subsistence wages made them most vulnerable to the rising cost of living, whilst they were the least likely to benefit from welfare legislation like old age pensions, with its disqualification clauses, and they were not covered at all by unemployment insurance despite the risk of irregular employment. A significant proportion of the estimated 30% of adult male workers earning less than 25s per week in 1911 were located in these categories of employment, and together with their dependents they numbered eight million people.[105] It is true that the boom in trade just prior to the First World War took much of the slack out of the labour market, but it was organised workers with their stronger bargaining position who stood to gain most from this. Much of the strike activity in the docks, for example, took the form of a 'general revolt', often spontaneous and independent of formal union organisation, with workers and their families parading through the streets. Their banners bearing inscriptions like 'Not Mere Alms but a Living Wage' testified to the existence of a kind of discontent that could not be readily ameliorated by the accepted assumptions and procedures of collective bargaining.

During the summer of 1911, a wave of strikes swept the country's ports and halted its railway system. This began in Liverpool where the largest companies were not members of the Shipping Federation, and this improved the workers' prospects of obtaining what they considered a basic right—union recognition. Yet the initiative behind this strike activity and the responsibility for its organisation relied primarily on unofficial committees of local militants, with the backing of experienced leaders like Tom Mann.[106] The key issue in dispute was the 'living wage', which could mobilise support from such disparate groups of workers as carters, dockers, railwaymen and seamen. The widespread deployment of police and later 5,000 troops to protect the movement of dock traffic against mass picketing in Liverpool deepened the resentment of the strikers and made them aware that they were not only in conflict with their employers but with the state itself. This was confirmed by the terms of settlement that was the direct result of government intervention. In Liverpool, for example, the procedure adopted by the newly appointed joint committee of employers and union officials included a no-strike clause, which made the parties represented on the committee liable to fines if they refused to observe its rules or accept its recommendations.[107] The outcome of the dispute in creating a powerful new Employers' Association in the port of Liverpool in 1913 increased the feeling among some of the rank and file that they had merely exchanged one form of oppression for another, made up of a coalition of union officials and employers' representatives. The impetus this gave to the tactics of 'direct action' was echoed in subsequent disputes, including the London dock strike of 1912 that was marked by street demonstrations, outbreaks of violence against blacklegs, and even gun battles on the steamship *City of Colombo*.[108]

It was the 'unofficial' character as much as the increasing incidence of industrial unrest after 1910 that caused alarm among many employers and in government circles. There was special concern about the challenge to established trade union leaders of moderate views, and the growing propensity of the rank and file to resort to direct action in contravention of agreed procedures. Liberal politicians like Sydney Buxton, President of the Board of Trade, looked askance at labour's reluctance in making use of the board's conciliation services, and he urged that 'an effort should be made to maintain a greater control over the position', i.e. by more positive government intervention.[109] Buxton expressed himself in favour of 'Canadian-type legislation' that would have required the submission of disputes to conciliation or arbitration boards before a stoppage of work could take place.[110] Other Board of Trade officials like Llewellyn Smith argued for compulsory conciliation and a statutory cooling-off period.[111] This was the background to the Board's setting up in 1911 of the Industrial Council, which was the brainchild of Sir Charles Macara, the Lancashire cotton magnate. This was to be composed of an equal number of prominent representatives of capital and labour, the responsibility for appointments resting with the Board of Trade. It was authorised to investigate disputes and make recommendations as to their settlement, but its decisions were binding only if both parties agreed that they should be.[112] Yet the council was never genuinely representative since its composition depended on government appointments, rather than reflecting the feelings of the respective parties of employers and employed, and it is significant that almost all the trade union members were identified with trades having highly organised procedures for collective bargaining.[113] It was this that in itself made the Industrial Council virtually useless in dealing with the new forms of labour unrest during the period 1910–14, and its record of intervention in disputes was one of almost complete failure.[114] The council was regarded by many as a 'packed jury', another example of a state-created institution designed to secure the 'servility' of labour.[115] To the extent that it had any influence at all, its involvement of government in industrial conflict served only to widen the opportunities for politicising the labour unrest of these years.

Although the New Liberalism had done little to alter in any fundamental way the allocation of wealth and power in British society, its radical rhetoric threatened to produce a dangerous convergence of industrial and political discontent, since it appeared to imply that an entire spectrum of economic and social problems was now the state's responsibility. At the same time, what many New Liberals did not perhaps fully appreciate was the underlying contradiction of a strategy that sought to ameliorate the condition of labour by state action, in a social context marked by massive inequalities in the distribution of wealth and income. Government intervention inevitably curtailed the freedom of action of working people, whether as the result of efforts to 'organise the labour market' as a means of alleviating unemployment, or as the consequence of attempts to strengthen the machinery for collective bargaining as a way of preventing unofficial strikes. The restrictions on working-class 'self-activity' that this entailed were perceived by many as extremely onerous, given the limited benefits of welfare reform. Britain's political system, moreover, was structured so as to give the wealthy and powerful a privileged position, while effective influence in governing circles was in practice denied to the majority of the population that was either voteless or dependent upon representatives who seemed to accept with equanimity their subordinate position beneath the 'progressive' umbrella.[116] Thus George Barker, a member of the miners' National Executive, described the House of Commons at the time of the 1912 coal strike as follows:[117]

> It consists of six hundred and seventy men, six hundred and thirty who were capitalists and landowners, and it will be the death knell to the liberties of this movement if we hand them over to a body of this character, therefore I say we cannot hope to get much from those who represent those great interests of the country, I say that we must hold the sovereign power in our own hands.

The possibility of a convergence of labour's political as well as industrial grievances had been anticipated late in 1909 by an action of the House of Lords. In the midst of the uproar generated by the People's Budget, it decided in favour of a member of the

Amalgamated Society of Railway Servants called Osborne who wanted an injunction to stop his union from spending its funds for political purposes. With the active assistance of the Anti-Socialist Union, which depended for its finance upon several prominent wealthy individuals, the Osborne decision was subsequently applied to other unions, with the result that by August 1910 thirteen had been restrained from using their funds for political purposes, including their support of 16 Labour MPs.[118] The controversy this caused emphasised the fragility of the alliance of Labour members and the Liberal Party in Parliament since several leading Liberals, including the whole of the Scottish Liberal Association, were opposed to any reversal of the Osborne judgement, regarding it as a legitimate part of a policy of 'standing up to the Socialists'.[119] Although its effect was to be nullified, at least in part, by the Trade Union Act of 1913, it cast doubt on the credibility of labour's parliamentary presence and the tactics of co-operating with 'advanced' Liberals. This was reflected in the constituencies where local labour groups found it less easy to maintain an alliance with Liberalism on the basis of the 1903 pact. In a series of by-elections between December 1910 and the summer of 1914, there were six instances of a triangular contest where the vote for the Labour candidate was greater than the margin between Liberals and Tories.[120] It was the latter, of course, who stood to gain as a result of the combined disadvantages of a limited franchise and divisions within the progressive ranks, which seemed to discredit even further the prospects for building a working-class presence in Parliament. The number of Labour MPs had, in fact, fallen to 37 by mid-1914, compared with 42 after the General Election of December 1910.[121] In this respect, the Liberal government's failure to resolve industrial conflict to the satisfaction of either capital or labour figured prominently as a cause of the dissensions within the progressive alliance, especially its Minimum Wage Act that settled the 1912 coal strike.

This was the background to growing fears that the working class might opt for direct action to achieve its ends, or even mount an extraparliamentary challenge to the established social order. Ruling opinion was afraid that the rising expectations generated by the *slogan* of 'Social Reform' was actually encouraging labour unrest, whereas welfare legislation sought ostensibly to prevent it.[122] The 1912 Minimum Wage Act affecting the coal industry was seen by many wage-earners as part of a natural progression, initiated by earlier legislation, that promised some kind of general minimum to which all were entitled, yet its limitations and loopholes illustrated the ambivalence of most Liberals to the entire issue of a national minimum guaranteed by government fiat, with the exception of a small group of self-conscious Radicals. The 1911 National Insurance Act, for example, not only imposed new forms of state compulsion on groups of workers who were relatively well organised and had long experience of making provision for their welfare through their own self-help institutions; the burden of contributions required by National Insurance fell most heavily on working-class families with incomes of less than 30s per week who were least able to afford this additional expense.[123] In practice, much welfare reform was punitive as well as 'regressive', creating regulations and restrictions, and a growing army of government bureaucrats with their inquiry forms, which many working people bitterly resented. Thus while state welfarism was conceived by the wealthy as leading inevitably down the slippery slope to socialism, the experience of those who were its supposed beneficiaries was often one of frustration and disillusionment. What made this especially menacing for the stability of society as a whole was the way welfare reform shifted the locus of social conflict from the arena of competing economic interests that could still be contained within the dominant social order to the pursuit of state power itself.

Despite the appearance of harmony between Liberals and Labour MPs in Parliament, this proved deceptive as an indication of what was happening in the constituencies where the local Liberal associations found a new generation of labour leaders increasingly unacceptable. The groundswell of militancy in the localities would have led, it is estimated, to the nomination of 150 to 170 Labour candidates had a General Election been called in 1914 or 1915, and most of these would have contested seats where the sitting member was Liberal.[124] The efforts made by Ramsay MacDonald during the General Election of 1910 to restrict the number of Labour candidates, as a means of maintaining the 'Radical' momentum of the Liberal government in the face of the 'revolt' of wealth, became a less convincing strategy after 1911 as the New Liberalism's ability to satisfy labour's rising expectations diminished. The Labour Party's by-election losses after 1910 were attributed by many socialists to its close identification with a government that was steadily losing its appeal as a progressive force, and led one trade union leader to disclaim any responsibility for electing Labour candidates—a not uncommon view in the ranks of organised labour.[125] MacDonald's opposition to 'wildcat' Labour candidates who did not suit the Liberal Party's electoral calculations, or fit the inclinations of its local constituency associations, was a particular cause of growing frustration among his own rank and file.[126] The contrasting editorial policies of the *Daily Citizen*, the moderately inclined official organ of the Parliamentary Labour Party, and the *Daily Herald* that relied more on voluntary subscriptions and organised '*Daily Herald* leagues' as local centres of political discussion on the dissident left, illustrate the tensions created within the labour movement by MacDonald's policy of co-operation with the Liberals.[127]

There were two alternative strategies available to those who felt constrained by the enforced 'moderation' resulting from MacDonald's pact with the Liberals. They could chose to 'socialise' the Labour Party by working *within* it, in order to force change in the policies of its leadership; or they could opt for activity centred on groupings *outside* that sought in different ways to construct a more explicitly 'socialist' connection between industrial militancy and the pursuit of political power in the interests of the working class. Both strategies were adopted in specific instances during the years 1910–14. In a by-election at Leicester in 1913, for example, local militants chose as their Labour candidate R. E. Hartley, a member of the British Socialist Party that had absorbed the old SDF in 1911. He was opposed by no less a person than Ramsay MacDonald who was the standing MP supported by the National Administrative Committee of the ILP. The latter decided to bow to local pressure and accept Hartley as the Labour candidate, but it refused any financial help and the subsequent campaign was fought without official support, with the result that Hartley received only 10.19 % of the votes cast.[128] In London, the rapid expansion in trade union membership after 1910 in what had previously been a badly organised area played an important part in the establishment of the London Labour Party in 1914. Unlike some other constituency associations, it showed some degree of tolerance towards other left groups like the British Socialist Party. The local branches of the BSP successfully sought affiliation to the London Labour Party, and five of their members were subsequently represented among the latter's 18 officers comprising its Executive Committee.[129] This gave the socialists an effective influence in the new party, although its electoral appeal was not put to the test before the First World War.

It might also be expected that working-class discontent would flow into extraparliamentary channels, direct action being preferred to the pursuit of representation in the House of Commons. The task of defining what 'syndicalism' actually means is probably an ultimately fruitless one, at least in the abstract, but in the British context it would seem that it emphasised industrial action as a means of mobilising mass support for a final 'general strike', which aimed to overthrow the state and the capitalist system it supported. The potential of industrial action for achieving revolutionary ends had traditionally been ignored by socialist groups like the SDF, and it is in this respect that syndicalists were singularly well placed to take advantage of the increasing incidence of strike activity after 1910. What made syndicalist propaganda especially effective was its practical appeal, particularly its campaign for 'industrial unionism' which bypassed the sectional institutions of collective bargaining and stressed the direct accountability of labour leaders to the whole of their rank and file, irrespective of their individual craft or job.[130]

The worsening state of industrial relations in coal-mining after 1908 created special advantages for those who sought to mobilise mass support for fundamental change. The coal industry was subject to an unprecedented degree of government regulation during these years, which might have been expected to yield political advantages for the Liberals in mining constituencies. It is true that the Labour Party had made surprisingly few breakthroughs into what had previously been Liberal strongholds by 1914, despite the decision of the Miners' Federation to affiliate to the Labour Party in 1908.[131] Yet the effect of legislation like the eight-hour day and the minimum wage had served to exacerbate discontent in the coalfields, and the Labour Party's support of these 'advanced' Liberal measures cannot have enhanced its popularity among the miners who remained loyal to the proven industrial record of their Liberal-inclined union leaders. The latter were an ageing group, however, and their steady disappearance from the political scene opened the way for a younger generation of leaders like Robert Smillie, elected President of the Miners' Federation in 1912, who was a professed socialist in addition to having an impeccable industrial record.

The erosion of Liberalism's popularity among the miners was a gradual and uneven process and, in the meantime, some of the rank and file chose to take matters into their own hands rather than wait for MacDonald's tactics of gradualism to bear fruit. In particular, the setting up of the Plebs League and the Central Labour College, which followed the dissensions at Ruskin College in 1908 over the character of working-class education, marked the creation of a new focus for popular propaganda that had as its underlying principle of instruction the teaching of the theory of class war. Militants like Noah Ablett carried this message into the South Wales coalfield, for example, and by 1910 the South Wales Plebs League had built up a network of some 50 activists working in local branches of the ILP, as well as in lodges of the South Wales Miners' Federation.[132] During the Cambrian Combine strike of 1910–11, the efforts of syndicalists to politicise the dispute were evident in the 'purposive way' crowds of strikers attacked not only employers and their property but also representatives of the state like the chief magistrate of the Rhondda.[133] The aftermath of the strike witnessed the birth of the Unofficial Reform Committee, a rank-and-file group organised within the South Wales Miners' Federation whose demands included a guaranteed minimum wage, direct accountability of union leaders to their members, and 'industrial democracy' based on workers' control of their respective industries. The last of these was posed as an alternative to the 'delusion and snare' of parliamentary democracy, which was regarded as merely a disguise for capitalist dominance.[134]

The extremely limited gains that labour had obtained from collective bargaining in the transport sector, including workers employed in the docks and on the railways, provided another focus for syndicalist activity. In Liverpool during the 1911 strike, for example, the influence of a leading militant like Tom Mann, recently converted to syndicalism, introduced a new spirit of 'anti-statism' among groups of workers who in the 1890s had looked primarily to government to improve their condition. Their experience of Board of Trade intervention in labour disputes and the forms of collective bargaining subsequently established led to unofficial and almost 'spontaneous' demonstrations of the rank and file, which not infrequently turned to violent direct action, as living conditions failed materially to improve.[135] Syndicalism's emphasis on industrial unionism and working-class solidarity proved especially effective during the general transport strikes on Merseyside in the summer of 1911, affecting seamen, dockers and railwaymen, which were to escalate into a nationwide stoppage on the railways despite opposition from the leadership of the Amalgamated Society of Railway Servants. Violence against railway property and attacks on police and troops were commonplace, while the strength of working-class solidarity was such that the Nottinghamshire miners held up the trains operating on the Midland Railway, and there were even strikes of schoolchildren in railway centres.[136] In the engineering industry, the influence of syndicalism was manifest in the prominent role played by the Workers' Union in organising the Black Country strikes of semi-skilled machine men in 1913, and the problems created by skilled labour substitution in the industry led to support for syndicalist policies of 'class war' in the workshop among the largest single group represented at the 1912 Delegate Meeting of the Amalgamated Society of Engineers.[137]

Syndicalism's emphasis on direct action and spontaneity could acquire specific organisational forms. Thus the Advocates of Industrial Unionism set up by the Socialist Labour Party were active in organising workers' resistance to a threatened wage reduction at the Singer Sewing Machine Works in Clydebank in 1911, and its propaganda was subsequently disseminated along the banks of the Clyde.[138] During the years 1912–14, the persistence of high levels of labour unrest produced new foci of syndicalist influence like the Industrial Democracy League and the *Daily Herald* leagues, which had a considerable presence during the 1913 Dublin lock-out and in the London building trades lock-out of 1914.[139] Yet in terms of its aim of spreading a revolutionary alternative to official trade unionism, and developing a worked-out scenario for the capture of state power, syndicalism's record prior to 1914 was one of almost total failure. Even in an area as apparently 'red hot' as South Wales, not only did Lib–Labism remain a dominant force politically, but most of the new generation of miners' leaders were inveterately hostile to syndicalist industrial policies that failed to generate sufficient support from the rank and file to wrench power from their control.[140]

The creation of the so-called 'Triple Alliance' of railwaymen, miners and transport workers in 1914 can be interpreted as a specific instance of how syndicalist notions of industrial unionism and working-class solidarity might be put into practice. The failure of the London transport strike in 1912, the continuing refusal of the railway companies to recognise the unions, and the ability of coalowners to disregard the spirit if not the letter of the 1912 Minimum Wage Act, all went to show that a sectional and unco-ordinated approach to workers' grievances yielded only limited dividends. Among the rank and file, there is evidence to suggest that the Triple Alliance was conceived in terms of syndicalist ideas of industrial unionism and direct action that aimed at a general strike.[141] Yet the text of the agreement setting up the alliance provided only for the respective parties to consult each other before deciding upon any unilateral action, and they were not obliged to act in unison. Among some trade union leaders, the Triple Alliance seems to have been regarded as a tactical device, which promised to realise their demands where unilateral action had failed, and they remained determined, above all, to preserve the autonomy of their organisations and not be drawn willy-nilly into disputes against their wishes.[142] The ambivalence if not confusion surrounding the underlying purpose of the Triple Alliance was consequently to prove disastrous for the British labour movement. Much depended on the ability of the grass-roots membership to force the hand of their leaders. This point was emphasised by the Unofficial Reform Committee of the South Wales miners:[143]

> At the present stage, the Triple Alliance is simply a concentration of the power of the leaders of the various unions involved... the courage to fight, the wit to devise how to fight, and the wisdom to decide what to fight for—must come from the rank and file itself.

It was in this connection, in terms of building an effective rank-and-file alternative to official union structures, that syndicalism's influence must ultimately be judged. And there was also the problem of how to prepare for the mobilisation of state power against any 'general' industrial confrontation. This was especially ominous given the enormous extension of the apparatus of government during the First World War, which was to overshadow altogether the 'Servile State' created by the New Liberalism.

Notes

1. This is the argument of George Dangerfield in his classic study, *The Strange Death of Liberal England* (London: Constable, 1935); a more recent interpretation along the same lines is Standish Meacham's '"The Sense of an Impending Clash": English Working-class Unrest before the First World War', *American Historical Review*, 77 (1972), no. 5.

2. E. H. Phelps Brown and Margaret H. Browne, *A Century of Pay* (London: Macmillan, 1968), Fig. 13, p. 142.

3. Marcello de Cecco, *Money and Empire. The International Gold Standard, 1890–1914* (Oxford: Blackwell, 1974), p. 125.

4. Ibid., pp. 127 ff. for a discussion of the financial crisis of 1914.

5. Philip Stanworth and Anthony Giddens, 'The Modern Corporate Economy: Inter-locking Directorships in Britain, 1906–1970', *The Sociological Review*, new series, 23 (1975), no. 1, pp. 6–10.

6. P. L. Payne, 'The Emergence of the Large-scale Company in Great Britain, 1870–1914', *Economic History Review*, 2nd series, XX (1967), no. 3.

7. Ibid., Table 1, pp. 539–40, compared with Stanworth and Giddens, *Corporate Economy*, Diagram 1, p. 9.

8. Derek H. Aldcroft and Harry W. Richardson, *The British Economy 1870–1939* (London: Macmillan, 1969), Table 1, p. 105.

9. Jürgen Kuczynski, *A Short History of Labour Conditions Under Industrial Capitalism* (London: Frederick Muller, 1972), p. 104.

10. J. H. Porter, 'Industrial Peace in the Cotton Trade, 1875–1913', *Yorkshire Bulletin of Economic and Social Research*, 19 (1967), Table 1, p. 60.

11. E. H. Phelps Brown, *The Growth of British Industrial Relations* (London: Macmillan, 1959), p. 26.

12. Parl. Papers, *Trade Disputes and Trade Combinations* (*Royal Commission*): *Minutes of Evidence*, LVI (1906), C. 2826, p. 311.

13. Ibid. See also B. C. M. Weekes, 'The Amalgamated Society of Engineers, 1880–1914. A Study of Trade Union Government, Politics, and Industrial Policy', unpublished PhD thesis, University of Warwick, 1970, pp. 101–2, 158.

14. Weekes, 'Engineers', pp. 212–15.

15. Brown, *British Industrial Relations*, p. 34.

16. Ibid., p. 35; see also p. 39 for class differences in the mortality rates of legitimate children.

17. S. B. Saul, 'House Building in England, 1890–1914', *Economic History Review*, 2nd series, XV (1962–3), no. 1, pp. 124–5.

18. Ibid., p. 126.

19. Joseph Melling, 'Clydeside Housing and the Evolution of State Rent Control, 1900–39' in the same author's edited volume, *Housing, Social Policy and the State* (London: Croom Helm, 1979).

20. Brown, *British Industrial Relations*, pp. 43–5.

21. Ibid., cited p. 51.

22. Brian Simon, *Education and the Labour Movement 1870–1920* (London: Lawrence & Wishart, 1974), pp. 296 ff.

23. H. V. Emy, *Liberals, Radicals and Social Politics, 1892–1914* (Cambridge: University Press, 1973), p. 146.

24. Ibid., pp. 146–8; see also Brown, *British Industrial Relations*, pp. 294–8, for a further discussion of the principles involved.

25. Parl. Papers, *Trade Disputes and Trade Combinations* (*Royal Commission*): *Minutes of Evidence*, LVI (1906), C. 2828, p. 287, for example, which was the view of Alexander White, representing the Lancashire, Cheshire and North Wales Building Trades Employers' Federation.

26. Emy, *Liberals*, p. 148.

27. A. H. Halsey (ed.), *Trends in British Society since 1900* (London: Macmillan, 1972), Table 4.14, p. 127, is a useful source of information concerning the extent of labour unrest.

28. Parl. Papers, *Trade Disputes and Trade Combinations*, LVI (1906), C. 2826, p. 333.

29. Keith Burgess, *The Origins of British Industrial Relations* (London: Croom Helm, 1975), pp. 60, 68–71.

30. Weekes, 'Engineers', pp. 200, 203–5.

31. Ibid., p. 266.

32. Bob Holton, *British Syndicalism 1900–1914* (London: Pluto Press, 1976), pp. 31–3.

33. J. H. Porter, 'Industrial Conciliation and Arbitration 1860–1914', unpublished PhD thesis, University of Leeds, 1968, Graph V/1, facing p. 396.

34. Ibid., see also Table II, p. 61; Ian G. Sharp, *Industrial Conciliation and Arbitration in Great Britain* (London: Allen & Unwin, 1950), p. 164.

35. P. F. Clarke, *Lancashire and the New Liberalism* (Cambridge: University Press, 1971), pp. 82–3.

36. A. J. Taylor, 'Labour Productivity and Technological Innovation in the British Coal Industry, 1850–1914', *Economic History Review*, 2nd series, XIV (1961–2), Appendix I, pp. 68–9.

37. J. E. Williams, *The Derbyshire Miners: a Study in Industrial and Social History* (London: Allen & Unwin, 1962), Chart 5, p. 355.

38. Porter, 'Conciliation', Table 4, p. 495.

39. Parl. Papers, *Trade Disputes and Trade Combinations*, LVI (1906), C. 2826, pp. 257–8, for the evidence of Reginald Guthrie, Secretary to the Coal-owners' Association of Durham and Northumberland.

40. B. McCormick and J. E. Williams, 'The Miners and the Eight-hour Day, 1863–1910', *Economic History Review*, 2nd series XII (1959–60), p. 227.

41. Ibid., pp. 233–4.

42. Halsey, *Trends in Society*, Table 4.12, p. 123; S. Pollard, 'Trade Unions and the Labour Market, 1870–1914', *Yorkshire Bulletin of Economic and Social Research*, 17 (1965), no. 1, Diagram 1, p. 101.

43. Halsey, *Trends in Society*, Table 4.14, p. 127.

44. Brown, *British Industrial Relations*, pp. 298–302.

45. John Lovell, *Stevedores and Dockers. A Study of Trade Unionism in the Port of London, 1870–1914* (London: Macmillan, 1969), pp. 150–5, for the background to this development.

46. Halsey, *Trends in Society*, Table 4.14, p. 127.

47. B. David Rubinstein, 'The Decline of the Liberal Party, 1880–1900', unpublished PhD thesis, University of London, 1956, pp. 522–3; Peter Fraser, 'Unionism and Tariff Reform: the Crisis of 1906', *The Historical Journal*, V (1962), no. 2.

48. D. W. Crowley, 'The Origins of the Revolt of the British Labour Movement from Liberalism, 1875–1906', unpublished PhD thesis, University of London, 1952, pp. 701–2.

49. Clarke, *Lancashire*, pp. 98–100.

50. C. J. Wrigley, *David Lloyd George and the British Labour Movement* (London: Harvester, 1976), especially pp. 3–9, 14–15, 25–6.

51. Frank Bealey and Henry Pelling, *Labour and Policies 1900–1906* (London: Macmillan, 1958), pp. 276–8.

52. C. L. Mowat, 'Ramsay MacDonald and the Labour Party' in Asa Briggs and John Saville (eds.), *Essays in Labour History 1886–1923* (London: Macmillan, 1971), p. 134; Kenneth D. Brown, 'The Labour Party and the Unemployment Question, 1906–1910', *The Historical Journal*, XIV (1971), no. 3, pp. 607 ff.

53. Paul Thompson, *The Edwardians. The Remaking of British Society* (London: Weidenfeld & Nicolson, 1975), especially Table 3, p. 14, which shows that there was a disparity in wages of more than 2:1 when comparing male and female workers.

54. Walter Kendall, *The Revolutionary Movement in Britain 1900–21* (London: Weidenfeld & Nicolson, 1969), p. 36.

55. A. Marwick, 'The Labour Party and the Welfare State in Britain 1900–1948', *American Historical Review*, LXXIII (1967), no. 2, pp. 384–7.

56. Roger Davidson, 'Llewellyn Smith, the Labour Department and Government Growth 1886–1909' in Gillian Sutherland (ed.), *Studies in the Growth of Nineteenth-century Government* (London: Routledge & Kegan Paul, 1972); Roy Hay, 'Government Policy towards Labour in Britain, 1900–1914', *Journal of Scottish Labour History Society*, 10 (June 1976).

57. Roy Hay, 'Employers and Social Policy in Britain: The Evolution of Welfare Legislation, 1905–1914', *Social History*, 4 (1977); this is examined in more detail in the forthcoming PhD thesis by Joseph Melling, 'Employers and Industrial Welfare in Britain: A Regional and Industrial Comparison, c. 1880–1920', Department of Economic History, University of Glasgow.

58. Hay, 'Employers', p. 8.

59. J. R. Hay, *The Origins of the Liberal Welfare Reforms 1900–1914* (London: Macmillan, 1975), p. 53.

60. Ibid., pp. 43–4.

61. Ibid., pp. 44–5.

62. Pat Thane, 'Non-contributory Versus Insurance Pensions 1878–1908' in the same author's edited collection, *The Origins of British Social Policy* (London: Croom Helm, 1978), especially p. 95.

63. Ibid., pp. 100–1.

64. See, for example, *Cotton Spinners' Annual Report*, 1899, p. 5.

65. Thane, *Social Policy*, p. 103.

66. Ibid., pp. 103–4.

67. John Brown, ' "Social Control" and the Modernization of Social Policy, 1890–1929' in Thane, p. 132.

68. Ibid., p. 131.

69. Ibid., p. 104.

70. J. H. Treble, 'Unemployment and Unemployment Policies in Glasgow 1890–1905' in Thane.

71. M. A. Crowther, 'The Later Years of the Workhouse 1890–1929' in Thane.

72. Ibid., p. 40.

73. Brown, ' "Social Control" ' in Thane, p. 136.

74. José Harris, *Unemployment and Politics* (Oxford: Clarendon Press, 1972), pp. 267–8.

75. Bruce K. Murray, 'The Politics of the "People's Budget" ', *The Historical Journal*, XVI (1973), no. 3, p. 563.

76. Wrigley, *Lloyd George*, p. 41.

77. Murray, ' "People's Budget" '.

78. Crowther, 'Workhouse'.

79. Harris, *Unemployment*, p. 285.

80. Hay, *Welfare Reforms*, p. 46.

81. Harris, *Unemployment*, p. 288.

82. This was the view, for example, of Sydney Buxton, President of the Board of Trade; Buxton Papers (Hassocks, Sussex): proof copy of Imperial Conference, 1911, fourth day, 2 June, p. 93; I am indebted to Roy Hay for making these materials available to me.

83. Harris, *Unemployment*, p. 354.

84. Ibid.

85. Hay, *Welfare Reforms*, p. 44.

86. Buxton Papers: Cabinet paper, November 1913, p. 130.

87. Ibid., file for May 1911: from an interview in the *Morning Post*, 12 May, p. 66.

88. Hay, *Welfare Reforms*, p. 44.

89. Harris, *Unemployment*, p. 317.

90. Hay, *Welfare Reforms*, pp. 54 ff.

91. See, for example, the case of the Leeds clothing firm of John Barran & Co., examined in Melling, 'Employers and Welfare'.

92. Cited from Hilaire Belloc, *The Servile State*, and discussed in Hay, *Welfare Reforms*, p. 46.

93. Harris, *Unemployment*, cited pp. 365–6.

94. John Foster, 'British Imperialism and the Labour Aristocracy' in Jeffrey Skelley (ed.), *The General Strike, 1926* (London: Lawrence & Wishart, 1976), pp. 21–2, 24–5.

95. Eric Wigham, *The Power to Manage. A History of the Engineering Employers' Federation* (London: Macmillan, 1973), p. 81.

96. Ibid., pp. 82–3.

97. *ASE Monthly Report*, August 1913; a valuable contemporary account is Alfred Williams, *Life in a Railway Factory* (Newton Abbot: David & Charles, reprint, 1969).

98. Porter, 'Conciliation', Table 4, p. 495; J. C. Stamp, 'The Effect of Trade Fluctuations upon Profits', *Journal of the Royal Statistical Society*, LXXXI (1918), Fig. 2, p. 572.

99. M. G. Woodhouse, 'Rank and File Movements Among the Miners of South Wales, 1910–1926', unpublished DPhil thesis, University of Oxford, 1970, pp. 21–2.

100. Ibid., p. 4.

101. Ibid., pp. 23–4.

102. David Evans, *Labour Strife in the South Wales Coalfield 1910–1911* (Cardiff: Cymric Federation Press, reprint, 1963), is a useful contemporary account.

103. Woodhouse, 'Rank and File', p. 71.

104. Ibid., p. 96; Holton, *Syndicalism*, pp. 119–20.

105. Rodger Charles, *The Development of Industrial Relations in Britain 1911–1939* (London: Hutchinson, 1973), p. 46.

106. H. R. Hikins, 'The Liverpool General Transport Strike, 1911', *Transactions of the Historical Society of Lancashire and Cheshire*, CXIII (1961), pp. 175 ff.

107. R. Bean, 'Employers' Associations in the Port of Liverpool, 1890–1914', *International Review of Social History*, XXI (1976), pt 3, pp. 377–8.

108. Holton, *Syndicalism*, p. 123; a detailed account of the 1912 London dock strike is contained in Lovell, *Stevedores and Dockers*, pp. 155 ff.

109. Buxton Papers: Cabinet paper, 15 August 1911, p. 71.

110. Ibid., p. 73.

111. Roger Davidson, 'War-time Labour Policy 1914–1916: A Re-appraisal', *Journal of Scottish Labour History Society*, 8 (June 1974), p. 5.

112. Charles, *Development of Industrial Relations*, pp. 60–1.

113. Ibid., pp. 57–8.

114. Ibid., pp. 61 ff.

115. See, for example, *Labour Leader*, 20 October 1911.

116. Martin Petter, 'The Progressive Alliance', *History*, 58 (1973), pp. 50–2.

117. Cited in Meacham, 'Impending Clash', p. 1354.

118. Emy, *Liberals*, p. 250.

119. Ibid., p. 251.

120. Roy Douglas, 'Labour in Decline 1910–14' in Kenneth D. Brown (ed.), *Essays in Anti-Labour History* (London: Macmillan, 1974), p. 121.

121. Emy, *Liberals*, p. 250.

122. Ibid., pp. 280–3.

123. Harris, *Unemployment*, Table 9, p. 380.

124. Petter, 'Progressive Alliance', p. 59.

125. R. I. McKibbon, 'James Ramsay MacDonald and the Problem of the Independence of the Labour Party, 1910–1914', *Journal of Modern History*, 42 (1970), no. 2, pp. 220–1.

126. Ibid., pp. 226–32; see also Mowat, 'Ramsay MacDonald' in Briggs and Saville, pp. 139–40.

127. R. J. Holton, '*Daily Herald* v. *Daily Citizen*, 1912–1915', *International Review of Social History*, XIX (1974), pt 3.

128. Douglas, 'Labour in Decline' in Brown, p. 120.

129. Paul Thompson, *Socialists, Liberals and Labour. The Struggle for London, 1885–1914* (London: Routledge & Kegan Paul, 1967), pp. 284–5.

130. Holton, *Syndicalism*, is one of the most recent studies of British syndicalism.

131. Douglas, 'Labour in Decline' in Brown, pp. 113–18; Roy Gregory, *The Miners and British Politics, 1906–1914* (Oxford: University Press, 1968), pp. 35–7.

132. Holton, *Syndicalism*, p. 50.

133. Ibid., p. 82.

134. See, for example, Kenneth O. Morgan, 'Socialism and Syndicalism: the Welsh Miners' Debate, 1912', *Bulletin of the Society for the Study of Labour History*, 30 (Spring 1975), especially p. 31.

135. Holton, *Syndicalism*, pp. 91 ff.

136. Ibid., p. 106.

137. Ibid., p. 151; Weekes, 'Engineers', p. 322.

138. Raymond Challinor, *The Origins of British Bolshevism* (London: Croom Helm, 1978), pp. 99–105.

139. Holton, *Syndicalism*, pp. 134 ff.

140. Kenneth O. Morgan, 'The New Liberalism and the Challenge of Labour: the Welsh Experience, 1885–1929', *Welsh History Review*, 6 (1973), no. 3, pp. 301–2.

141. Holton, *Syndicalism*, pp. 171–5.

142. G. A. Phillips, 'The Triple Industrial Alliance in 1914', *Economic History Review*, 2nd series, XXIV (1971), no. 1, p. 63.

143. Cited in Woodhouse, 'Rank and File', p. 111.

CHAPTER 5

1914–20: A New Social Order?

The Demands of War and the Extent of State Control

The outbreak of war in Europe during July–August 1914 found Britain with its pre-war class antagonisms still largely unresolved. In consequence, it is clear that the new forms of social unrest manifest during the years 1914–18 had their origins in the preceding period. Yet what led to their culmination was the vastly increased control wielded by the multiplicity of government agencies created to meet the demands of twentieth-century warfare. The mobilisation of people and resources was on a scale that was unprecedented and largely incomprehensible in terms of pre-war assumptions. It was expediency that dictated government policy, and the *ad hoc* way in which the state was forced inexorably to extend its scope of action meant that major changes were set in motion in a context where there was little understanding of the principles of wartime mobilisation, and even less of an appreciation of the social consequences that could have scarcely been anticipated. At the same time, the experience of state control in Britain during the First World War did little to alter fundamentally the allocation of wealth and power in society as a whole, despite the development of policies in this direction that were largely abortive, and in spite of the efforts made by wartime governments, especially the Lloyd George coalition, to *represent* state control as an engine of 'social reconstruction'.

In the ranks of organised labour, there was little outright opposition to Britain's participation in the conflict. The dependence of Labour MPs, for example, on the Liberals was at its most extreme in the sphere of foreign affairs, and although the Parliamentary Labour Party had passed a resolution in favour of Britain staying out of the war, the small anti-militarist group that included Ramsay MacDonald was powerless to prevent the subsequent vote for war credits.[1] Labour members also agreed to an electoral truce for the duration of hostilities, any seat becoming vacant to be retained by the former member's party. This marked the closure of a safety valve for expressing popular feeling in Parliament and was important subsequently in directing social unrest into extraparliamentary channels. Again, there were prewar precedents for this but these paled in comparison with the social unrest that began to increase during 1915 as hopes for a quick victory dimmed and the earlier euphoria subsided. Even more important in this respect was the declared opposition of both the TUC and the Labour Party to strikes in wartime. This helps explain why so much labour unrest during the war was unofficial in character. Both Keir Hardie and MacDonald himself argued, despite the latter's anti-militarism, that strikes in wartime were an act of betrayal undermining the sacrifices of the 'sons of toil' who were fighting their country's battles.[2] And the *Daily Citizen* used its position as the official organ of the labour movement to stress the contribution of the 'common soldier' as the 'backbone of the war effort'.[3] These efforts to identify working-class interests with the 'national interest' did not, therefore, deny class consciousness but sought to mobilise it in the interests of military victory. It was for this very reason that the Labour Party's policy in opposing strikes was initially very successful: between April and June 1914 more than five million days had been lost in disputes affecting 250,000 workers, compared with only 161,437 days lost involving a mere 21,128 workers during the period from October to December.[4]

The outbreak of war also found the 'rebel' groups of left dissidents who had flourished before 1914 in serious disarray as a result of their conflicting attitudes to the war. The Hyndmanite rump controlling the British Socialist Party singled out 'Prussian militarism' as the biggest enemy of the socialist cause and campaigned actively for an Allied victory.[5] In this respect, it echoed the sentiments of influential trade union leaders like Ben Tillett and social critics like G. K. Chesterton, who used the 'rebel' *Daily Herald* as a platform for their views. The latter's officially anti-war stance was vitiated by its contraction to a weekly paper as a result of economic conditions and wartime restrictions, which left strongly pro-war newspapers like the *Daily News* firmly in control of the mass circulation press.[6] The only left groups containing a significant anti-war element centred around the *Daily Herald* leagues and the Socialist Labour Party, although even the latter included prominent activists like David Kirkwood and John Muir who were to succumb to 'social patriotism'.[7] This was a source of weakness that was to continue to plague the attempts made by revolutionary socialists to mobilise mass support for fundamental change when social unrest intensified later in the war.

The demands of war confronted the British state with three major problems that were interrelated. The first of these was how to finance the mobilisation of men and materials on the scale required. This led, secondly, to the problem of organising production in a way designed to optimise the economy's capacity to sustain a huge increase in the output of munitions, whilst at the same time ensuring the necessary inputs of raw materials, food and other civilian production that was outside the armaments sector but remained essential to it. And, thirdly, government had to devise means of maintaining the flow of men to the armed forces, as determined by the ever-increasing needs of the military, without reducing the economy's ability to produce or otherwise obtain the arms, raw materials, food and a whole range of other commodities and services deemed necessary for the prosecution of the war. As the conflict dragged on, the focus of government policy began to concentrate on the state's need for manpower, and it was in this sphere that efforts to reconcile rising losses at the front with the necessity of meeting wartime demands in terms of production led the state to become increasingly involved in the direction, control and disciplining of the labour force. It was the imposition of these external forms of authority upon what had traditionally been a relatively voluntaryist structure of labour market relations that was the underlying cause of much of the social unrest of the war years.

The overriding problem immediately facing the government was scarcity: scarcity of funds, scarcity of materials, scarcity of manpower and, above all, scarcity of organisation.[8] While conditions of scarcity are inherent in an economic system geared to maximising private profit, rather than being the fortuitous result of physical or human limitations, these were aggravated by wartime demands because of the need to mobilise a significant proportion of the country's resources for non-productive use. The first task of government was to establish the principles and practice of wartime finance, hence the importance attached by the Liberal government in getting Labour MPs to vote for war credits. The experience of financial policy in Britain during the war was relatively successful by international comparison, at least in terms of raising the required funds, but the generally orthodox means employed led to serious consequences not anticipated in 1914. Even during the early phase of the war, government expenditure rose considerably above peacetime levels, and by 1916 this represented an increase of 562% on the first War Budget.[9] Government income covered substantially less than one-third of total expenditure until the very last year of the conflict and the size of the deficit steadily grew. Tax revenues provided for only 28% of the total expenditure during the fiscal years 1914/15–18/19.[10] Government relied on a combination of credit expansion, begun on 1 August 1914 when the Bank of England was authorised to exceed the fiduciary issue laid down by the 1844 Bank Act, and a succession of War Loans that were snapped up in the absence of other profitable investment opportunities like overseas issues.

The financial cost was high, however, and the social consequences immeasurable. Since a large proportion of the massive increase in government indebtedness was earmarked for non-productive uses, the fires of inflation were allowed to rage almost out of control. Yet this seemed the only means of harnessing the resources of capital in the service of the war effort, short of the complete collectivisation of the factors of production that was unlikely to be acceptable to their owners. It has been estimated that government expenditure during the war would have been no more than 50% of its actual amount if this 'ransom' to private capital had not in fact been paid.[11] There is no denying the size of the return going, for example, to the owners of the means of exchange. At the end of the war, the amount of interest required to service the National Debt exceeded an *entire* pre-war budget.[12] The inequality of 'sacrifice' this implied, is clear when compared to the experience of death or mutilation in the trenches, and in comparison with the burden of long working hours and more intensive labour utilisation carried by workers on the 'Home Front' whose real earnings were, moreover, continually jeopardised by rising prices and shortages of basic essentials.

The Liberal government's major concern was not whether the consequent rise in profits was justifiable, but its fear of the damage rising prices would cause to orthodox wartime finance. Lloyd George regarded the customary practice of competitive tendering for government contracts, which contributed to the rising trend of prices during a period of war-induced scarcity, as an obstacle to a closer and more systematic relationship between government and industry that would seek to direct war profits into new investment. The first step in this direction was the laying down by the government's purchasing agencies of criteria for establishing standardisation and quality control, in close liaison with the various trading and employers' associations.[13] This encouraged horizontal and vertical-type trust combinations, which usually preserved the integrity of the individual enterprise, although in some areas more thoroughgoing forms of amalgamation were achieved. In this respect, private capital benefited from guaranteed orders at price levels that of necessity had to take into account the unit costs of the least efficient firms, while patterns of share-ownership and managerial control were not seriously disturbed. The contribution this subsequently made to improved efficiency is doubtful, but its effect on profitability suggests that for many companies the period of the First World War marked a 'Golden Age'.[14]

An innovation that was a more tangible inducement to improved efficiency was the Excess Profits Duty, introduced following investigations made by the Ministry of Munitions into comparative costing after the summer of 1915. Although useful as a means of meeting the enormous growth in government spending, Lloyd George launched the scheme as a concession to the trade unions in the hope of getting them to accept his manpower policies, *and* as a means of modernising British industry. The latter was encouraged by the provision allowing firms to write down new investment out of their excess profits, the rate of duty averaging 63 % on profits exceeding the levels of 1913–14 (a relatively prosperous year). It is estimated that only 34 % of the Excess Profits Duty was collected, the rest being written off against new investment.[15] Thus the First World War created the opportunity for implementing the quest for 'national efficiency' that had been a significant strand in the thinking of the New Liberalism, and the interests of private industry benefited considerably as a result.

Elsewhere in the economy, the extension of state control proceeded in an *ad hoc* and piecemeal fashion, reflecting the lack of any underlying organising principles other than the power of particular vested interests, and the relative importance of the contributions they made to the war effort. In recognising its need to retain the goodwill of the banking system, which was crucial to the government's programme of wartime finance, the state guaranteed the solvency of the banks and discount houses by authorising the Bank of England to relieve from all liability the holders of discount bills of exchange drawn before the outbreak of hostilities. Funds were also advanced to acceptors to pay off bills as they matured, and any claim for repayment was postponed until a year after the end of the war.[16] The railways were also taken under state control, although this was essentially a book-keeping technicality since their ownership remained in private hands and their existing management retained. Shareholders did not fare badly as a result. Railway profits were guaranteed at their levels of 1913, and subsequently the companies were also paid interest on any additional capital expenditure undertaken since the beginning of 1913, with the result that government payments to the railways during the war amounted to more than £95 million.[17] It was not until 1916 that the government enforced economies like the discontinuance of competitive trains on different lines. Shipping was another sector of the economy that was, at the same time, crucial to the war economy and dominated by powerful private interests. A scheme of State Insurance against War Risks, which involved a government partnership with the existing private War Risk Association on a 4:1 basis, insured all ships and fixed premiums for all voyages begun after the outbreak of war. By March 1915, the government was also forced to insure for ship cargoes, since losses had made the rates offered on the open market prohibitive, and government insurance rates were generally only one-quarter of private ones.[18] In the meantime, a combination of war losses and government requisitioning had forced freight rates as high as five times their pre-war level by 1918, which yielded record profits and large capital gains for the shipping companies.[19] State intervention in the coal industry was roughly similar to its organisation of the railway system, i.e. government control coexisted with private ownership that was paid a guaranteed dividend. The net effect of state intervention during the war was that industrial production in Britain fell only slightly, despite losses of manpower, materials and markets overseas.[20]

This brief survey of the closer relationship between the state and private capital achieved during the war suggests that the outcome was generally beneficial as far as the latter was concerned. Private ownership and managerial prerogatives remained largely intact, even in the context of government control. Yet the *forms* of control adopted to mobilise the resources of capital could be expected to differ significantly from those employed to harness manpower. This was rooted in the wage system itself and the inequalities arising between the sellers of labour and the owners of capital. State intervention during the war did little to alter in any fundamental way this underlying characteristic of all capitalist societies. In fact, it might be argued that the effect of state manpower policy was to *increase* the subjection of labour to capital, since there developed an entire battery of government controls that sought to complement if not replace the disciplines of the market place with a system based upon administrative fiat. While this seriously curtailed the freedom of working people to protect their interests by voluntary action, private capital continued to expand and flourish with state backing.

It was to be expected that state control would impinge most immediately and directly on workers in trades who were engaged in the manufacture of war materials. The production of munitions depended on the application of a wide range of skills, particularly in the engineering industry. Yet it was in this very sector of the economy where relations between capital and labour had been especially strained during the pre-war years, and where the prospects for industrial peace seemed remote. One leading employer acknowledged that by 1914 the means of resolving disputes in the engineering industry, which had been remarkably successful in the decade after 1897–8, had become virtually inoperative and that a large-scale confrontation was imminent.[21] It was in this context of rising militancy among engineering tradesmen that war intervened. At the same time, it became clear as the hopes for a quick military victory receded that the output of the engineering and munitions trades could not be increased on the scale required without fundamental changes in working methods. The system of voluntary recruitment to the armed forces, for example, had meant that 19.5 % of male workers in the engineering industry had enlisted by June 1915, creating severe shortages of skilled labour as munitions production was increased.[22] Voluntary schemes for directing skilled labour to where it was most needed had palpably failed.[23] Some form of state compulsion seemed the only alternative.

The methods used to implement state manpower policy during the war became apparent in the course of the first year of hostilities. In the same way that a combination of *laissez faire* and high prices failed to increase the output of materials required by the war effort, so the voluntary schemes improvised to attract scarce labour to where it was most needed foundered against the sheer scale of mobilisation demanded by the war. The Defence of the Realm Act of August 1914 constituted the legal basis for state control. As amended subsequently, this conferred wide powers upon the government in harnessing the factors of production for 'the public safety and the defence of the Realm', but what this meant in practice was arrived at in an *ad hoc* fashion that had to take into account the respective class positions of capital and labour. Government was careful, for example, to provide compensation for requisitioned property and private capital was assured the 'usual' rate of profit when supplying its needs.[24] Employers were left free to hire and organise labour in the best way they saw fit, but in the process the state began increasingly to restrict labour's ability to protect its interests by voluntary action. During the early months of 1915, a succession of orders not only made strikes illegal on government work but also prescribed all 'restrictive practices or customs calculated to affect the production of munitions of war'. This was incorporated in the famous Treasury Agreement signed in March 1915 by the government and the officials of the leading unions involved.[25] The government's approach in negotiating separately with the employers and then with labour gave credence to the view that its role was ostensibly an impartial one, although it took some time for practical experience to demonstrate that in terms of consequences, at least, this was far from the truth. It was labour's experience of the subsequent Munitions of War Acts that lent weight to a growing body of opinion within the labour movement in regarding state manpower policy during the war as the embodiment of the Servile State.

In the first instance, the trade unions were deceived by the purpose of the local munitions committees set up to carry into effect the Treasury Agreement. Composed of an equal number of representatives of employers and workers, and an additional number of 'impartial persons' appointed by the state, their brief was not only the settlement of wages questions but also 'the management and control of industry' itself.[26] This was represented by Lloyd George as 'the great charter of labour', and was regarded even by some socialists like G. D. H. Cole as a major step towards workers' control of industry.[27] Yet the behaviour of the munitions committees was to depend very much on the attitude of the government and its representatives appointed to them. In fact, these committees were soon to disappear after the passage of the first Munitions of War Act, to be replaced by the more overtly coercive Munitions Tribunals. In the meantime, the power of the munitions committees to settle wage questions, especially the clause in the Treasury Agreement specifying that semi-skilled 'dilutees' should receive the 'usual rates of the district' when performing work done previously by operatives 'of higher skill', had to cope with the proliferation of output-linked methods of wage payment during the war years that provided employers with ample opportunities for fixing wages on the basis of individual performance, rather than in accordance with established rates negotiated collectively in the district. This was to become an important instrument for strengthening managerial prerogatives to the detriment of collective bargaining.

The development of closer links between the state and private capital received additional impetus as a result of the notorious 'Shells Scandal', which undermined the credibility of the Asquith government during the early months of 1915. The new coalition government formed in May saw as its central task the improvement of the administrative machinery for mobilising the resources of the economy. Accusations of bureaucratic incompetence, particularly in the War Office, led to demands that businessmen should be more directly involved in running the war economy. This was the background to the setting up of the Ministry of Munitions in June 1915, under the direction of Lloyd George who drew subsequently on the 'fund of goodwill' he had accumulated with the business community before 1914 in persuading men of business to accept prominent positions in the state apparatus. It is estimated that more than 90 directors and managers were 'loaned' to the Ministry of Munitions for the duration of the war, although many were to remain on the payrolls of their respective firms, and the instances where leading figures like Alfred Herbert administered sectors of productions which also happened to coincide with their own business interests strengthened the relations between private capital and the state. According to James Hinton:[28]

> In such an organization it was difficult to tell where business control ended and state control began.

This interlocking relationship between the forms of state control and the interests of private capital had a special significance as it affected the subsequent development of government manpower policy. There were, however, important elements of continuity with pre-war precedents, particularly the 'national efficiency' argument of the New Liberalism advocating some form of state organisation of the labour market. In fact, leading New Liberals like Llewellyn Smith and William Beveridge were recruited to key positions in the Ministry of Munitions.[29] The wartime emergency was the ideal opportunity for putting their policies into practice. The crucial problem facing the government was that voluntary schemes for attracting scarce tradesmen to sectors of employment where they could be most usefully occupied in the production of war materials had fallen foul of market forces, with employers bidding up the price of labour in order to retain their skilled personnel. The Treasury Agreement in confining its attention to firms directly engaged in government work had failed to tackle the challenge posed by the war in terms of the labour market as a whole. The creation of the Ministry of Munitions was the necessary outcome of this failure. Yet the dilemma it faced was that in recruiting the skills of the business community required to organise war production more efficiently, it became inevitably influenced by the class attitudes rooted in the private ownership of capital and the wages system. It was because of this that the class conflict generated consequently came to focus on the quest for power and influence *within* the apparatus of the state itself. This was to create a dangerous point of convergence for all manner of working-class grievances.

The main aim of the Munitions of War Act was to control and discipline the labour market in order that the required momentum of armaments production could be sustained. Llewellyn Smith analysed the problem facing the government in June 1915 as follows:[30]

> The shortage of labour directly delays production. It is however, at the present time having indirect effects perhaps even more serious. Practically any workman of any pretensions to skill at all in the engineering and ship building trades has so little difficulty in finding work the moment he wants it that he has little economic motive left for remaining with his employer... The ordinary economic control of the individual workman has practically broken down. The result is that to a very considerable extent men are out of the control both of the employers and of their own leaders. The question is whether some exceptional form of control or motive not of a purely economical character can be effectively substituted.

The outcome was that the provisions of the Munitions of War Act severely limited the workers' scope for voluntary action in defence of their interests, although as a *quid pro quo* the rights of employers were also curtailed.[31] Strikes and lock-outs were declared illegal, and heavy penalties were imposed for any breach of the law, while the settlement of differences was left to compulsory arbitration. In the context of labour scarcity, the prohibition of lock-outs as well as strikes did little to undermine the authority of employers.

The Act also created a new industrial category—the so-called 'controlled establishment'—defined as any plant considered essential for the manufacture of munitions. In controlled establishments, all restrictive practices or customs concerning the employment of skilled and unskilled labour were suspended, and wages and discipline became the direct responsibility of the Ministry of Munitions. The government's imposition of a Munitions Levy on the profits of controlled establishments, to be merged later with the more widely applied Excess Profits Duty, was like the latter measure used as a means of writing off tax against capital expenditure and depreciation. The clauses in Section 4 of the Act emphasise that it was not only wages that were now subject to government control. Every aspect of factory organisation related to maximising output, including manning levels, the choice of operatives to be employed, and the more general 'ordering of work', was not subject to direct state control.[32] In order to prevent the 'poaching' of scarce labour by firms other than those categorised as controlled establishments, workers could be assigned to their place of employment according to the wishes of the Ministry of Munitions, and they were not allowed to seek work elsewhere unless in possession of a leaving certificate issued by the previous employer. Finally, Section 10 of the Act gave the state very wide and undefined powers of control in case any of the more specific provisions proved inadequate. It authorised the government[33]

> to regulate or restrict the carrying on of any work in any factory, workshop or other premises or the engagement or employment of any workman or all or any classes of workmen therein or to remove the plant therefrom with a view to maintaining or increasing the production of munitions in other factories, workshops or premises.

It was generally accepted that the Munitions of War Act represented the maximum degree of control the state could exercise over the labour market, short of outright 'industrial conscription'. This is shown in Section 10 of the Act, although the efficiency of the other provisions was such that it was never invoked. Yet it is important to appreciate that the impact of the Act, especially in terms of popular perceptions of it, extended beyond those firms with plants designated as controlled establishments, i.e. directly engaged in the manufacture of munitions. In fact, what 'munitions work' meant was never clearly defined although the Act as amended early in 1916 specified, in addition to armaments, 'any other articles or parts of articles intended or adapted for use in war'.[34] Thus the repair of railway wagons belonging to a colliery was classified as munitions work since the wagons were being used for war purposes.[35] In terms of the administration of the Act, a considerable degree of discretion was left to the specially appointed Munitions Tribunals that were empowered to proceed against offences committed under the jurisdiction of the Act.[36] The potential authority of the Munitions Tribunals was very great indeed in light of the vagueness concerning the meaning of munitions work in controlled establishments. This was regarded as a serious threat by many working people, including those outside what may be narrowly defined as armaments production, and must be taken into account when considering the new forms of social unrest that emerged during 1915–16.

An assessment of the Ministry of Munitions need not reduce to a crude version of the 'conspiracy theory', which argues that senior government officials consciously connived with representatives of private capital in exploiting the wartime emergency as the occasion for 'smashing' the labour movement.[37] In analysing the motives and activities of the Munitions Ministry, there is no need to go any further than the terms of the Act itself, which in effect intensified the contradiction inherent in capitalist society arising from the private ownership of capital and the employment of wage labour. This is illustrated by the fact that whereas under the Act employers were entitled to refuse workers their leaving certificates, there was no reciprocal restriction on the right of employers to dismiss them if they were so inclined.[38] Thus employers' prerogatives were strengthened by government fiat to an extent that could not be achieved by market forces alone. In consequence, private capital was left free to reap record profits and renovate obsolescent plant and working methods, with assistance from guaranteed government contracts. Although the developing links between the state and private capital were initiated in an *ad hoc* and unplanned way, the process once begun had an internal logic based upon generally accepted assumptions. This denies the relevance of any 'conspiracy theory' form of explanation.

The Beginnings of Labour's Challenge to the State, 1915–16

The objective conditions created by the First World War constitute the background to the new forms of social unrest that appeared during the course of the hostilities, particularly the government's initiatives in the sphere of manpower policy. Yet it would be misleading to conceive of this unrest as simply a mechanistic 'response' of labour to what was regarded as state coercion. The character of the labour movement itself underwent a significant transformation during the war, and it was this that determined the *forms* of unrest arising during the period. An especially striking development was the profound effect that the demands of war had on the participation by working people in the labour process. The almost insatiable demand for manpower meant that unemployment among trade unionists virtually disappeared and the formerly abundant residuum of casual underemployed were able to secure regular jobs for the first time.[39] Nearly 800,000 additional women were employed in industry, particularly in metal-working occupations and government establishments where the rate of growth of female employment was greatest, although commerce, local and national government, and transport also recruited many more women workers.[40] In total, the effect of these changes in employment marked a degree of working-class integration into the labour process that had not existed since the early phase of industrialisation. The fact that this coincided with the implementation of new forms of control over labour by the state, which in effect increased the subjection of labour to capital, led to a period of intense instability in labour's relationship with British society and had unforeseen economic and social consequences. One of the most important of these was the boost that the war gave to trade union membership, which climbed steadily from 4,145,000 in 1914 to 6,533,000 by 1918, and the immediate post-war boom took the total to a record figure of 8,348,000 in 1920.[41] Among women workers, the growth of unionisation was in the order of 130% between 1914 and 1920.[42]

This striking increase in the number of trade unionists gave their organisations an official presence with government that had not existed before the war. The great efforts made by Lloyd George to cultivate friendships with trade union leaders, to agree to separate negotiations with them, and to 'manage' the implementation of government policy in a way that would win the unions' active co-operation—the 'Great Charter of Labour'—all emphasise the importance attached by government to the numerical growth of the trade unions. Trade union officials were also recruited to a variety of government posts, commissions and committees, including prominent figures like George Barnes and William Brace who became members of the new coalition government. These moves were designed, of course, to help smooth the working of industrial relations during the war emergency and formed an essential part of state manpower policy. What the government did not fully appreciate was the effect of the rapid growth in union membership in weakening the control exercised by union leaders over their rank and file. This problem was aggravated further as union officials were given positions within the state apparatus. It was the government's rather belated recognition of this that lay behind the Munitions of War Act, which sought to complement the tactic of persuasion with the force of state coercion.[43] At the same time, the expansion of union membership led to the development of industrywide or nationwide collective bargaining, which sat uneasily with the traditions of local autonomy and rank-and-file militancy that had flourished before the war. The Triple Alliance of railwaymen, coal-miners and transport workers, for example, signed an agreement in April 1915 whereby 'joint action' could only be taken after the issue in question had been put before the membership of each of the unions, 'by such methods as the constitution of each organisation provides'.[44] It was barriers like this to the effective co-ordination of trade union power at the centre that contributed to the isolation of individual union officials from the workplace, following their incorporation into the agencies of government. This was why so much of the social unrest emanating from the workplace during the war was unofficial in character; and unlike much of the militancy of the pre-war period, this wartime labour unrest was to take a more menacing form as the institutions of 'civil society' were steadily embraced beneath the umbrella of government tutelage. In consequence, the scope of social unrest became circumscribed to attacks on state power itself.

The greater integration of Britain's population into the labour process during the First World War was also accompanied by the spread of new forms of control at the workplace. It was one of the major long-term effects of the war that it marked the widespread implementation in Britain of the methods of 'scientific management'.[45] New machinery and the employment of 'dilutees' meant that management control in its formal unitary sense was no longer sufficient. There was a need as 'an absolute necessity for adequate management the dictation to the worker of the precise manner in which work is to be performed'.[46] At the same time, the scarcity of skilled labour highlighted the problem of maintaining discipline which justified greater managerial supervision. The tendency of scientific management was to disassociate the aptitude and skill of the operative from the labour process as a whole. Of course, the extent to which there was a uniform process of deskilling in Britain during the First World War should not be exaggerated. A minority of highly skilled tradesmen was required to set up, superintend and maintain the new machinery, and its actual manufacture remained a heavily skill-intensive occupation. In fact, it was precisely this double-edged effect of the scientific-technical revolution that has to be understood, especially in the British context where a distinctive craft tradition had been so well entrenched. While it is admitted that perhaps a majority of tradesmen with average levels of aptitude were exposed to some of deskilling, particularly in the munitions industries, an important minority also acquired more responsibility in the labour process, even if the overall demand for manipulative skill or dexterity was reduced.[47] This arose not only from the need to superintend the work of semi-skilled machine-operators, but also resulted from the necessity of maintaining the safety of the equipment, the product and, above all, of the other workers involved. Thus the changes in the labour process threw up a new contradiction that juxtaposed, on the one hand, greater management control, and on the other, additional responsibility for a highly skilled minority.

It was this shift in the locus of conflict between capital and labour from the actual *performance* of work to questions of *responsibility* for organising work that helps explain the changing course of social unrest during the First World War. Its significance lies in its effect upon working-class consciousness. One kind of workers' response to this development might take the form of a narrowly defensive struggle to maintain occupational autonomy by defending craft prerogatives. Yet, at the same time, an influential minority of working-class militants located mostly in highly skilled trades abandoned this approach, which was appropriate when conflict between capital and labour arose primarily during the actual performance of work, and adopted a different perspective that sprang from an experience of greater responsibility for organising work. This perspective was grounded in an awareness of the social needs served by the system of production, which grew as levels of responsibility increased. And those militants who were eventually to become revolutionary socialists reasoned further that insofar as the scope for greater responsibility justified the control of industry by workers themselves, in order to ensure that production served social needs rather than private profit, then it followed logically that the agencies of workers' control in industry should become the instrument for organising not only production but also the means of distribution and exchange. In the context of increasing state control during wartime, moreover, the effect of this change in the labour process directed social action to the pursuit of state power:[48]

> The new consciousness questions not only the organisation of work but that of society as a whole. The labour movement becomes aware that the worker will only regain control over his work through a measure of control of the firm, which itself is dependent on its participation in government power.

The potential for change from craft consciousness or solidarity to class consciousness and class action also created opportunities for community-type forms of social action that transcended the workplace. This was especially likely in relatively non-diversified communities where there is a greater possibility that working life is merged with life outside the community.[49] In regions of Britain that were to become heavily dependent on munitions production during the war, particularly Clydeside, the local occupational structure made for comparatively non-diversified communities, marked by a considerable degree of overlap between working life and community. The latter is a product of a localised network of social relations based upon a common area of residence, close ties of family and friendship, and participation in the 'civil society' of the locality, e.g. local politics. The extent of this kind of 'interconnectedness' implies that community-type forms of social action are possible, which may include groups who are not affected in the same way by changes in the labour process. Thus once class consciousness arises from workers' changing experience of the labour process, this can also articulate a focus of identity for class action in the community since the latter tends to be conceived in class terms when its occupational structure is relatively non-diversified. In the case of Clydeside, for example, not only was it the single biggest and probably most rapidly expanding centre in Britain for manufacturing munitions of war, it was also characterised by overlapping forms of workplace and community association that could bring together different groups who were not uniformly affected by changes in the labour process. Above all, it was the extension of government control culminating in the Munitions of War Act that helped generate forms of social unrest based upon a generalised class consciousness, mobilised in the pursuit of state power, which was not confined to those workers employed in specialised engineering firms directly engaged in munitions production where the impact of the scientific-technical revolution was most striking.[50]

The fusion of the various trades employed in 'controlled establishments' under the Munitions of War Act during the latter part of 1915 emphasises the role of state control as the final catalyst of labour unrest. Skilled-labour substitution or dilution in the engineering shops was but one aspect of this development. The demands of war required that the state had to 'regularise' the labour market, in the interests of maximum output. This involved restrictions on labour mobility, the imposition of controls to ensure workplace discipline, the introduction of training schemes to make good the losses of skilled manpower, and the regulation of wages. Section 6 of the Munitions of War Act gave statutory force to an earlier voluntary scheme designed to attract skilled labour to munitions work.[51] Special employment exchanges were opened and existing ones taken over to assist in the recruitment and transfer of labour. Once employed in controlled establishments, workers became subject directly to the restriction on mobility arising from the system of leaving certificates. To many of them, the latter bore a sinister resemblance to the system of 'character notes' used traditionally by Clydeside shipbuilding and engineering firms, for example, as a means of disciplining their labour force, and it is noteworthy that this was a major issue underlying the strike at Fairfield's shipyard in August 1915, which marked the beginnings of a period of increasing labour unrest.[52]

It is important to appreciate that of all workers transferred under government direction the proportion of shipbuilding trades involved was almost as great as the number of fitters and turners employed directly in armaments production who were the most seriously threatened by the spread of new working methods.[53] In those trades where dilution was practical, a rising number of women workers were also subject to the restrictions imposed by leaving certificates.[54] It was the recruitment of increasing numbers of women workers under these conditions that gave further impetus to the community dimension of social unrest during the war years. Thus while the system of leaving certificates was an effective lever used by firms to impose whatever forms of workplace discipline they thought appropriate, the Ministry of Munitions also drew up its own 'model' set of rules governing the behaviour of employees in controlled establishments during August 1915, and by January 1916 copies had been posted up in 1,168 plants.[55] These were often complementary to existing rules drawn up by the individual firm or employers' association.[56] The ministry's own rules included provisions for 'regularity and diligence', and required the working of a 'reasonable' amount of overtime, the 'suspension of restrictive practices', and the maintenance of 'sobriety and good order'. The greater integration of the working-class population into the labour process coincided, therefore, with the introduction of more formal means of subjecting labour to capital. The result was that long hours of work, as many as 70 or 80 and even 100 hours per week, were not uncommon and were officially legitimated by government fiat.[57] This was rationalised further by the work of the Ministry of Munitions' Welfare Section where specially appointed welfare and medical officers introduced new forms of control in an attempt to prevent 'carelessness' arising from long hours and arduous conditions.[58] Many workers bitterly resented the activities of these people who were often regarded as the servants of management. It is in this wider context that the new forms of social unrest developing during the latter part of 1915 have to be considered, including the activities of the Clyde Workers' Committee that became more specifically concerned with the consequences of dilution.

The extension of state control during the war, moreover, also had definite limits. Whilst the implementation of state manpower policy imposed restrictions on the freedom of working people to chose their place of employment, and negotiate their wages and working conditions, the government's wartime financial policies led to a steep rise in the cost of living that bore heavily on wage-earners, especially in the case of families where the sole bread-winners were adult males who had enlisted in the armed forces. Until the spring of 1916, the levels of wage increases guaranteed to men were in the order of an additional 4s on time rates, or 10% on piece rates, and it was only by working systematic overtime that enabled earnings to keep abreast of the rising cost of living.[59] Many women workers whose wage became the major source of family income, as military recruitment proceeded, were guaranteed a minimum of only £1 a week if they were fortunate enough to find jobs in controlled establishments, as laid down in Circular L2 issued by the Central Munitions Labour Supply Committee in October 1915.[60] The fact that this minimum was reissued during 1916 suggests that it was not always adhered to by individual firms.[61] It was below the level required to maintain a family's subsistence, even in terms of pre-war prices, yet the government's own figures indicate that retail food prices had risen by 32% during the first twelve months of the war in large towns where the controlled establishments were mostly located.[62] And women workers employed outside the munitions sector where wage levels were in the order of 10–14s per week in 1914 did not benefit from this minimum specified by the Ministry of Munitions.[63] This latter group was clearly hard pressed to maintain even an adequate level of individual subsistence, let alone provide for a family in the absence of a male wage-earner.

The cost of living included, of course, other items besides food. The latter, whilst not directly creating a focus for social unrest, did begin to bear indirectly on other areas of expenditure like rents where there was considerably more scope for resistance and protest. Particularly in relatively non-diversified communities, an issue like rents could mobilise the potential for class solidarity and class action in districts where overlapping forms of association at the workplace and outside in the community created a body of shared experience that cannot be explained exclusively in terms of a response to changes in the labour process.[64] Housing provision reproduces capitalist social relations on the basis of the distinction between the property-owner and the propertyless tenant. Yet the variety of workers' experience of the labour process, reflected in differences in bargaining strength, wages and working conditions, also reproduces important differences in the kind of housing available to the propertyless tenant. Research into the character of Glasgow's housing stock, for example, has emphasised the role of housing as a dimension of working-class differentiation before the First World War, with artisans, clerks and other 'respectables' living in rented accommodation that was markedly superior to the property occupied by the poorer classes.[65] Even prior to 1914, however, a combination of rising interest rates, the movement of capital into overseas issues, and a lack of effective demand had led to a worsening housing shortage, despite an absolute surplus of unoccupied accommodation.[66] This situation was aggravated, of course, by the expansion of the munitions industries on Clydeside during the war, with the population of Glasgow alone increasing by almost 65,000 between 1912 and 1915, although only 1,500 of the 14,000 new homes estimated to have been required were in fact built during this period.[67] The government's wartime financial policies had the effect of bringing almost to a halt what little house-building that had been undertaken specifically for the working class in the period 1900–14.

The result was to intensify pressure on Glasgow's existing stock of working-class housing, more than two-thirds of which consisted of accommodation with two or fewer rooms per unit.[68] The competition for the remaining housing comprising the city's stock of 'superior' accommodation was especially intense, as the war led to an increase in the proportion of the population earning regular and rising money wages. It is noteworthy, in this respect, that during 1914–15 the highest rent increases, varying from 11.67% to 23.08%, affected housing in Partick and the Govan and Fairfield Ward where a large concentration of artisan tradesmen lived adjacent to expanding munitions firms.[69] This was the basis for the community character of the rent strikes, which began in October 1915.[70] And it is significant that these coincided with the government's efforts to shackle labour at the workplace. Yet conflict over rents was a manifestation of a collective consciousness that for a time overcame the sectional attitudes springing from different experiences at the point of production. Organisations like the local wards of the Independent Labour Party and the Glasgow Women's Housing Association were especially active in leading the rent strikes.[71] The government was particularly concerned about a possible conjuncture of community protest over rents and opposition to its manpower policies, which might lead to a major social crisis, and it seems clear that the rent strikes had obtained a wide circle of support, including munitions workers like William Reid who was leading shop steward at Parkhead Forge.[72]

The government's task, therefore, was to resolve the rents question before it could generate a wider movement of opposition threatening its wartime policies. It regarded the prospect of sacrificing the interests of small capitalists investing in house mortgages as the lesser of the evils when compared to the threat of widespread disruption and social unrest, and in this respect, there was pressure from some prominent industrialists for some form of state rent control.[73] It was in this context that the government acted quickly and passed into law a Rent Restriction Bill in December 1915, which froze all rents at their pre-1914 levels. Although this left the more deep-seated housing problem unresolved, its effect was to nip in the bud a developing social movement that threatened to link up community protest with class action in the workplace. The government was subsequently able to concentrate its attentions on the 'management' of its manpower policies, especially dilution, without the attendant danger of triggering a widely-based challenge to employers' prerogatives and property relations that could have posed a serious menace to the authority of the state itself. The settlement of the rent strikes was thus an important turning-point in the development of social unrest during the First World War.

While the government was moving towards a resolution of the rents issue, opposition to its manpower policies was gathering increasing momentum. By the end of September 1915, it had become clear that the War Munitions Volunteer Scheme had failed to attract the required numbers of skilled tradesmen to armaments work, and that as an alternative to the introduction of industrial conscription, the government decided on the systematic pursuit of dilution as a means of avoiding a head-on collision with a working class united in its opposition.. In this task, Lloyd George used his personal influence with the trade union leaders who had already signed away any *official* right to oppose dilution, after they had agreed to the provisions of the Munitions of War Act. The government had thus driven a wedge between the trade union leadership and the rank and file, which it exploited in the aftermath of the unofficial strike of shipwrights at Fairfields.[74] This gave to social unrest an increasingly workplace orientation, particularly after the passage of the Rent Restriction Act, yet the existence of distinctions and divisions among munitions workers, arising from objective conditions at the point of production, made it difficult to generalise their experience at a wider level of class action. This was reflected in the official policy of the Executive of the Amalgamated Society of Engineers, which sought to restrict the employment of dilutees by insisting that they be paid the normally recognised skilled wage rate when performing work done previously by skilled tradesmen.[75] Yet the position of the ASE Executive ignored the 'technological dynamism' of the engineering industry where the introduction of labour-saving techniques had the effect of widening the labour supply available to employers and undermined the long-term viability of craft unionism.

In contrast, the new principle developed by the shop stewards' movement, following the formation of the unofficial Clyde Workers' Committee, accepted the fact that dilutees could not expect to receive the standard skilled rate because they only worked on part of the process that had once been performed wholly by skilled operatives.[76] Furthermore, the dilutees continued to rely on the new *responsibilities* of a smaller proportion of highly skilled workers who 'set up', superintended and maintained the new machinery. The shop stewards' aim was, therefore, to prevent the employers from using dilution as a means of reducing *overall* labour costs and thus maximising their share of the industry's output at the workers' expense. The agreement negotiated subsequently in the major Clydeside munitions factories specified that dilutees once fully trained should receive rates of pay that,[77]

> with the wages paid to the necessary supervisor and the increased wages paid to the men who now solely perform the difficult portion of the operation, will make the cost of doing the work not less than it was before.

It was this approach that formed the kernel of the demand for workers' control of industry since it could not be expected that employers and managers would willingly surrender their prerogatives and refrain from using the opportunity presented by deskilling to buy their labour as cheaply as possible.

Despite the potentially divisive effect of the dilution issue, it was left primarily to the majority of skilled craftsmen with their new responsibilities for organising work and trade union tradition to provide the leaders of the shop stewards' movement. What encouraged an awareness among some of them as to the potential of the dilution controversy for mobilising the mass of workers to demand a fundamental transformation of society was the propaganda of a handful of revolutionary socialists, who had been active in areas like Clydeside before the war. They found the expanding munitions districts fertile ground for their arguments after 1914 in the context of rising prices and rents, food shortages, and state control of the labour market, which appeared to exacerbate class distinctions and antagonisms. John Maclean of the British Socialist Party had first come into prominence as one of the leaders of the 1915 rent strikes. Important firms like Weir's of Cathcart and the Albion Motor Works had an active core of BSP and Socialist Labour Party members, including William Gallacher who was to become President of the Clyde Workers' Committee, and J. M. Messer of the Independent Labour Party who was its Secretary. In fact, the setting up of the Clyde Workers' Committee during the last week of October 1915, representing a fusion of shipyard and arma- ments factories, increased the employers' reluctance to make ener- getic use of their new power to manage bestowed on them by the Munitions Act. Many remained sceptical about the efficacy of dilution in the industry, especially the efficiency of women workers.[78] It was the government faced with a growing manpower crisis that forced the employers' hand, although some leading firms like Weir's were only too willing to do the government's bidding.

The government was disposed initially to persuasion rather than coercion. Lloyd George intervened personally and toured the muni- tions districts trying to get the local union officials to accept dilution. In line with earlier government policy, he refused to treat with the shop stewards, with the important exception of Clydeside where the strength of local feeling was such as to leave him with no other alternative. His talks with a deputation of the Clyde Workers' Committee on 24 December 1915 and his speech at a tumultuous public meeting at St Andrews Hall the next day proved abortive. This marked the turning-point in the government's handling of dilution, although the possibility of resorting to legal coercion had been mooted earlier.[79] In January 1916, three government- appointed Dilution Commissioners were dispatched to the Tyne and Clyde to 'supervise' the implementation of dilution. On Clydeside, they worked closely with William Weir who was not only a major employer but had been Director of Munitions for Scotland since August 1915. The government was prepared to take legal action against strikers or any incitement to strike under regulations of the Defence of the Realm Act.[80] Even then, it was not until February 1916 that the government considered the Clyde Workers' Committee sufficiently isolated for it to precipitate a showdown. During February and March, a series of strikes at Parkhead Forge, Weir's, the Albion and several other works led to the arrest and deportation of their leaders, and in the process the left-wing journal *Forward* was suppressed.[81] With their leaders gone, and amidst the introduction of strike-breakers, the opposition of workers to dilu- tion on the Clyde collapsed.

This defeat was in marked contrast to the victorious conclusion of the rent strikes in the previous year, which relied on a much larger circle of working-class support. Yet the outcome was not entirely negative. Later in 1916, the shop stewards' movement spread to Sheffield where it was successful in negotiating the so-called 'trade card scheme' that allowed the unions a voice in controlling the recruitment of skilled operatives to the armed forces.[82] Many skilled tradesmen also found that their new position as administrators of work broadened their perspective on the relationship between the worker and the productive system as a whole. This was the background to the negotiation of new agreements in the munitions factories on the Clyde during 1916, which led to a more sophisticated reformulation of workers' control as a *class* demand.[83] This was to be taken up again later in the war in the form of more overtly revolutionary shop stewards' activity. By then, the issue of dilution that had so bewildered the efforts of the Clyde Workers' Committee to widen the scope of its struggles during 1915–16 had become an accomplished fact, and the focus of social unrest had shifted to the legitimacy or otherwise of the war itself. In the meantime, workers' rank-and-file organisations revived as they discovered that voluntary 'slowdowns' were often a safer and more effective means of giving vent to their grievances, compared with outright strike action.[84]

'War Socialism': The Imperatives of Survival, 1916–18

The creation of the Ministry of Labour in December 1916 was a direct consequence of the fall of Asquith and the accession of Lloyd George as Prime Minister. Lloyd George's administration was bound to be more systematically interventionist, having none of the inhibitions of Asquith's visibly Whiggish régime. The change in government was particularly significant as an indication of the shifting balance of class interests or the factions of capital who were most directly served by the state. Until December 1916, it could be argued that historically it had been financial capital or the rentier bourgeoisie centred in London and the south-east of England who had continued to retain the ear of government, absorbing within their ranks the plutocratic elements of industrial capital. The accession of Lloyd George marked a turning-point in the sense that the balance of class interests controlling the state shifted in favour of industrial capital, located primarily in the factories and workshops of provincial Britain outside London 'where the war was being won'.[85] Thus the most striking feature of Lloyd George's govern-

ment was the recruitment of his so-called 'new men', mostly industrialists, to head the powerful ministries that subsequently were to
increase considerably the effectiveness of the state in its handling of
the war.[86] They included Joseph Maclay who became Shipping
Controller, Eric Geddes as the 'Napoleon of Transport' and Lord
Rhondda who was appointed Minister of Food. They were mostly
without political experience and had no firm attachment to either
party. Yet it was left to them to carry through the practical implementation of collectivist policies which prior to 1914 had aimed
to moralise capitalism in the interests of social cohesion and
stability.

The contradictions of the New Liberalism, arising from the
restrictions state control imposed on the ability of working people
to protect their interests by voluntary action, were thus brought to a
head in the experience of 'war socialism'. The question as to whether
state control would proceed along socialist lines or on the basis of
the assumptions of private enterprise was to be resolved in favour of
the latter. The wartime outcome of the New Liberalism was not,
therefore, a kind of *socialism*, as its spokesmen like Hobson had
envisaged, but approximated more closely to a form of *corporatism*,
which has been defined as 'the unification of self-governing industries by a national committee representing them and other interests,
including the state'.[87] The appointment of Arthur Henderson as
Minister of Labour with the responsibility for 'managing' industrial
unrest, which was regarded at the time as a major concession to
organised labour, has to be seen in this context of a developing
corporatism that sought to preserve rather than transform the
existing social order. Leaders of representative bodies of the labour
movement set up to protect working-class interests during the war,
like the War Emergency Workers' National Committee, were
individually offered influential posts in the state apparatus, but the
result when these were accepted was usually to reduce their effectiveness as representatives of working-class interests.[88] The years
1917–18 thus produced new opportunities for the expression of class
solidarity and class action among working people, but the climax in
the wartime extension of state control was to affect profoundly what
this was going to achieve.

The realities of war socialism were reflected in the intensity of
labour unrest during 1917. Underlying this were the rising expectations nourished by the rhetoric of Lloyd George's government.
Pledged to the more efficient prosecution of the war, Lloyd George

had necessarily to be more 'thorough' in his handling of issues like conscription and dilution. At the same time, he had also to respond to demands like the 'Conscription of Riches', put forward by the War Emergency Workers' National Committee, which indicated the strength of feeling that wartime sacrifices were not being equally shared. The conscription issue, in particular, generated widespread opposition as the war's demands for manpower and materials continued to escalate, with the trades councils becoming a focus for agitation against the class 'bias' of the recruiting drive that it was feared would lead to industrial conscription in the interests of employers.[89] By the early months of 1917, the situation had become critical owing to the success of Germany's intensive submarine campaign. It became imperative to restrict the production of non-essential products and services, especially if they had a high import content, whilst economising on the use of manpower in a way that would contribute, first, to maximum production for military purposes, and secondly, maintain the export trade.[90]

This gave rise to measures leading to the most serious labour unrest of the war. The first was a bill proposing to extend dilution to private non-munitions work, and the other was the government's decision to end the trade card agreement with the trade unions and substitute in its place a more rigorous Schedule of Protected Occupations administered directly by the state. The proposal to extend dilution to private non-munitions work was regarded as an unacceptable surrender of hard-won privileges, in an area that had been outside the scope of the war emergency, and where established practises would be difficult to restore in peacetime. The imposition of the Schedule of Protected Occupations, moreover, in removing the mediating function performed by the unions under the trade card scheme, left the worker defenceless in the face of the combined power of the state and the employers who now ran its various new ministries. At the same time, rising prices were beginning to take their toll of morale and there was growing war-weariness, which was aggravated further as the pace and intensity of work continued to increase.[91] During the first six months of 1917, retail prices exceeded by a ratio of more than 2:1 the levels prevailing in 1914, while wage rates for most workers were rarely more than 50% above their pre-war levels.[92] The situation by 1917, therefore, had become less of a problem of government policy threatening the craft privileges of engineering tradesmen, but had shifted instead to the implications of war socialism for munitions workers as a whole.

This was the background to the unofficial and almost spontaneous wave of strikes that starting in the Lancashire textile machine-making districts spread subsequently to engineering centres in Sheffield, the West Midlands and London.[93] Beginning at the end of April 1917, they had by the end of May involved 200,000 workers and led to the loss of 1,500,000 working days. For the first time, a 'Joint Engineering Shop Stewards' Committee' was formed to co-ordinate the strikes, which sought to negotiate directly with the government and repudiated any 'interference by the union executives of the workers in the present dispute'. Henderson warned the government that the unrest had been 'deepened by the Russian Revolution', and Lloyd George acknowledged that the War Cabinet was aware of the existence of 'a very considerable and highly organised labour movement with seditious tendencies'.[94] W. C. Anderson, MP for Sheffield Attercliffe, reported to Parliament on 14 May that the unrest was more general than the extent of the strikes would suggest, with 70,000 people marching through the streets of Glasgow 'wearing the revolutionary colours', although the Clydeside munitions workers who had fought a lone struggle during 1915–16 now refused to join the strike movement in the south.[95] Clydeside's absence from the disputes of April–May 1917 highlighted the almost insuperable problems encountered by the Joint Engineering Shop Stewards' Committee in co-ordinating the strikes and preventing divisions within its own ranks. Craft exclusiveness remained the prime source of motivation for many of the rank and file, although prominent members of the committee like George Peet and William McLaine, who were members of the British Socialist Party, aimed to extend the principle of workshop organisation to link up with all unions in the workplace. In districts like the West Midlands, moreover, where the progress of new technology had probably gone furthest in undermining the pretensions of skilled tradesmen, the local union officials had a relatively easy task in regaining control of the movement from the unofficial shop stewards.[96]

The government's strategy was, in fact, to re-establish the authority of the union officials and this was eventually successful in bringing the strike wave to an end.[97] With arrest and the threat of imprisonment facing several of its leaders, representatives of the Joint Engineering Shop Stewards' Committee attended a meeting with Ministry of Labour officials, at which the ASE Executive was also present. The outcome was that Lloyd George agreed to withdraw the charges against the strike leaders, provided they promised to adhere to the terms already accepted by the ASE Executive. There was some modification of the proposed Schedule of Protected Occupations, which included a. pledge to call up all dilutees for military service before the recruitment of skilled men or apprentices, and the government promised to consult the unions in implementing the schedule. This tactic of giving preferential treatment to the skilled tradesmen served to reaffirm the lines of differentiation among munitions workers and applied the brake to a developing class movement. Furthermore, Lloyd George's willingness to share some of the responsibility with the union officials in helping to formulate and implement government policy was in line with his wider corporatist strategy based upon state agencies interlocking with 'self-governing' industries. In so doing, he succeeded in isolating the 'revolutionary' elements in the shop stewards' movement. The latter, of course, suffered from its own inherent weaknesses. Not only did much of its momentum derive from the bedrock of craft exclusiveness, but unlike the unrest on Clydeside during 1915–16, the strikes of 1917 lacked a focus in the community (the rents issue) that might have helped generalise the movement on a broader basis. The question of achieving political power in the interests of the working class as a whole was entirely overlooked by the shop stewards' movement.[98] Its policy of ever-increasing workers' control was *in the abstract* a class demand, but *in practice* it was flawed by the craft exclusiveness of many of the rank and file, and it failed completely to grasp the implications of the interlocking of the state with private capital that made workers' control of industry impossible without the abolition of existing property relations by political means.

The problematic of creating a political dimension to industrial unrest during 1917 was complicated further by Lloyd George's astute handling of the labour situation. What he termed 'constructive co-operation' had led, for example, to the appointment of the Whitley Committee in November 1916, and its interim report published during the following March recommended the formation of joint standing Industrial Councils.[99] This was passed on to the new Ministry of Reconstruction for further consideration. The latter was to be a 'thinking ministry' rather than an instrument for specific legislation. The device of the consultative committee was adopted to allow full participation by the various interests, including labour, but in practice the ministry's own Advisory Council controlled the specialist sections like Commerce and Production, Labour and Industrial Organisation, and Social Development. It is difficult to escape the conclusion that what Lloyd George was engaged in was a massive public relations exercise. As one historian has written:[100]

> The original inspiration and the continuing stimulus for reconstruction came from the need to urge the people on at the very time when they were tending to lag... Little was expected in this direction during the war, and very little was accomplished.

Yet in the context of an apparently endless war, there is no doubt that the promise of 'reconstruction' represented a tremendous propaganda victory for the government. As a slogan it almost acquired a life of its own, divorced from the practical concerns of the bureaucrats and men of business who were running the state's war machine.

The government's opportunism in relation to its promise of reconstruction was evident in October 1917, for example, when the Cabinet formally adopted the Whitley Committee report on Industrial Councils but subsequently delayed its implementation.[101] In the meantime, the government acted swiftly to slow down the wartime rise in the cost of living. The Food Controller introduced a scheme that actually reduced the prices of some basic necessities, which involved the appointment of food control committees by the local authorities with statutory powers to fix maximum retail prices and ensure an equitable distribution of commodities. The result was that the upward trend of retail food prices was brought to a halt during the latter half of 1917, and the price of some food items like bread, potatoes and meat was reduced.[102] In the administration of the Munitions of War Acts, important amendments were made authorising the Minister of Munitions to abolish the much-hated leaving certificates and correct discrepancies between skilled time rates and unskilled piece rates, which had been a major source of unrest in the munitions industries. What became known as the 'common rule' was also enforced, making wage increases binding on all firms in a sector covered by a government award. Substantial increases were granted after the summer of 1917, particularly in the engineering and shipbuilding trades, and even more significant, greater uniformity was introduced into wage negotiations, with the result that during 1917–18 money wages rose rapidly and began to keep pace with the cost of living for the first time during the war.[103]

On the housing issue, George Barnes at the Local Government Board promised a 'far-reaching' programme of housebuilding by the local authorities after the war, as part of the government's commitment to reconstruction. Finally, the government did not hesitate to mobilise the panoply of its coercive powers against any 'left' opposition to the war, illustrated by the arrest of exiled political refugees in Britain and the authorisation of police raids on the offices of organisations like the Socialist Labour Party.[104] In a sense, the October Revolution in Russia resolved a difficult problem for Lloyd George because it had the effect of completing the isolation of the revolutionary left from most Labour MPs and official union leaders who regarded the Bolshevik takeover as a 'tragic' mistake.[105]

Despite the concessions made by the government to organised labour after the summer of 1917, there was no immediate cessation of industrial unrest. In fact, disputes caused the loss of 5,875,000 working days during 1918—the highest number for any year of the war. Again, it was the critical manpower shortage that came to a head during the winter of 1917–18, after the huge losses sustained in the Passchendaele campaign, which precipitated another crisis of civilian morale, and the situation worsened further during March 1918 when the beginning of the German offensive on the Western Front seemed to signal the coming of outright industrial conscription.[106] Yet despite the industrial unrest of 1918 the government did not fall and the 'revolution' failed to occur. In this respect, it can be argued that the rising momentum of unrest during 1918 had outrun the political development of the shop stewards' movement; while, in contrast, the government had established a strong political position in the latter half of 1917 that enabled it to manage successfully the disturbances of the following year. In objective terms, the shop stewards' movement was by 1918 in direct confrontation with the state and the class interests it supported, following the Military Service Act of January 1918 that made *all* workers fit for military service eligible for enlistment. Its everyday *practice* was no longer confined to opposing dilution in the interests of craft exclusiveness. Yet opposition to the government's manpower policies required a level of politicisation among the rank and file that clearly did not exist. The consensus of workshop meetings, for example, was against strike action to end the war.[107] This feeling grew after the Germans launched their last great offensive in the West. Militancy dwindled and employers used this as the occasion for victimising many of the leading shop stewards.[108] The reconstruction of the

Labour Party during 1917–18, with clause four of its new constitution being widely interpreted as indicating its commitment to socialism, appeared to offer working people hope in the constitutional road to a better future after the war, which only a complete military victory could secure.

The victorious conclusion of the war did not, however, allay the government's fears of a major social upheaval. The expectations of a better future that were fed by the wartime sacrifices endured by the mass of the population, and which were raised further by the government's promise of reconstruction, led to a serious upsurge in social unrest during the winter of 1918–19. There was a strike in the previously quiescent cotton industry, much of the coal industry lay idle, and there were menacing disputes in the engineering centres of Glasgow and Belfast. Even more alarming for the government, unrest spread to the agencies of the civil power itself. There were mutinies in the armed forces over the slowness of the War Office's initial scheme for demobilisation and the meagre levels of service pay compared with domestic cost of living. Trade unionism began to infect the police force and there were police strikes in London and on Merseyside. Meanwhile, the allied intervention in Russia against the Soviets made the authorities doubtful about the loyalty of the armed forces, and fearful of a possible conjuncture of civilian unrest and disaffection in the military. The leaders of the shop stewards' movement appeared to have learned their wartime lessons and influential activists like Jack Murphy had become fully committed to direct action based on shop committees that were now regarded as embryonic 'social committees' or soviets. The latter were now seen as the means for overthrowing capitalist society, rather than as bodies that by working within capitalist society could establish 'encroaching workers' control'.[109]

Yet at the same time, there were also stabilising factors at work which in the long run proved to have a more lasting effect. The focus on the industrial unrest engendered by state intervention during the war must take into account the instances where government control had been remarkably successful. In cotton textiles, for example, the Cotton Control Board had managed a detailed scheme of output restriction linked to unemployment benefits, which succeeded in releasing labour for essential war work, without leading to any significant industrial disputes.[110] A legacy of wartime state intervention was the enlarged corporatist bureaucracy now gathered together under the aegis of the Ministry of Reconstruction. In this respect, it is important to appreciate how the ideology of reconstruction and its vision of a more 'harmonious' social order had acquired a momentum of its own, which did not derive directly from the class interests represented in the Lloyd George government. Leading figures as varied in background as Milner, Salisbury, Morant, J. H. Thomas and the Webbs all shared in 'an authentic enthusiasm for reform', and who took it for granted that the increased scope of government created during the war would now be used positively to assist in the process of social advance.[111] The close links some of them had with the trade unions and the Labour Party attracted support from many working people in the critical period of transition to peacetime conditions during 1918–20. Thus the government appeared set on policies that promised to consolidate and extend further the very real improvement in the quality of life registered during the war years, which became clearly visible once the burden of wartime restrictions and sacrifices was steadily lifted. With imports gradually becoming available again and employment incomes maintained by the pent-up demand for civilian production, both at home and overseas, real gains were made in terms of higher wages during the years 1918–20 compared with the levels obtaining in 1914 (itself a boom year), especially among the unskilled and semi-skilled.[112] Even more striking, wartime experience had proved beyond conclusion that a reduction in working hours to eight per day was compatible with optimum levels of labour efficiency, and there was no going back to pre-1914 norms after 1918.[113] This was important in making possible the widespread dissemination of new forms of leisure, particularly organised professional sport, which before 1914 had been available only to a minority working-class audience concentrated largely in the industrial north.[114] It also ushered in the era of mass popular travel and generally lessened the burdens on family life.

The postwar improvement in real wages and working conditions compared with 1914 was part of a wider process of occupational change that had a stabilising effect on social relations in the context of rising expectations. There had been a definite shift of labour into relatively well-paid and new industries, which combined comparatively high wages with reduced vulnerability to unemployment, while low-paid, seasonal or casual occupations in agriculture, clothing and domestic service had contracted.[115] Occupations in the electrical industry, cycle-making and the manufacture of motor vehicles had increased more than 100% by 1921, compared with

1911, and opportunities for secure employment in national and local government, including public utilities, had risen by about 50% in the same period.[116] Many of these were semi-skilled jobs where wage rates had also increased relative to other trades.[117] At the same time, the effect of government manpower policy had been to reduce permanently the nineteenth century army of 'labourers' who were mostly unskilled and casual, while its emphasis on the organisation of work had led to an expansion of the so-called 'white-collar' grades of supervisory and technical workers, who formed a relatively privileged stratum within the wage-earning class.[118] In traditional trades in heavy industry like iron and steel, innovations like the introduction of the eight-hour day could have an upgrading effect since additional key personnel were required to run production on the basis of three eight-hour shifts, compared with the pre-war system of two twelve-hour shifts.[119] In general, the outline of a recognisably 'modern' occupational structure can be discerned emerging from the First World War.

Finally, the war had witnessed a marked extension of welfarist activity, contributing further to improved living and working conditions. The extent of industrial unrest had led employers' organisations like the West Yorkshire Coal Owners' Association, for example, to set up comprehensive welfare programmes for their supervisory employees as a means of ensuring their loyalty to the firm.[120] Schemes providing pensions, sickness allowances, and educational and canteen facilities for *all* workers had been initiated or expanded during the war years by some companies.[121] In this connection, the welfare activities of the Ministry of Munitions helped generalise the practice of some of the pioneering employers in setting up canteen facilities, for example, which often followed as a result of the growth in female employment. Post-war reconstruction promised, moreover, to expand welfare provision further. The notion of a national minimum was in vogue during the years 1918–20, and it was widely expected that the Ministries of Labour and Housing would build further upon legislation like the Trade Boards (Amendment) Act and the Wages (Temporary Regulation) Act of 1918, which seemed to indicate the government's intention of establishing a national minimum.[122]

What the government thus required was breathing space or, more precisely, time to restore a viable social order in peacetime. With the spectre of revolution haunting countries throughout Europe, and with the Bolsheviks already installed successfully in Russia, the government's task was essentially a political one—to win back the loyalty of the people to existing institutions. The promise of reconstruction was part but not the whole answer. The credibility of the autonomous institutions of civil society had to be restored, as distinct from the formal structure of government and its agencies that during the war had appeared to engulf all society and con-centrate social conflict in a struggle for state power itself. It was advisable that this exercise in the management of the climate of opinion should not be the responsibility of either the government itself, which had already done so much to erode the autonomy of civil society, or those associations directly representing the domin-ant class interests. It was an awareness of this that underlay the anti-Bolshevik campaign launched during the last year of the war, and sustained in the immediate post-war period.[123] This was organised by a plethora of propaganda or 'educational' societies active at this time, which were continually at pains to stress their 'independent' and 'non-political' stance, although most of their leading figures as well as their financial resources derived from business origins.[124] It was in the midst of this campaign that the government felt suffi-ciently confident to pass into law the Representation of the People Act of 1918. This did more than any other single measure since the 1832 Reform Act to realise genuinely universal suffrage, granting the vote to all males over the age of 21, and to women over the age of 30 who were either householders, married to householders, or gradu-ates, thus almost trebling the size of the electorate. How the latter might vote was not regarded as that serious a problem in the General Election held in December 1918, shortly after the armistice was signed, because it was staged as a vote of confidence in the personal leadership of Lloyd George who had brought the war to a victorious conclusion.[125]

During the 1918 election campaign, Lloyd George staked his formidable personal reputation firmly in favour of reconstruction. The outcome was a resounding victory for his coalition government. At the same time, the Labour Party had prepared its own version of post-war reconstruction, which in proposals like 'the universal enforcement of the national minimum' shared common ground with the government's programme.[126] To the public at large, therefore, there appeared to exist some degree of consensus between the government and the Labour Party over the course of Britain's economic and social development. The election of 57 Labour MPs, secured by a poll of 2,244,948 votes, also testified to the resurgence of the constitutional left after the extraparliamentary alarms of the war years. A relatively peaceful transition to peacetime conditions was assisted by the flexibility of the government's handling of demobilisation, enabling more than four million members of the armed forces to return to civilian life during 1919 whilst unemployment stood at only 2.4%.[127] The latter was made possible by Britain's formal departure from the gold standard in peacetime, recognised officially on 31 March 1919. With the interest rate on Treasury bills fixed at $3\frac{1}{2}\%$ until October, a share boom ensued lifting money incomes by an estimated 25–35% between April 1919 and April 1920, with the result that it could be argued that 'cheap money' thus helped save Britain from a possible revolution during this critical period.[128]

It was in this mood of expansion and easy profits that the government began the job of dismantling the wartime apparatus of the corporate state. The prosperity of 1919–20 was regarded as a prelude to what was presented as just the beginning of a new 'Golden Age' for British capitalism; and its timing to coincide with the increasing momentum of decontrol was interpreted as a vindication of the 'British genius' deriving from individual effort, which would be extinguished if state ownership continued to prevail.[129] The authorities were also concerned, of course, that the expanded machinery of government might fall into the hands of a radicalised working class and used in a way that had not been intended. The process of re-educating the British public in the 'laws of the market' and the 'principles of sound finance' was thus begun, after the experience of wartime 'excess'. This was the remit of the Cunliffe Committee of 1918, which recommended a return to balanced budgets and the gold standard as the basis for a post-war policy of deflation designed to reduce the production costs of industries competing in overseas markets. The boom of 1919–20 made the immediate implementation of these recommendations undesirable and potentially suicidal for the government, in the political context of the period, not least because wartime wage increases formed a large part of industry's total costs of production; *and*, these had to be whittled away *before* price levels and the overall cost of living could be reduced. Industrial capital had also benefited enormously from cheap credit and increased purchasing power at home that had resulted from the government's economic policy of 'frank opportunism'. Yet the latter, if continued, threatened to break the City of London's hold on world trade, which had proved so profitable to its financial institutions before the war and depended on stable exchange rates linked to the gold standard. The Treasury, needless to say, was bound to represent these interests, and it was, moreover, determined to reassert its authority in policy-making following what it saw as the wartime aberrations of 'Lloyd-Georgism'.[130] It also argued that a deflationary policy, involving cuts in public expenditure and the rapid repayment of the national debt, would reduce inflation by stabilising price relations, thus releasing more funds for private investment.[131] Private capital, it was argued, could then exploit lower production costs when competing in overseas markets that were expected to reappear as international trading relations returned to 'normalcy'.

At the beginning of 1919, however, few grasped the fact that one of the few lessons of the war government which was to apply consistently in the post-war years was the experience it had acquired in breaking strikes. In fact, it was Lloyd George's confidence in the state's organisation for coping with industrial unrest that helps explain his enthusiasm for decontrol and his conversion eventually to deflationary policies.[132] Thus the establishment of the Industrial Unrest Committee in February 1919 marked the beginnings of an important shift in emphasis from concession to coercion in the government's handling of labour problems. It was in this context, for example, that the government withdrew from its wartime commitment to set up Joint Industrial Councils, with authority to fix 'fair' or minimum wages.[133] The coercive powers of the state were mobilised to the full during the 40-hours' strike on Clydeside in January–February 1919, and effectively stifled what some regarded as the beginnings of a nationwide 'insurrection' against the civil power.[134] The danger posed by the Triple Alliance of miners, railwaymen and transport workers receded after the government had successfully isolated the moderate leadership of the National Union of Railwaymen by persuading the companies to postpone their demands for wage reductions and agree to recognise the rail unions, despite evidence of militancy and radical politicisation amongst the rank and file.[135] Thus the government's handling of labour unrest in the aftermath of war proved especially astute, based upon a judicious choice of concession and coercion, with the latter veiled in secrecy and used only as a last resort.

A combination of factors explains, therefore, why the government's fears of a Soviet-style extraparliamentary challenge to the dominant social order failed to materialise. The boom of 1919–20 that was planned deliberately in the interests of social stability created the illusion of permanent prosperity at a time when the government was moving to decontrol the economy and return productive resources to private capital. This short-lived period of affluence also served to revive the lines of differentiation within the working class that had been increasingly submerged during the wartime emergency. The recently acquired economic and social status of semi-skilled occupations in new industries, and the growth of intermediate grades of white-collar supervisors and technicians forming a revitalised labour aristocracy, made these groups especially susceptible to the 'Red Scare' propaganda campaign orchestrated during this period. In this respect, it is important to appreciate that the real gains in wages and working conditions won during the war and its immediate aftermath were not eroded all at once, but survived in varying degrees throughout the 1920s and 1930s, particularly in areas of the country like the West Midlands and the south-east of England where the inter-war depression of the staple export trades had little impact.

Yet attention must also be centred on the weaknesses of the extraparliamentary left in Britain that was unable to grasp the opportunity presented to it. The revolutionary movement made serious errors at a critical time, and these were not entirely unavoidable. The Russian Revolution, in particular, had the effect of exacerbating the internecine sectarianism of the extraparliamentary left, dividing revolutionary socialists among a number of tiny groups whose limited capacity to intervene effectively in everyday struggles deprived them of the *practice* that was essential to the development of a dynamic and relevant *theory* of revolutionary politics. Furthermore, the decision of the Russian Communists to use as the basis for a new revolutionary alignment in Britain the British Socialist Party, which shared many of the same illusions about the potential of parliamentary politics in furthering the cause of socialism as its parent Social Democratic Federation, formalised the fragmentation and subsequent isolation of revolutionary socialists.[136] This is attributable, in part, to a mistaken assessment of the British political scene made by Lenin himself, whose call for revolutionaries to affiliate their organisations to the Labour Party rested on a superficial analysis of the latter's recent reconstruction in 1918. But it was also the result of illusions entertained by British socialists themselves about the potential of revolutionary trade unionism and direct action.[137] The tortuous 'unity' negotiations leading up to the creation of the Communist Party of Great Britain during 1919–20 merely consolidated previous divisions, which left the CPGB with no more than 5,000 members at the beginning of 1921.[138] This was hardly an instrument capable of posing a major challenge to the existing social order.

Notes

1. C. L. Mowat, 'Ramsay MacDonald and the Labour Party' in Asa Briggs and John Saville (eds.), *Essays in Labour History 1886–1923* (London: Macmillan, 1971), p. 141.

2. Raymond Challinor, *The Origins of British Bolshevism* (London: Croom Helm, 1978), p. 124.

3. R. J. Holton, '*Daily Herald* v. *Daily Citizen*, 1912–1915', *International Review of Social History*, XIX (1974), pt 3, p. 371.

4. Samuel J. Hurwitz, *State Intervention in Great Britain. A Study of Economic Control and Social Response, 1914–1919* (New York: Columbia University Press, 1949), pp. 225–6.

5. Walter Kendall, *The Revolutionary Movement in Britain 1900–21* (London: Weidenfeld & Nicolson, 1969), pp. 84, 86–8.

6. Holton, '*Herald* v. *Citizen*', pp. 372–3.

7. Ibid. See also Kendall, *Revolutionary Movement*, p. 111; Challinor, *Bolshevism*, pp. 151–2, 154–6.

8. R. H. Tawney, 'The Abolition of Economic Controls, 1918–1921', *Economic History Review*, XIII (1943), pp. 1–2.

9. Gerd Hardach, *The First World War* (London: Allen Lane, 1977), p. 151.

10. Ibid., p. 165.

11. A. H. Gibson, 'A Criticism of the Economic and Financial Policy Pursued by the Government During the War' in A. W. Kirkaldy (ed.), *British Finance During and After the War 1914–21* (London: Pitman, 1921), p. 396.

12. Hardach, *First World War*, p. 166.

13. E. M. H. Lloyd, *Experiments in State Control* (Oxford: Clarendon Press, 1924), pp. 348–54, 367–71.

14. Simon Litman, *Prices and Price Control in Great Britain and the United States during the World War* (New York: Oxford University Press, 1920), pp. 71–7, contains some useful information on the profitability of commerce and industry during the First World War.

15. Sidney Pollard, *The Development of the British Economy 1914–1967* (London: Edward Arnold, 1969), p. 63.

16. Hurwitz, *State Intervention*, p. 67.

17. Ibid., pp. 68–9.

18. Ibid., p. 72.

19. Pollard, *Development of Economy*, p. 48.

20. Ibid., p. 54.

21. J. R. Richmond, *Some Aspects of Labour in the Engineering Industries* (1917), p. 6.

22. Humbert Wolfe, *Labour Supply and Regulation* (Oxford: Clarendon Press, 1923), p. 14.

23. Hurwitz, *State Intervention*, pp. 98–101.

24. Lloyd, *State Control*, pp. 50 ff.

25. Wolfe, *Labour Supply*, Appendix 9, pp. 361–4, for the text of the agreement.

26. M. B. Hammond, *British Labor Conditions and Legislation during the War* (New York: Oxford University Press, 1919), p. 79.

27. G. D. H. Cole, *Labour in War Time* (1915), p. 198.

28. James Hinton, *The First Shop Stewards' Movement* (London: Allen & Unwin, 1973), pp. 29–30.

29. Ibid., pp. 30 ff.

30. Ibid., cited p. 33.

31. Wolfe, *Labour Supply*, pp. 100–14, discusses in detail the provisions of the Munitions of War Act.

32. Ibid., pp. 104–6.

33. Ibid., cited pp. 108–9.

34. Ibid., Appendix 13, p. 378.

35. Hammond, *Labor Conditions*, p. 89.

36. Wolfe, *Labour Supply*, pp. 110–11.

37. Roger Davidson, 'War-time Labour Policy 1914–1916: A Reappraisal', *Journal of Scottish Labour History Society*, 8 (1974), June, who criticises the view of Hinton, *Shop Stewards*, that the ministry's labour department was influenced if not directly controlled by business interests.

38. Wolfe, *Labour Supply*, p. 109.

39. M. A. Crowther, 'The Later Years of the Workhouse 1890–1929' in Pat Thane (ed.), *The Origins of British Social Policy* (London: Croom Helm, 1978).

40. Arthur L. Bowley, *Prices and Wages in the United Kingdom, 1914–1920* (Oxford: Clarendon Press, 1921), Tables LXXIII, LXXIV, pp. 184–5.

41. Henry Pelling, *A History of British Trade Unions* (Harmondsworth: Penguin Books, 1967), pp. 262–3; the unskilled and semi-skilled were special beneficiaries: in the engineering industry, for example, whilst the major craft unions grew by 76% between 1914 and 1918, the two largest general unions organising the semi-skilled and unskilled in the industry increased by 216% and 137% respectively; see Hinton, *Shop Stewards*, pp. 49–50.

42. Sheila Lewenhak, 'Women in British Trade Unions during Two World Wars', paper presented to the Anglo-Dutch Labour History Conference, University of London, September 1979, p. 3.

43. See Hinton, *Shop Stewards*, p. 33, for Llewellyn Smith's justification of the Munitions of War Act.

44. P. S. Bagwell, 'The Triple Industrial Alliance, 1913–1922' in Briggs and Saville, pp. 100–3.

45. Pollard, *Development of Economy*, pp. 53–6, 81–2.

46. Harry Braverman, *Labor and Monopoly Capital* (New York: Monthly Review Press, 1974), p. 90.

47. Ibid., pp. 216–19.

48. A. Touraine *et al.*, *Workers' Attitudes to Technical Change* (Paris: OECD, 1965), pp. 30, 41–2.

49. Ibid., pp. 119–21.

50. Wolfe, *Labour Supply*, p. 198.

51. Ibid., pp. 196–8.

52. Hinton, *Shop Stewards*, p. 114.

53. Wolfe, *Labour Supply*.

54. Irene Osgood Andrews, *Economic Effects of the War Upon Women and Children in Great Britain* (New York: Oxford University Press, 1918), pp. 84–5.

55. Wolfe, *Labour Supply*, pp. 175–6.

56. Ibid.

57. Ibid., p. 179.

58. Barbara Drake, *Women in the Engineering Trades* (London: Allen & Unwin, 1917), p. 117.

59. Wolfe, *Labour Supply*, p. 244.

60. Hurwitz, *State Intervention*, p. 141.

61. Ibid., pp. 141–2.

62. Litman, *Price Control*, p. 32.

63. Wolfe, *Labour Supply*, p. 295.

64. Bert Moorhouse, Mary Wilson and Chris Chamberlain, 'Rent Strikes—Direct Action and the Working Class', *The Socialist Register* (1972), pp. 133–6.

65. Joseph Melling, 'Clydeside Housing and the Evolution of State Rent Control, 1900–39' in the same author's edited collection, *Housing, Social Policy and the State* (London: Croom Helm, 1979).

66. Ibid.

67. Ibid.

68. Ibid.

69. John McHugh, 'The Clyde Rent Strike, 1915', *Journal of Scottish Labour History Society*, 12 (February 1978), p. 62 (footnote).

70. Ibid. See also Joseph Melling, 'The Glasgow Rent Strike and Clydeside Labour—Some Problems of Interpretation', *Journal of Scottish Labour History Society*, 13 (May 1979).

71. Ibid.

72. McHugh, 'Clyde Strike', pp. 59–60; Hinton, *Shop Stewards*, pp. 125–7, insists that the rent strikes and munitions struggles were unrelated, a view criticised by McHugh and Melling.

73. Melling, 'Clydeside Housing'.

74. Wolfe, *Labour Supply*, pp. 127–30; Hinton, *Shop Stewards*, pp. 118–19 ff.

75. Hinton, *Shop Stewards*, p. 68.

76. Ibid., p. 69.

77. Ibid.

78. Ibid., p. 145; Iain McLean, 'The Ministry of Munitions, the Clyde Workers' Committee, and the Suppression of the "Forward": An Alternative View', *Journal of Scottish Labour History Society*, 6 (December 1972), pp. 6–7.

79. Hinton, *Shop Stewards*, pp. 140–3.

80. James Hinton, 'The Clyde Workers' Committee and the Dilution Struggle' in Briggs and Saville, pp. 172 ff.

81. Ibid., pp. 177 ff. McLean, 'Ministry of Munitions', p. 13.

82. Wolfe, *Labour Supply*, Ch. IV.

83. Hinton, *Shop Stewards*, p. 69.

84. Hammond, *Labor Conditions*, pp. 237–8.

85. A. J. P. Taylor, *English History 1914–1945* (Oxford: University Press, 1965), p. 67.

86. Peter K. Cline, 'Eric Geddes and the "Experiment" with Businessmen in Government, 1915–22' in Kenneth D. Brown (ed.), *Essays in Anti-Labour History* (London: Macmillan, 1974).

87. L. P. Carpenter, 'Corporatism in Britain, 1930–45', *Journal of Contemporary History*, 11 (1976), no. 1, p. 3.

88. Royden Harrison, 'The War Emergency Workers' National Committee, 1914–1920' in Briggs and Saville, pp. 236–8.

89. Alan Clinton, 'Trade Councils during the First World War', *International Review of Social History*, XV (1970), pt 2, p. 215.

90. Lloyd, *State Control*, Ch. XXII.

91. Parl. Papers, *Commission of Enquiry into Industrial Unrest*, North-Western Area, 1917 (Cd. 8663), pp. 19–20; Yorkshire & East Midlands Area, 1917 (Cd. 8664), p. 5.

92. Bowley, *Prices*, especially pp. 7–9, 105 ff.

93. Hinton, *Shop Stewards*, Ch. 7, contains a full discussion.

94. C. J. Wrigley, *David Lloyd George and the British Labour Movement* (Hassocks: Harvester Press, 1976), p. 189.

95. Ken Coates, Anthony Topham (eds.), *Industrial Democracy in Great Britain* (London: Macgibbon & Kee, 1968), cited p. 115.

96. Hinton, *Shop Stewards*, Ch. 8.

97. Wrigley, *Lloyd George*, pp. 196–8.

98. J. T. Murphy, *Preparing for Power. A Critical Study of the History of the British Working-Class Movement* (London: Pluto Press, reprint, 1972), pp. 159–60.

99. Rodger Charles, *The Development of Industrial Relations in Britain, 1911–1939* (London: Hutchinson, 1973), pp. 94 ff.

100. Hurwitz, *State Intervention*, p. 290.

101. Charles, *Development of Industrial Relations*, pp. 115–16.

102. Bowley, *Prices*, pp. 35, 44.

103. Ibid., pp. 105 ff.

104. Challinor, *Bolshevism*, pp. 184–5.

105. Ibid., p. 175; see also J. M. Winter, *Socialism and the Challenge of War. Ideas and Politics in Britain 1912–18* (London: Routledge & Kegan Paul, 1974), pp. 244–52, for the effect of Arthur Henderson's visit to Russia in confirming his anti-Bolshevik position.

106. Hinton, *Shop Stewards*, pp. 255 ff.

107. Ibid., pp. 262–3.

108. Ibid., p. 266.

109. Ibid., pp. 312–18.

110. Hurwitz, *State Intervention*, Ch. XII.

111. P. Abrams, 'The Failure of Social Reform, 1918–20', *Past and Present*, 24 (1963), pp. 48–50.

112. Bernard Waites, 'The Effects of the First World War on the Economic and Social Structure of the English Working Class', *Journal of Scottish Labour History Society*, 12 (February 1978), pp. 8, 14–15.

113. Pollard, *Development of Economy*, p. 91.

114. Waites, 'Effects of War', Table 6, p. 21, shows that occupations in entertainment and professional sport had expanded by 63 % between 1911 and 1921.

115. Ibid.

116. Ibid.

117. Ibid., pp. 3–4, 6–8.

118. B. A. Waites, 'The Effect of the First World War on Class and Status in England', *Journal of Contemporary History*, 11 (1976), no. 1, p. 37, for the precocious flowering of white-collar trade unionism during 1917–20.

119. Bowley, *Prices*, pp. 145–7.

120. Joseph Melling, 'Employers and Industrial Welfare in Britain: A Regional and Industrial Comparison, c. 1880–1920', forthcoming PhD thesis, Department of Economic History, University of Glasgow.

121. Ibid.

122. Rodney Lowe, 'The Erosion of State Intervention in Britain, 1917–24', *Economic History Review*, 2nd series, XXXI (1978), no. 2, pp. 271–3.

123. Stephen White, 'Ideological Hegemony and Political Control: The Sociology of Anti-Bolshevism in Britain, 1918–20', *Journal of Scottish Labour History Society*, 9 (June 1975).

124. Ibid., Table 1, p. 13, for a list of societies and their business connections.

125. Trevor Wilson, 'The Coupon and the British General Election of 1918', *Journal of Modern History*, XXXVI (1964), no. 1.

126. Hammond, *Labor Conditions*, pp. 308–17, provides a concise treatment of the Labour Party's plans for reconstruction.

127. Stephen Richards Graubard, 'Military Demobilization in Great Britain Following the First World War', *Journal of Modern History*, XIX (1947), no. 4.

128. Susan Howson, 'The Origins of Dear Money, 1919–20', *Economic History Review*, 2nd series, XXVII (1974), no. 1, pp. 88–91.

129. Tawney, 'Abolition of Controls', pp. 11 ff.

130. Howson, 'Dear Money', pp. 91–2.

131. Ibid., pp. 93–4.

132. Ralph Desmarais, 'Lloyd George and the Development of the British Government's Strike-breaking Organization', *International Review of Social History*, XX (1975), pt 1, pp. 1–4.

133. Charles, *Development of Industrial Relations*, pp. 121 ff.

134. Kendall, *Revolutionary Movement*, pp. 169 ff. For the 'insurrectionary' quality of the 40-hours' strike see, for example, Highton Collection, Department of Economic History, University of Glasgow: *Strike Bulletin*, 30 January, 1919, p. 3; 11 February, 1919, p. 1.

135. Bagwell, 'Triple Alliance', pp. 106–10, 116.

136. Kendall, *Revolutionary Movement*, pp. 296–9, 433; Challinor, *Bolshevism*, pp. 221–4.

137. Hinton, *Shop Stewards*, pp. 298–304, 306–8.

138. Kendall, *Revolutionary Movement*, pp. 303–5, provides a detailed calculation.

CHAPTER 6

The 1920s: The Challenge Contained

British Capitalism on the Defensive: Its Implications for Social Stabilisation

Britain emerged from the boom of 1919–20 to face an economic environment that did not augur well for the claims of labour. The demands of the First World War had led to a massive extension of heavy industry which bore no relation to 'normal' market conditions, even assuming that a return to the pre-war status quo was possible. The war had also produced a huge deficit in Britain's merchandise account of its overseas trade, which stood at $4.1 billion by 1920.[1] The end of hostilities found the USA in the position as the world's leading creditor, with Britain's dollar indebtedness estimated at nearly 3.7 billions.[2] This burden of wartime indebtedness made it impossible for Britain to lend abroad on the same scale as before 1914, and the export prospects of its industries were thus seriously jeopardised.[3] What made the situation even worse was the method of funding the huge growth in indebtedness by the expedient of government loans. The national debt had risen to £7.8 billion by 1920, compared with £650 million in 1914, and the speculative excesses of 1919–20 had given an additional twist to the inflationary spiral that had reduced sterling to one-half of its pre-war value.[4] This disordering of the relationship between domestic and world price levels and costs was to harm severely the international competitiveness of British industry in the post-war period.

It was the central role it was assumed Britain's financial institutions played in relation to the development of the economy as a whole that was the major consideration affecting government policy in the 1920s. This was most clearly evident in the decision to return to the gold standard. In principle, the gold standard specified a fixed rate of exchange based upon the free convertibility between sterling on the one hand, and gold and all other currencies on the other. This implied not only that Britain's domestic currency was linked to the level of its gold reserves but also that the total volume of the world's gold reserves constituted an international medium of exchange. In practice, what had made this system so beneficial to Britain before the First World War had been the strength of its balance of payments, which had led simultaneously to an accumulating gold hoard in London and the continued extension of credit abroad. This had meant, in effect, that although gold was nominally the international medium of exchange, it was sterling that was in fact most commonly used as a 'reserve' currency. The willingness of other countries to hold sterling in lieu of gold had proved immensely profitable to the finance houses of the City of London, placing them at the centre of the world market for money and commodities. Yet the extent of the sterling bloc's indebtedness to the USA after the war made it no longer possible for Britain to maintain its gold hoard and at the same time invest heavily overseas. A return to the pre-war system could not be achieved without great sacrifice and cost to the economy as a whole.

It is difficult to disentangle the economic, social and political motives that lay behind the decision to return to the gold standard. A narrowly conceived self-interest in the prosperity of London as a financial centre is part but not the whole of the explanation. There was, first of all, a strong desire in high financial circles for 'distributive justice' after the inflationary experience of the war and the speculation of 1919–20, which was regarded as having benefited industrialists and wage-earners at the expense of bankers and rentiers.[5] The traditional power and prestige of Britain's rentier bourgeoisie had been eroded as a result of Lloyd George's war socialism, and it is conceivable that their desire for revenge cannot be explained exclusively in terms of economic rationality. The intensity of the struggle between the government and the permanent staff of the Treasury and their advisers prior to the victory of the 'dear money' party during the winter of 1919–20 emphasises the importance of 'irrational' factors like institutional jealousy and just plain snobbery.[6] What is clear is that the government's conversion to deflation in 1920 was seen as the basis of a long-term plan to restrict the growth of the domestic money supply, and thus bring down internal prices to a level at which free convertibility between gold and sterling could be restored.[7] And the means adopted to achieve this end reflected the dominant assumptions of international bankers and rentiers, rather than the interests of industry or the welfare of its employees.

Cuts in government spending combined with a high bank rate were the principal means used to reduce domestic price levels during the early 1920s. The 1921 Budget Speech led to the appointment of a powerful committee chaired by Sir Eric Geddes, which had as its remit, 'to make recommendations to the Chancellor of the Exchequer for effecting forthwith all possible reductions in the National Expenditure of Supply Services'; and its subsequent influence led one civil servant to claim that the Geddes Committee became practically the Cabinet of the day.[8] The burden of the Committee's attentions fell upon the armed forces and the spending of other civil departments, and it arranged for the transfer of financial responsibilities from central government to the local authorities. Expenditure on the armed forces, for example, was reduced from £353.6 million during 1920–1 to £134.3 million by 1923–4, while spending by other departments was cut from £465.6 million to £278.6 million during the same period: much of the latter resulted from educational economies and the running-down of public works. Interest on the National Debt began to absorb as much as 40% of government expenditure and was higher in absolute terms during 1924–5 than in 1920–1, despite the downward trend of prices during the intervening period.[9] In the meantime, the bank rate that had been raised to 7% during 1920–1 was reduced only slowly to 3% by June 1922, and the note issue was also curtailed.[10]

It is pertinent to explore the reasoning behind this strategy and consider whether any alternative policy was available. In this respect, there is no doubt that the relative homogeneity of the powerful financial interests represented on the Court of the Bank of England gave them a position of influence that could not be easily challenged. Of the court's 26 members in 1924–5, at least 15 were connected with overseas banking, mainly in the Empire and Latin America, five were in insurance and shipping, whilst only two could be described as industrialists.[11] The fact that many of these individuals had traditionally been among the richest and most powerful men in Britain provided further weight to the assumption that what was good for the City of London was good for the economy as a whole. Moreover, they had a highly articulate spokesman in the figure of Montagu Norman, Governor of the Bank of England. In his view, the basic task of government policy was to maintain equilibrium in the money market. In the context of the 1920s, this meant that the expansion of credit and the growth of the money supply had to be restricted in order to compensate for the weakening of London's position as an international creditor and its tendency to lose gold to the rest of the world. He thus argued, for example, that it was 'the international consideration' rather than the domestic 'state of trade' that should determine the bank rate.[12] His assumptions did not take into account the relationship between monetary policy and its effect on domestic levels of savings, investment and employment. It was for this reason that Norman was so insistent on returning to the gold standard at the pre-war parity of $4.86 to the pound sterling. This would restore 'discipline' to the international exchanges, enabling overseas bankers and merchants to lend and trade without political 'interference' arising from domestic considerations.

Norman's reasoning implied that there would have to be a significant reduction in domestic prices and costs. He also accepted that this might lead to an overvaluation of sterling on the foreign exchanges, but he stressed the beneficial effects of a strong currency in reducing the cost of imported food and raw materials, as well as the contribution it would make to maximising the 'invisible' exports earned by London's financial institutions.[13] In regard to the detrimental effect of overvaluation on Britain's export industries, Norman believed overseas demand to be relatively price inelastic, and he argued that the benefit of exchange stabilisation in reestablishing international confidence in London as a financial centre would assist the export trades. It would be wrong to conclude, therefore, that Norman's emphasis on returning to the gold standard at the pre-war parity indicated any principled abdication of responsibility for its impact upon industry; rather, it would appear that he considered industry's prosperity to be dependent upon restoring confidence in London as a financial and trading centre, and it was this premiss that explains his determination to return to gold. After all, his analysis showed a shrewd appreciation of how Britain's financial and trading dominance had supported its export industries before the First World War.

With the benefit of hindsight, it is easy to fault Norman's failure to realise that Britain's wartime indebtedness had permanently impaired its ability to invest abroad on the pre-war scale. And his experience as a banker may have led him to overestimate industry's flexibility in restructuring its mix of capital, labour and products in response to the spread of industrialisation overseas. It was in this latter respect that the deflationary measures required before the gold standard could be restored had such a damaging effect on the economy, particularly industry and the welfare of wage-earners, yet many employers as well as figures in the City of London itself were not unaware of the implications of deflation for industry.[14] But these doubts lacked the logical coherence of the arguments so lucidly marshalled by Norman and other prominent bankers having the ear of government.[15] The attitudes of some industrialists were often articulated in a tentative if not contradictory fashion. Thus Sir William Larke, Director of the National Federation of Iron and Steel Manufacturers, complained about the detrimental effect of credit restriction, yet at the same time he warned of the dangers of international exchange instability—a view shared by the Federation of British Industry.[16] It was John Maynard Keynes, of course, who was almost alone in advocating a coherent alternative to orthodox monetary policy, whilst accepting the legitimacy of a capitalist market economy.

Keynes was engaged in a running war of words with the authorities throughout the 1920s. He argued for a managed currency, not tied to a fixed rate of exchange, that would make possible cheap money conditions at home and allow for a programme of capital development involving the large-scale transfer of labour away from the traditional export industries.[17] Yet this made him very much the outsider in relation to the hallowed circle of international bankers and merchants close to the government. It has also been suggested that Keynes's difficulty in winning converts to his views was a product of his failure to demonstrate convincingly that the gold standard and deflation were necessarily and inevitably linked.[18] Where he left his audience in no doubt at all was the effect of the restoration of the gold standard on Britain's price and wage structure, which he estimated in May 1925, after the return to gold had been achieved, to be 10–11 % higher than the level justified by the international price of sterling.[19] The inevitable consequence of this was that not only had the *general* level of prices and wages to be reduced, but the brunt of this was bound to fall initially and most heavily on the so-called 'unsheltered' export trades, which were tied most directly to the international gold price of sterling. And, because the output of the so-called 'sheltered' trades fed as an input into the unsheltered or export sector, the deflationary effect of price and wage reductions would subsequently have to be diffused throughout the economy. Yet it is not clear that Keynes's advocacy of exchange depreciation would in itself have prevented the industrial decay, rising unemployment and labour unrest resulting from deflation and the return to gold. It is almost certain that had Britain allowed sterling to float downwards, or returned to gold at less than $4.86, the monetary authorities of other countries would have acted to maintain their relative undervaluations existing when the pre-war parity was restored, thus strengthening the deflationary spiral on a worldwide basis. Furthermore, Montagu Norman's contention that overseas demand was relatively price inelastic in the 1920s has never been convincingly refuted. Was it not the actual composition of Britain's exports, committed as these were to a comparatively narrow range of traditional staples, rather than price considerations, that was at the heart of the economy's difficulties in the 1920s?

The problems of British capitalism were far more deep seated than Keynes himself was willing to concede, and demanded a measure of control, direction and planning that at the time was politically unthinkable. What was required was a massive shift of capital and labour from the old export industries to newer sectors like chemicals, electricals and motor vehicles, where British industry had been especially deficient before the war. Yet the priorities of financial orthodoxy made this transformation a particularly slow and painful process. Export industries like shipbuilding and textiles embodied highly specialised forms of interdependence between capitals, having intricate backward and forward linkages in relation to other sectors of the economy. The extent of this 'indivisibility of plant' made it virtually impossible to cut back output by shifting to a smaller scale of plant, for example, without the attendant risk of permanent undercapacity working, because of the internal and external economies associated with the existing mix of productive techniques. British industry had developed since the 1870s on the basis of 'a gradual succession of small adaptations', but what was required in the 1920s was a 'revolutionary leap' in re-equipment.[20] But market factors and, more particularly, the financial environment of the 1920s made this very difficult to achieve because of the restrictive policies implemented by the monetary authorities, and the structure of the British capital market with its historic orientation towards overseas issues rather than long-term investment in domestic industry.

In the meantime, the degradation of the lives and work of many ordinary people was the consequence of accepting as 'inevitable' what was politically unthinkable. Given the constraints on the employers' ability to shed labour as a means of reducing their costs of production, arising from factors like indivisibility of plant, it was to be expected that their efforts to overcome rigidities in labour costs should focus in the 1920s on cutting down the 'inflated' wage settlements inherited from the 1914–20 period.[21] This was the background to much of the labour unrest that was to culminate in the General Strike of 1926. Yet, in this respect, it was wage-earners who reaped the most bitter harvest from capital's own earlier profligacy. The share boom of 1919–20, for example, had accelerated the wartime increases in capital values that were to bear little correspondence with market realities during the 1920s. Moreover, the extent to which this rise in capital valuations was achieved by borrowing at low rates of interest during 1919–20 left many firms with heavy overhead charges when restrictive monetary policies were applied after 1920.[22] At the same time, the effect of credit restriction and high interest rates in increasing the cost of re-equipment impeded the development of a more productive relationship between finance and industry that was necessary if the 'revolutionary' leap to new processes and products was to be realised during the 1920s.[23] Meanwhile, unfavourable market conditions did not prevent a strong recovery in the economy's profitability after 1921 as capitalists adjusted to tighter monetary policies.[24] The wage–income ratio in all sectors, excluding agriculture, fell on trend during the decade.[25] Yet in the context of pre-war expectations, when the share of profits in the national income had been rising, levels of profitability in the 1920s were generally regarded as unsatisfactory, and particularly in industry, equity yields compared even more unfavourably than had been the case before 1914 with the returns obtained by rentiers from fixed interest securities.[26] This represented a strong disincentive to re-equipment and investment in new sectors of manufacturing industry required to maintain employment and wage incomes.

In industry, efforts to maintain prices and profits took the form of concentration and 'rationalisation' as a means of eliminating less viable concerns and 'excess' capacity. This was evident in the trend towards monopolisation, which was often *represented* as rationalisation although in practice this was not necessarily the case. The inter-war period was marked by the spread of trade associations, for example, where the main priority was fixing minimum prices, achieved either by a quasi-monopolistic firm acting as price-leader or by patents and international agreements to share out markets.[27] Since a trade association preserved the existence of individual firms, which meant that prices had to be fixed in light of the cost structure of its less efficient members, the opportunities for rationalisation were often seriously restricted. The degree to which a trade association was successful in stabilising prices would imply a greater propensity to invest, yet re-equipment within the monopolised sphere might threaten its protected rate of profit, hence the growth of trade associations led frequently to ossification of existing techniques rather than rationalisation.[28] Any surplus consequently generated within a monopolised sphere could be diverted into 'free' areas of production, like the manufacture of new consumer durables, but the result tended to create overcrowding in the latter and contributed to the generally low yields on industrial equities in the 1920s. This explains the painfully slow process of restructuring in industry during this period, the persistence of excess capacity and high unemployment, and why the downward trend of the wage–income ratio was not reversed during the 'recovery' of the 1930s.[29] At the same time, the extent of industrial concentration was by no means uniform, and spectacular instances like the formation of Imperial Chemical Industries were not representative of the situation in many of Britain's staple export industries.[30] Many of the latter were crying out for rationalisation but market conditions did not encourage the pursuit of economies of scale, and the complex interdependence of small-scale enterprise often made concentration difficult to achieve, with falling wages and poor employment prospects frequently cited as the outcome of monopoly pricing imposed on a reduced volume of output.[31]

Despite the constraints on the growth prospects of British industry in the 1920s, what continues to strike the historian of this period is the economy's capacity to adapt, change and expand in the face of great difficulties. It is true that the effect of cost rigidities and depressed demand did not encourage a high rate of capital accumulation. Thus total investment as a percentage of gross national product averaged 12% during the years 1920–9, compared with 13.3% during 1900–9 when investment in Britain was already relatively low by international comparison.[32] Yet it has been argued that more emphasis needs to be placed on how efficiently capital is utilised and less on the actual quantities of investment made. Recent calculations have shown, for example, that gross domestic product per head (at constant prices) rose as fast if not faster in the 1920s than during most of the second half of the nineteenth century, and considerably faster than in the decade or so before the First World War.[33] The trend towards monopolisation, for example, implied that firms had a greater propensity to invest in labour-saving technology, given their cost rigidities, and this is illustrated by the rise of 37.2% in the capacity of electric motors employed in all trades between 1922 and 1930, with the exception of electricity supply undertakings.[34] Innovation was assisted further by the favourable movement in the terms of trade, with food and raw material prices falling, which increased demand for new consumer goods among the middle class and upper strata of the working class in areas of the country like the south-east of England that were relatively unaffected by unemployment. Depreciation as a proportion of gross fixed capital formation was 80% in the 1920s and 85% during the 1930s, and this allowed for considerable technical improvement as old equipment was replaced, despite historically low levels of total investment in industry.[35]

Productivity in British industry was clearly rising faster during the inter-war period than in the years just prior to the war, but technical progress was not by itself responsible for the fall in industry's unit wage costs during the 1920s and 1930s.[36] The latter must be considered in the wider context of the downward shift in the wage–income ratio. High unemployment weakened the bargaining strength of wage-earners, especially after the 1926 General Strike, and this enabled employers to keep down wages and introduce more intensive methods of working that were as important as technical progress in raising productivity.[37] Moreover, the striking decline in family size during the inter-war years encouraged a 'shake-out' of labour from depressed industries, where productivity was generally low, since the burden of family responsibilities discouraging occupational mobility was reduced.[38] The steady decline in the proportion of very old and very young dependants, whilst the reservoir of labour between the working ages of 15 and 64 increased, provided a powerful inducement to structural change in industry as its traditional export sectors contracted. At the same time, the wartime acceleration in the growth of the white-collar salariat was sustained during the 1920s, with the result that by the early 1930s salary-earners comprised one-fifth of Britain's occupied population and consumed one-quarter of its national income.[39] The expansion of the salariat was a consequence not only of the comparative resilience of the banking, financial and distributive sectors, in contrast to industry's economic difficulties, since these employed a high proportion of salaried employees; the trend towards monopolisation and the growth of the large-scale company in manufacturing led to changes in technical processes and work organisation requiring more white-collar supervisors relative to manual workers. The former approximated most closely to the 'running overhead costs' incurred by firms and not readily shed when market conditions were depressed.[40] Their position of comparative privilege was evident in the ways they were becoming more formally differentiated from the manual grades of wage-earners, reflected in distinctive career structures linked to specific technical or professional qualifications and strengthened by selective benefits like company welfare schemes.[41]

It is no coincidence that the semi-skilled grades of wage labour were expanding at the same time as the white-collar salariat was growing.[42] This marked the quickening in the pace of change in the labour process that had its origins in the pre-war years and had increased further after 1914. The wages of many of the rising numbers of semi-skilled workers employed during the war had risen more than the rates of skilled tradesmen, and a considerable share of this improvement was retained in the post-war period.[43] This was because the semi-skilled tended to be concentrated outside the staple export sectors where unemployment was greatest; they were also in some cases directly replacing old skills; and it was they who benefited from the wages minima established by the government's Trade Boards.[44] It was the spread of 'scientific management' in combination with the more specialised semi-skilled workers that also made the latter less vulnerable to unemployment. The spread of what has been called 'Fordism' in the 1920s, with its capacity to provide *regular* work, created the basis for a new labour aristocracy where skill alone was no longer a primary consideration.[45] The view taken by the growing army of scientific management and salaried staff envisaged labour as 'an organic whole', rather than as discrete 'hands' or factors of production who could be dispersed or readily assembled together again at will. The need to co-ordinate and supervise the specialised components of this organic whole had led to an early expansion of the office staff in American manufacturing industry during the early twentieth century, yet what has often been overlooked is the extent to which the same phenomenon gathered momentum in Britain during the inter-war period.[46]

In the most general sense, it is not clear whether these developments had a stabilising or destabilising effect on labour's relationship with British society. In the wider context of deskilling, for example, the extensive introduction of electric motors during the 1920s increased enormously the scope for adopting powered control systems of production, where machines can preselect and supply their own control signals.[47] This made possible a significant dimunition in the decision-making authority of the operative, and was unlike much of the deskilling during the First World War that had actually increased the responsibilities of some highly skilled operatives. Much of this authority now fell to the growing numbers of office staff. This often reduced the capacity and inclination of many engineering workers, for example, to defend whatever craft autonomy they had managed to regain, whilst a not insignificant minority aspired, of course, to positions as salaried office staff. At the same time, the advent of high levels of unemployment in those very areas and sectors of industry where craft autonomy had been most entrenched proved an obstacle to generalising the skilled workers' experience in terms of trade solidarity or class action. What often resulted was that previously militant sections of the traditional labour aristocracy became demoralised, withdrawing from their earlier close identification with the work situation.[48] This occurred especially when there was enforced migration from the occupational communities typical of the centres of declining export industry to areas of expanding industry like the south-east of England.[49] The phenomenon of 'withdrawal' from the workplace was frequently accompanied by a shift to a more home-centred lifestyle, which was encouraged by the decline in family size and the availability of better housing in new industrial areas; or it was evident in an obsession with having 'a good time', as the antithesis of work, that was strengthened by the reduction in working hours, the spread of night or shift-working, and the expansion of public entertainment during the inter-war period.[50] This development helps explain why a distinctively 'labourist' subculture not only survived in Britain, but had by the 1930s reproduced itself in new forms.

It is in this connection that some discussion of the changes in wages and living conditions during the inter-war years is justified. The impact of the war had been to disrupt established norms that had provided inter-class reference points for legitimating what were regarded as 'acceptable' standards of living. The combined effects of wartime inflation, occupational mobility, the virtual disappearance of the underemployed residuum, and the narrowing of wage differentials, had raised significantly the aspirations and expectations of wage-earners as a whole. Notions like the 'national minimum', for example, had intensified what has been called the 'relative deprivation' felt by many workers, because it assumed an abstract reference-point for determining whether living standards were acceptable or not, without regard to the existance of class relations that had restricted the terms of reference for comparability according to *intra*-class criteria. In contrast, proposals like the demand for a national minimum implied the existence of criteria based upon comparisons *between* different social classes.[51] Labour's sense of relative deprivation had somehow to be reduced if the stability of British society in the post-war period was to be ensured. In explaining how this was achieved, what needs to be emphasised is the context of this period that must include an appreciation of the regional unevenness of depression and high unemployment; the degree to which their effects were ameliorated; and how this tended to magnify contemporary perceptions of any improvement in living standards taking place during these years. These wider issues are central to an understanding of why the industrial unrest culminating in the 1926 General Strike was eventually resolved, and how a new modus vivendi in labour's relationship with British society was subsequently established.

Recent research into the distribution of wealth in Britain shows that a small downward redistribution *within* the top 20% of wealth-holders took place during the 1920s.[52] Yet in 1930 the top 10% of wealth-holders still had 86.6% of the total wealth, in comparison with 92% of the total wealth possessed by the top 10% in 1911–13. Contemporary estimates of *income* distribution, on the other hand, indicate a more striking redistribution from the very largest to the more moderate income-earners, largely because of the effect of price and tax changes.[53] Yet most of the latter were not wage-earners but were drawn either from the self-employed or the increasingly numerous body of salaried employees who had been marginal taxpayers in 1913.[54] It was they who were most likely to have close and regular contact with wage-earners, thus contributing to the latter's sense of relative deprivation in the 1920s. What must have made this even more intolerable was the extent to which the wage increases obtained in the period 1914–20 were eroded during the years 1920–5. Money wage rates fell faster than the cost of living, and real wage rates were actually lower in 1923, 1924 and 1925 than they had been in July 1914, leaving aside the effect of unemployment and short-time working on wage-earnings as distinct from rates.[55] The magnitude of the reduction in money wages in Britain during the 1920s appears unique in comparison with the experience of other advanced economies.[56] Above all, wages were reduced more than the incomes of salaried employees in the same industry or sector, or in comparison with the incomes of professional groups.[57] It seems clear that it was not until 1927–8 that there was any sustained recovery in real wages from the low levels of 1923–4.[58]

The government's abandonment of its commitment to reform after the First World War limited the extent to which the effect of wage cuts in reducing living standards could be cushioned by social welfare provision. The increase in unemployment presented government with an especially intractable problem, with the proportion of insured workers unemployed rising from 3.9 % in 1920 to 16.9 % in 1921, and unemployment remained in double figures until 1927.[59] In centres of traditional export industry, unemployment was particularly high, thus the local employment exchange at Alexandria near Glasgow registered a figure of 58 % unemployed in the middle of 1922, and as entitlement to insured benefits was rapidly exhausted many 'respectable' wage-earners had to resort to the Poor Law.[60] This forced the government to introduce unconvenanted benefits on a non-contributory basis, yet civil servants had considerable discretion in deciding whether these should be paid or not, including stringent tests for determining if the applicant was genuinely 'seeking' work.[61] Instructions issued in May 1922 also stipulated that unconvenanted benefits were only to be paid if household incomes were less than 13s per week.[62] Statistical calculations of inequality in Britain during the 1920s fail to take into account the humiliation and loss of self-respect that figured prominently as a cause of the widespread sense of relative deprivation in this period, and the consequent resentment was felt even more bitterly given the grandiose promises made only a short time earlier.

The commitment made during 1917–19 to an ambitious post-war programme of state-subsidised housebuilding was similarly emasculated in the early 1920s. The implications of the slogan 'Homes *Fit for Heroes*' meant the construction of between 500,000 and one million additional houses during the immediate post-war period.[63] It was the assumption of housing need that had led to the enactment of Addison's 1919 Housing and Town Planning Bill, which introduced the radical principle of Treasury subsidies to local authorities in an attempt to encourage them to build homes at the prevailing level of rents paid by the working class. Whilst conditions during 1919–20 had been favourable to the implementation of Addison's Act because interest rates were relatively low, the coming of 'dear money' in 1920–1 made local government borrowing increasingly prohibitive, at the same time that building costs proved difficult to reduce.[64] A proposal for licensing or rationing housebuilding according to need had been rejected in 1918. The outcome was that local authorities were left to compete with private enterprise for the available funds, which were being deliberately diminished and made more expensive after 1920.[65] This marked a reaffirmation of the ideology of private ownership, as distinct from public provision, and formed part of the government's wider aim of re-educating labour in the laws of the market, the legitimacy of private property, and the desirability of individual self-help. This was to be confirmed in the more cautious approach adopted by the Chamberlain and Wheatley subsidies, with the result that during the decade after 1923 twice as many houses were built by private enterprise than by the local authorities, and more were built without subsidies than with them, largely for the middle and lower-middle classes.[66] Subsequently, rising rents and subletting became commonplace after 1923, when the government moved piecemeal to decontrol rents fixed by the 1915 Act, and contemporary evidence points to increasing overcrowding in the 1920s compared with 1913.[67]

Thus the popular image of growing working-class affluence in communities like Greenwich and Dagenham during the inter-war period is qualified by its coincidence with urban degeneration in areas of export industry like Lancashire and Clydeside.[68] What made this decay even less acceptable than it might otherwise have been in the 1920s was the contrast it posed to the pre-war vitality of 'respectable' working-class self-help in regions of staple export industry. It was probably this as much as anything else that made the latter so prominent in the labour unrest of the period. Yet the very unevenness of Britain's industrial development, together with surviving peculiarities in the community forms of social relations, worked against an effective co-ordination of working-class unrest required to challenge effectively the combined power of private capital and the state.[69]

The Employers' Offensive and Reformism Recast, 1920–4

The labour unrest of the 1920s illustrates the unevenness of Britain's economic development during these years. The conjuncture of nearly full employment and the momentum of wartime militancy had made the years 1918–20 a critical period in the government's strategy for post-war stability. What was especially dangerous from the government's point of view was the extent to which industrial conflict had become overtly political, with local Councils of Action, for example, threatening strike action to end the economic blockade of the Soviet Union and force the withdrawal of troops from Ireland.[70] It has been argued that activity of this kind represented a 'confusion' of the industrial and political spheres of working-class action, and encouraged a false sense of immunity from the charge of 'unconstitutional' behaviour that was to have a direct bearing on the policies pursued by the trade unions during the period leading up to the 1926 General Strike.[71] The use of terms like 'confusion' and 'unconstitutional' in this context assumes, of course, an *a priori* legitimacy for the British labourist tradition, based upon a strict separation of the industrial and political spheres of working-class action, which during the years 1918–20 was seemingly on the point of disintegration. The government's own intelligence service regarded this prospect as dangerous and potentially 'revolutionary', hence its efforts to rehabilitate the traditions and practices of labourism during the 1920s. This task of depoliticisation was seen as particularly crucial since it would again make feasible the resolution of industrial problems in accordance with 'natural' market forces, bereft of the political overtones that had earlier provided a focus for co-ordinated activity by wage-earners as a *class*.

The labour unrest of the 1920s was to be marked by the resurgence of sectional divisions as groups of workers sought to preserve wartime gains in the face of rising unemployment and demands from employers for wage reductions. This focus of activity on sectionalised self-defence helped, in turn, to revitalise a labourist outlook as worsening economic conditions weakened the capacity of local rank-and-file organisations to mobilise workers' resistance along class lines, whilst the authority of an expanding trade union bureaucracy was consequently strengthened. This development was rooted in the contrasting situation confronting workers in the unsheltered as distinct from those in the sheltered trades who did not suffer immediately from the effects of the return to monetary orthodoxy.[72] The demands of the First World War had intensified further nineteenth-century patterns of regional specialisation, with the result that workers in the unsheltered export trades were concentrated in areas like Scotland's central belt, the north-east of England, South Wales and Lancashire. With the possible exception of the West Midlands, these areas also contained a disproportionately large share of the total trade union membership, but they were not growth points for the development of new comparatively sheltered industries during the 1920s and 1930s. It is this that highlights the central paradox of labour militancy in Britain during the immediate post-war years: namely, that the best-organised and potentially most militant section of labour was geographically and industrially concentrated, whilst remaining comparatively isolated from the rest of the occupied population. It was the former, of course, who had traditionally been most dependent on export markets and who were now the first to suffer the brunt of the employers' attempts to reduce their working costs at labour's expense, as overseas demand fell away and the squeeze of financial orthodoxy tightened during the years 1921–3. There was thus an objective logic of inevitability in the tactics of sectionalised self-defence adopted by workers in these years, which proved a major obstacle to broadening the lines of resistance on a class basis.

The collapse of the Triple Alliance during the course of 1921 and the consequences of decontrol in the coal industry illustrate the sectional fragmentation of workers' resistance and the way in which labour unrest was depoliticised. The miners, in particular, had good reason to doubt the commitment of the railwaymen's and dockers' leaders to call out their members in the event of a widespread dispute. Not only were the railwaymen and dockers less well organised in comparison with the miners, their leaders were also acutely aware of the efficiency of the government's strike-breaking organisation. This had already been put to the test during the 1919 railway strike and was thereafter extended to all forms of transport, including the mobilisation of military vehicles for deliveries to and from the docks.[73] Moreover, the successful outcome of the 1919 railway strike and the award made to the dockers by the Shaw Inquiry in 1920 had strengthened the authority of union leaders like J. H. Thomas who had little sympathy with the Triple Alliance as a strike weapon. Yet more important was the fact that workers in transport and communications remained relatively unaffected by the slump of 1921, which led to rising unemployment and substantial wage reductions in unsheltered export trades like coal-mining.[74] This was the background to the decision of the Executive of the Triple Alliance not to support the miners in resisting wage reductions, which was announced on 15 April 1921—'Black Friday'. The last-minute equivocation of the leadership of the railwaymen and transport workers seems to have been decisive in isolating the miners since it is probable that both the dockers and railwaymen would have supported a sympathetic strike had one been called.[75]

The desertion of the miners by their erstwhile allies did not prevent a national stoppage in the coal industry that lasted until July 1921 when the miners returned to work on the owners' terms. Yet it soon became clear that wage cuts could not alone restore the fortunes of the coal industry.[76] Modest proposals were made for rationalisation or the concentration of production in the most efficient units, but these faced implacable resistance from the coal-owners whilst at the same time falling short of what the miners themselves wanted.[77] In the face of this seemingly unbreakable deadlock, the discontent and militancy of the rank and file was left to smoulder unassuaged as conditions worsened.[78] But the combined effect of rising unemployment and demoralisation, which was especially evident after the miners had returned to work on the owners' terms, weakened the resistance of rank-and-file opposition to the official line of Miners' Federation that supported the terms of settlement of the 1921 dispute. At the 1922 Annual Conference of the MFGB, Herbert Smith spoke on behalf of the Executive justifying the 1921 agreement which had restored wage bargaining on a regional basis, and he blamed low wages on the depression rather than the agreement itself. Smith argued for closer co-operation within the Miners' Federation in order to raise productivity, which he maintained was the only avenue to future improvement.[79] This testifies the degree to which labour had been re-educated in the laws of the market during the 1920s.

The experience of industrial strife in the coal industry is an extreme example of how the unevenness of Britain's economic development tended to segregate labour unrest in areas removed from other major centres of the working population. The location of the engineering industry was also relatively concentrated, although to a lesser extent than coal-mining. Engineering was also more heterogeneous in character, yet the dependence of its heavy sector on overseas trade meant that it too suffered from the contraction of demand abroad during the 1920s, and its rate of profit fell steadily between 1921 and 1923.[80] During 1921–2, the employers who had recently consolidated their collective strength by establishing a widely-based Engineering and Allied Employers' National Federation felt able to demand the termination of wartime bonuses and the withdrawal of increases made only the year before. Rising unemployment undermined the workplace strength of the wartime shop stewards' movement, despite the creation of the Amalgamated Engineering Union in 1921, with the result that between 1921 and 1922 wages in the engineering industry were reduced more than during any corresponding period in its experience of collective bargaining.[81] At the same time, employers sought to maximise the gains obtained from deskilling and more systematic managerial supervision since 1914, by attacking 'restrictive practices' and increasing productivity. This was the setting for a nationwide lock-out in the engineering industry in 1922, fought ostensibly over the extent of overtime working, but was in reality a struggle over 'managerial functions', particularly the manning of machinery.[82] The outcome of the dispute marked a noteworthy victory for the employers since the terms of settlement provided that managerial decisions were to be adhered to, without a stoppage of work, until questions of disagreement had passed through the procedure for resolving disputes established in 1898.[83] Moreover, the employers made use of the reservoir of unemployed available in 1922 in refusing to re-engage union members and victimising known militants.[84]

The phasing of the employers' counter-offensive during 1921–2, following the wartime concessions to labour, had the effect of isolating in turn the best-organised and most militant groups of workers in the unsheltered trades who had earlier posed the most serious challenge to the dominant social order. In the process, labour's rank-and-file organisations were also emasculated, which increased the authority of the full-time union officials whose numbers rose following the amalgamations like the AEU and the Transport and General Workers' Union.[85] The reorganisation of the TUC after 1920 strengthened their authority further. Ernest Bevin had prepared a memorandum in November 1919 where he set out proposals for a new TUC General Council to replace the old Parliamentary Committee, to be composed of the leaders of unions selected on the basis of economic groups, which was later enlarged to take into account the numerical size of a few big unions.[86] Its duties included the co-ordination of industrial action when more than one union was involved, especially on general questions like minimum wages and hours of labour. The view of some left-wingers was that this reorganisation would make it easier to arrange sympathetic strike action, including the much-discussed general strike, yet like the defunct Triple Alliance, the new General Council represented no more than a concentration of authority in the hands of the full-time officials comprising the executives of its constituent bodies.[87] This fact was not fully appreciated by left-wing groups like the Communist International who continued to retain illusions about the 'revolutionary' potential of the TUC General Council until the 1926 General Strike, and reflected their failure to work through the 'labourist' implications of Bevin's original memorandum, which stressed at the outset that the General Council was to develop the 'industrial' rather than the 'political' side of the trade union movement.[88]

The revitalisation of trade union sectionalism during the 1920s was to present a serious problem for the tiny minority of revolutionary socialists who sought to harness industrial militancy for their political ends. The recently formed Communist Party of Great Britain (CPGB), with its organic links with the Russian-dominated Communist International, was persuaded that its aim was to create a mass revolutionary party on the Bolshevik model. In the British context, however, the prospects were not encouraging. In the first place, the heavy-handed tactics that had been used to weld together the various socialist groups into one united and disciplined Communist Party during 1919–20 had alienated many revolutionaries like Sylvia Pankhurst of the Workers' Socialist Federation, who found it impossible to reconcile the ostensibly revolutionary aims of the CPGB with its advocacy of affiliation to the Labour Party and its refusal to run candidates in local elections solely on a platform of 'class war'. The dialectical juggling that subsequently led the CPGB to proclaim its support for the Labour Party and a strengthened TUC General Council, whilst at the same time insisting on the need for a mass revolutionary party, was not likely to appeal to more than a small minority of 'true believers'. This was an indication of the party's inability to intervene effectively in industrial struggles during a period when militancy was in retreat. Thus although many of the leading lights of the shop stewards' movement joined the CPGB, the fact remained that more than 80% of its minuscule membership was, with the exception of London, concentrated in areas of staple export industry like Lancashire, Clydeside, Fife and South Wales.[89] The objective conditions of nearly full employment that had sustained these districts' reputation for militancy during the period 1914–20 disappeared in the wake of rising unemployment, defeat in industrial disputes, victimisation and demoralisation during the 1920s. To an increasing extent, therefore, the CPGB became a *substitute* for genuine forms of working-class self-activity, and this has led to the view that the party's central aim of building a mass revolutionary party during the 1920s was mistaken.[90]

Despite the failings of the Communists, what was more important in completing the depoliticisation of labour unrest in the 1920s was the rise of Labour as a party that aspired to govern Britain in its own right, rather than as a junior partner in alliance with the Liberals. Liberalism's popular appeal had depended upon the subtle nuances of status, indicated by the use of terms like 'deserving' and 'residuum', which has described the complex hierarchy of distinctions within the working class in pre-war society. The effect of the First World War had been to erode these distinctions and reduce social perceptions to more straightforward formulations based upon class, at least insofar as these were articulated in the rhetoric of parliamentary politics.[91] The new semi-skilled workers enfranchised in 1918 had little inclination to vote for the Liberal Party, which they more often than not identified with the 'selfishness and craft pride' of the 'so-called aristocracy of labour'.[92] At the same time, the expanding army of white-collar salaried workers was more likely to identify with the economic self-interest of their employers, most of whom were deserting Liberalism for the safer havens of the Conservative Party, while the newly enfranchised women voters had no reason for having any special liking for the Liberals who had been so equivocal in their attitude to demands for universal suffrage before the war. Finally, what was to complete the demise of the Liberals as a party of government during the post-war years was the phenomenon of Lloyd George's leadership of the coalition government, which triggered a Conservative revolt in October 1922 and led to the isolation of those Independent Liberals alienated by Lloyd George's sudden changes in political direction and the sycophancy of his 'camp followers'.[93]

In the 1920s, therefore, it was the Parliamentary Labour Party (PLP) that aspired to the role of 'progressive umbrella' analogous to the pre-war position of the Liberal Party in British politics. It was the Webbs who had stressed when framing the 1918 Constitution of the PLP that it should not be an exclusively working-class party, and this aim was reflected in the provision creating a new category of individual membership complementing the earlier structure of Trades and Labour Councils. The entry of former New Liberals into the party was thus facilitated, and they subsequently acquired considerable influence in proportion to their numbers because of their political experience and the freedom of most of them from the demands of arduous wage labour. They shared the traditional progressive aim of moralising capitalism in the interests of the 'community'. There was generally a remarkable absence of any conversion to socialism, while slogans like 'class war' and 'revolution' were anathema. Some even adhered to a 'technical determinist' conception of social development, based upon the systematic application of science to industry, which would provide a volume of production sufficient to meet the needs of all, and accepted the existing means for generating wealth in capitalist society via the market mechanism.[94] The task of politics was thus to moralise humanity in anticipation of the 'inevitability' of a new social order. Ramsay MacDonald and Philip Snowden, in particular, were influenced by these views, and this helps explain the curious blend of 'utopianism' and 'reformism' underlying much Labour Party policy-making during the 1920s.

The result was that it fell to the leaders of the Parliamentary Labour Party rather than the Communist Party of Great Britain to define politically the terms of reference for industrial conflict during the 1920s. In consequence, the traditional separation of the political and industrial spheres of the labour movement was preserved formally intact.[95] Paradoxically, this separation was reinforced further by the degree of control of the Labour Party by the trade union leadership, provided for in the 1918 Constitution, since the latter was determined to protect its independence, authority and funds from the interference of middle-class outsiders seeking careers as Labour Party politicians.[96] It was MacDonald's accession to the leadership of the party in 1922 that provided the essential 'symbol' of unity it had previously lacked.[97] He set a precedent for subsequently successful Labour Party leaders, appealing at the same time to left-wingers like the Clydeside MPs and moderate trade union leaders, while his eloquence and debating skills attracted the party's intelligentsia. Yet he had no hesitation in deploying its centralised organisation against the 'entryst' tactics of revolutionary groups like the CPGB seeking to work within it.[98] This was the background to the advent of the first minority Labour government in 1924, following the Conservative's conversion to protectionism that reunited the progressive ranks in defence of traditional free trade principles. Although there were some who regarded the prospect of a Labour government as calamitous for the country, wiser heads in both the Liberal and Tory camps prevailed. They recognised as a matter of the utmost importance that it should be

Parliament itself rather than a rising tide of socialist sentiment in the country at large that should create the precedent of Labour in office.[99] It was this as much as Labour's minority position in Parliament that was to confirm its evolution into a constitutional reformist party shorn of extremist influence. What is more, this exactly fitted MacDonald's own personal inclinations.[100]

Thus the development of independent labour politics since the First World War had seemingly been transformed from a commitment to socialism *represented* by the 1918 Constitution to the parliamentary calculations of the 1924 General Election. The latter appeared to some as justifying the pursuit of political power almost as an end in itself, especially in light of the very limited achievements of the first Labour government.[101] The outcome was to recast the British labourist tradition on a recognisably modern basis, yet rooted in the long-established distinction between the industrial and political spheres of working-class action. The realisation of a fully integrated working-class culture was thus effectively prevented, which subsequently was to enervate the menace of labour unrest to the dominant social order.[102] The consequent isolation of industrial militancy in the context of the unevenness of Britain's economic development was to end in the defeat of the 1926 General Strike. The rise of the Labour Party had played a crucial role in depoliticising labour unrest after the experience of 1918–20, and in the process, it had become reconciled to the norms and values of bourgeois social democracy. As Anthony Eden declared on the floor of the House of Commons in 1928:[103]

> We have not got democratic government today. We have never had it and I venture to suggest to Honourable members opposite that we shall never have it. What we have done in all progress of reform and evolution is to broaden the basis of oligarchy.

The 1926 General Strike

The period in office of the first Labour government had coincided with a temporary revival in the prospects for Britain's export industries.[104] Unemployment that had reached a peak of 1,828,000 in 1922 fell to 1,244,000 in 1923 and 1,135,000 in 1924. Yet the benefits of this revival were very unevenly spread. Employers representing the sheltered trades complained of high wages, which in industries like public utilities and transport were 14–17% higher in real terms in 1924 than in 1920.[105] This complaint was echoed by employers in the unsheltered trades who argued that wage cuts in the sheltered industries were necessary because prices in the latter comprised a major input of their production costs, and they would help restore 'appropriate' differentials between the skilled and unskilled and generally improve labour discipline.[106] A policy of reducing wages in the sheltered trades whilst resisting demands for wage increases in the export industries was regarded as especially imperative in the economic context of 1924–5 because of the continuing squeeze imposed by the financial authorities, in anticipation of an imminent return to the gold standard.[107] Yet its effect was to create a base for united action by the working-class that had previously been much more comprehensively divided by the uneven impact of the depression. This made the likelihood of a large-scale confrontation between organised labour and the combined power of the state and private capital increasingly probable during 1925–6.

It was the probability of a confrontation of this kind that was a particularly alarming prospect for the trade union leadership. This was likely to begin in the export industries, especially since the return to the gold standard implied further reductions in export prices, but the attitude of employers as a whole seemed to suggest that demands for wage cuts would subsequently be made throughout the economy. This posed a serious threat to the union amalgamations only recently formed, including a high proportion of unskilled, semi-skilled and transport workers who unlike the miners, for example, were very vulnerable to blacklegging and victimisation in the event of a general and prolonged dispute. It explains the attempts made to strengthen the powers of the TUC General Council during 1924–5, in order to improve the organisation for joint industrial action after the fiasco of Black Friday. Thus when the Mining Association presented their proposals for a new wage agreement to the Miners' Federation on 1 July 1925, the issue at stake was more than just the level of miners' wages. The owners' demand for the abolition of the national minimum standard was estimated by the Miners' Federation as having the effect of reducing wages by 2s per shift—equivalent to about 20%—in all districts except Yorkshire, Nottinghamshire and Derbyshire.[108] The magnitude of this reduction was alarming even to moderate trade union leaders on the TUC General Council because there was abundant evidence to indicate that this would signal a more general attack on working-class living standards.[109] On 10 July, therefore, the General Council resolved to give the miners their 'complete support' in helping them to resist the owners' proposals. It appointed a Special Industrial Committee, chaired by Alonzo Swales of the AEU, to maintain contact with the Miners' Federation and jointly prepare a plan of action.

Despite its declaration of support, the TUC General Council was clearly not going to commit itself to a nationwide sympathy strike in the summer of 1925, and it is not difficult to understand why. Walter Citrine, the TUC General Secretary, emphasised the need for time to organise support, yet although this was self-evidently necessary, he had in mind much more than the issue of miners' wages. The trade union leadership was determined, above all, to resist being drawn haphazardly into a general stoppage that it did not effectively control. What it desired was to organise support for the miners in such a way that the mere *threat* of sympathetic industrial action would be sufficient to force the government to intervene, and thus produce a compromise settlement, without endangering its own position. This was distinctly different from a scheme for 'the definite merging of existing unions', which had been the demand of the Miners' Federation, as formulated by Communist militants and pressed by the South Wales Miners' Federation at the 1924 TUC.[110] Although Congress had accepted this proposal in principle, the General Council was only prepared to accept 'a united front' so long as this preserved the autonomy of individual unions and the authority of their leaders. It continued subsequently to resist proposals emanating from the Communist left that it organise a National Congress of Action to draw up plans with the Co-operative Movement in the event of a mining dispute. The practical work and responsibility for organising the 'response' of the TUC General Council to the crisis in the coal industry was delegated to its own bodies like the Special Industrial Committee, which strengthened even further the independent authority exercised by the full-time officials appointed to them. It was only with the benefit of hindsight that activists on the revolutionary left were later to recognise that the General Council's preparations during 1925–6 represented the actions of 'a diplomatic corps to prevent struggle and not a general staff to lead the struggle of the workers'.[111]

While the TUC General Council was making its plans for dealing with the mining crisis, the Tory government set in train its own preparations. Although there were members of Baldwin's administration who were inclined to believe that the TUC's plans formed part of some sinister 'revolutionary' plot, Baldwin himself appreciated the potential malleability of the trade union leadership, A. J. Cook and the Miners' Federation notwithstanding. The return of right-wing labour leaders like J. H. Thomas to the industrial relations scene, following their term of office in the first Labour government, strengthened Baldwin's case for seeking to isolate the miners from the rest of the trade union movement, rather than run the risk of a fight to the finish with a united trade union bureaucracy that would have only served to play into the hands of the militants. Baldwin's analysis was confirmed by the efforts made by the TUC's Special Industrial Committee to persuade the government to set up a general inquiry into the coal industry and produce the basis for a settlement of the crisis.[112] Yet such was the militancy of the miners and the extent of popular sympathy on their behalf that the General Council felt compelled to commit itself to a national embargo on the movement of coal, to take effect from midnight on 31 July. It was at this critical stage that the government's own Macmillan Inquiry on the coal industry was published, which was generally favourable to the miners, accepting the principle of a national minimum and rejecting the owners' argument for a longer working day. It was in response to this dilemma that the majority of a divided Cabinet decided in favour of a government subsidy to the coal industry on the evening before the threatened embargo was due to begin—'Red Friday'.

In the government's official statement announcing the subsidy, Baldwin was careful to stress the temporary character of this subvention, and it seems clear that its timing to coincide with his promise of a Royal Commission to inquire into the coal industry was designed to create the conditions in which wage cuts would be generally acceptable as 'fair', not only in the coal industry but elsewhere as well. The government was particularly concerned about the serious damage a miners' lock-out combined with sympathetic industrial action would have done to the economy during the summer of 1925, especially in light of the deterioration in industry's export competitiveness since the gold standard had been restored in April. In addition, the unpreparedness of the government's emergency organisation has been widely cited as a factor contributing to the grant of the subsidy and the promise of a Royal Commission.[113] The government worked purposively during the rest of the year and the early months of 1926 to mobilise the civil power in the event of a future confrontation. These plans included the stockpiling of resources, the establishment of volunteer service and haulage committees, and the recruitment of employers' representatives in ports and railway centres, with instructions to collaborate with the local authorities there, including the police. The government also gave encouragement to the creation of an ostensibly independent body for enlisting volunteer labour, the Organisation for the Maintenance of Supplies, founded by an eminent group of former civil servants and retired military officers. The government's full access to BBC radio facilities was officially revealed to the Cabinet in November 1925.[114] Finally, as a last resort, the strength of the armed forces stationed near the principal urban centres was steadily increased, and major units of the Home Fleet were despatched to all the important ports.[115]

In conventional political terms, the selection of Sir Herbert Samuel as Chairman of the government's promised Royal Commission was an indication of its determination to avoid radical schemes for the reorganisation of the coal industry, including nationalisation. Samuel had been Liberal Home Secretary in 1916 during the labour unrest, and was ex-Governor of Palestine, while the other members of the commission did not suggest that it would be favourably inclined to fundamental change in the coal industry.[116] Although Baldwin was careful not to commit the Cabinet to any specific course of action, prior to the commission's report, his refusal to intervene as miners' wages were reduced and hours lengthened on a district basis after August 1925 seemed to indicate that the government had become convinced in advance of the necessity for 'adjustments' on the employers' terms. The TUC General Council, for its part, refused to recognise the government's complicity in this respect, and even Ernest Bevin who became increasingly influential after he attended his first council meeting in October 1925 was slow to appreciate that the mining issue was no longer a strictly industrial question, which called for 'disciplined leadership' and 'passive resistance', but had political ramifications that implied a challenge to state power.[117] Just as important was the General Council's failure to reach agreement with the co-operative societies for the feeding of workers in case of a general stoppage.[118] This meant that official TUC policy in regard to the provision of food for strikers was to depend on the government's own emergency organisation, which was designed precisely to *minimise* the effect of sympathetic industrial action. At the same time, J. H. Thomas was in the process of building for himself an ascendant position on the TUC's Special Industrial Committee, which was responsible for negotiating directly with the government on the miners' behalf, yet he was also especially hostile to proposals for drawing up contingency plans, regarding the mining crisis as one that had to be resolved by the miners' own efforts.[119] Needless to say, the leadership of the Labour Party was even more opposed to any form of industrial action that might endanger the constitutional order of the state, despite the sympathetic response of many of the rank and file in the constituencies to the outcome of Red Friday.

The unanimous report of the Samuel Commission published on 11 March 1926 implied that the protection of existing capitals in the coal industry should be the government's first priority.[120] Yet this was not necessarily coterminous with its argument that only higher productivity and lower costs would restore the industry's prosperity. The commission's vagueness as to how the latter might be realised is emphasised in its treatment of the conditions of employment in the industry. Any doubts it may have had about the coal-owners' capacity or willingness to tackle the problem of 'excess' capacity were to be resolved in the short-term at the expense of miners' wages and working conditions. The Commission's censure of the government's subsidy was untypically positive and decisive, and its assumption that coal-mining should be subject to the disciplines of the market meant inevitably that the 1924 minimum wage agreement had to be abandoned. The notion of miners' wages as 'a standing charge' on the industry, irrespective of price and profit levels, was explicitly rejected when the commission suggested that a 10% reduction in the wage bill might be sufficient to balance costs against proceeds, and it admitted that larger cuts would be needed to restore 'equilibrium' in the export districts. Although it agreed with previous enquiries in rejecting the alternative of a lengthened working day, it did not rule out that this might be implemented if the industry 'agreed'.

In declaring the government's public acceptance of the Samuel Report in principle on 24 March 1926, Baldwin hoped to shift the onus of responsibility for causing a stoppage to the TUC General Council. Yet it is probable that the latter had already tacitly accepted the need for wage cuts in the coal industry, as the price to be paid for some form of undefined 'reorganisation'.[121] Otherwise, it is difficult to believe how the experienced negotiators comprising the TUC General Council could have been so credulous or gullible when they seized upon the commission's proposals for reorganisation as the basis for future negotiations.[122] What must, of course, be appreciated during the crucial weeks of March–April 1926 is that the trade union leadership, like the government, had to 'manage' its own rank and file in the interests of unity and discipline. However reluctant Thomas and company might have been to become involved in strike action in support of the miners, earlier promises could not simply be reneged upon without risking not only a permanent breach with the Miners' Federation, but also the alarming prospect of the trade unions being driven into the hands of the 'wild men' of the left. The government, for its part, appears to have become increasingly aware of the dilemma facing the TUC General Council, and during the negotiations that followed it made every effort to help loosen the noose the General Council had placed almost unwittingly around its own neck.[123] In this respect, the government's astuteness was probably decisive in preventing what might have become a serious social crisis if the trade union leadership had lost control of its members to a possibly spontaneous upheaval organised from below. It is noteworthy in this respect that the crucial move in the General Council's 'preparations' for the General Strike was the Special Industrial Committee's decision to call a conference of trade union executives for the 29 April. No lead was to be provided until this conference had met, while in the meantime, the General Council proceeded 'almost casually', having no clear strategy in mind.[124] At the conference of union executives, it was given complete authority to define the limits of any intended stoppage; to call out or order back to work any group of workers, as it saw fit; and, above all, to decide on what terms it would resume negotiations in the hope of finding a settlement.[125]

It is an interesting reflection on the General Council's intentions that it was not until 30 April that a plan 'for co-ordinated action' prepared by its Ways and Means Committee was presented to the delegates who had attended the conference of union executives. It was Bevin, in particular, who appreciated that the successful outcome of the sympathetic industrial action that began on 3 May 1926 would be critically dependent on the stoppage of transport services. Workers in this sector were thus called out in support of the miners, together with the printers and the other trades employed in construction or maintenance in the industries affected. The purpose behind this strategy was to achieve maximum impact at the minimum cost to the trade union movement as a whole, although the so-called 'second line' of heavy industry trades was kept in reserve to reinforce the 'first wave'. It is significant that all the unions whose members were withdrawn in the first wave possessed well-developed structures of authority that made them amenable to General Council directives. None had the experience of unofficial workplace organisation manifest in the shop stewards' movement in the engineering industry, which might have challenged centralised control. Yet what is remarkable, nevertheless, was the extent of support for the stoppage, although this was by no means uniformly solid.[126] More than 1,650,000 workers were involved, excluding the second line of engineering and shipbuilding trades who were not called out until the last day of the strike.

The government's handling of the General Strike was in marked contrast to the TUC's efforts to limit its scope and define its purpose in strictly 'constitutional' terms. The entire armoury of the civil power was mobilised to discredit and defeat what Baldwin claimed was a direct challenge to the 'constitution'.[127] The government's own newspaper, the *British Gazette*, systematically attacked the principle of the General Strike and made no claims as to its impartiality, whilst the government's requisitioning of all the available newsprint seriously interfered with the publication of the TUC General Council's own newspaper, the *British Worker*.[128] The BBC, on the other hand, retained the appearance of independence but in practice this was largely nominal.[129] In maintaining the flow of essential goods and services, the government's emergency organisation was sufficiently prepared to run a basic system of transport, relying mostly on road haulage where trade unionism was especially weak.[130] Outside the coalfields and some northern industrial towns, these services were allowed to operate largely unhindered. Where there was a threat of confrontation, as in the transport of goods from the London docks, the deployment of military convoys was sufficient to guarantee that goods were moved unimpeded. It is important to understand the relative absence of violence during the General Strike in the light of the government's overwhelming coercive presence, which included the mobilisation of more than 200,000 'second reserve' police in England and Wales alone, and supported ultimately by troops and naval units stationed deliberately at strategic points as if to overawe the strikers. Nevertheless, the Home Office reported 1,760 arrests made under the government's emergency regulations between 1 and 12 May. Perhaps as much as one quarter of the Communist Party's pre-strike membership suffered from some form of government repression, and its communications and printing facilities were subjected to continuous harassment and successive police raids.[131]

The numerous local studies made of the General Strike emphasise the unevenness in the scope and character of working-class organisation, reflecting the localisation of traditions of militant self-activity largely in centres of staple export industry.[132] Thus the Methil Council of Action in the Fife coalfield, for example, created an especially comprehensive network of control based upon the use of mass pickets and transport permits, and backed by a Workers' Defence Corps or 'workers' police'.[133] A similarly organised system of 'dual power' was also set up in other coalfields like North Lanarkshire and South Wales.[134] At Mardy in South Wales, the extent to which dual power had replaced capitalist social relations is evident in the instructions given by the strike committee to local shopkeepers regulating the sale of certain goods and fixing maximum prices. This was clearly more difficult to establish in large urban centres where the full weight of the government's resources was generally committed. Yet there was considerable improvisation, in the absence of detailed preparations made prior to the strike, which became particularly necessary as it continued because of the lack of rapid communications facilities with the TUC General Council in London. In Glasgow, for example, a subcommittee of the Trades Council was responsible for deciding in cases where the undertaking of 'essential' work deserved the granting of special permits.[135] Yet even in London, where the government's coercive presence was concentrated, the militant local district of the Amalgamated Engineering Union called out all its members except those employed in health, sanitary or social services during the first week of the stoppage, refusing to wait for the General Council's instructions to the 'second line'.[136] In fact, the extent of the unofficial withdrawal of labour in defiance of instructions, particularly in the engineering industry and among electrical workers, gave rise to serious concern in TUC circles and explains why the General Council called out the second line *after* it had already decided in private to terminate the strike.[137]

The radio announcement made at about 1.0 p.m. on Wednesday 12 May by the TUC General Council, calling off the General Strike 'immediately and unconditionally', was at first interpreted by many strikers to mean a victory for the miners. As the details of the settlement became known, which included 'sufficient' assurances from the government that it would reorganise the coal industry, a sense of bewilderment often turned to anger in the more militant areas.[138] Yet many were not immediately aware of the extent of the TUC's capitulation, and this undoubtedly assisted the return to work.[139] In deciding to end the strike, the General Council seems to have been intimidated by the success of the government's transport organisation and the threat of a major collision between the state and the developing forms of dual power in the locally militant districts, and these fears were increased further by the government's preparation of coercive legislation.[140] The trade union leadership also feared the consequences of the drain on its financial resources that if exhausted might not only leave the unions bankrupt but fatally undermine the authority of their leaders in relation to the rank and file, with the resulting danger of widespread civil disorder and the menace this posed to the very existence of trade unionism.[141] In the event, the campaign for an orderly return to work did not reckon with the employers' determination to use this as an opportunity for worsening conditions of employment and victimising leading militants.[142]

The miners' dogged resolution in continuing their resistance alone did not reduce the likelihood of an inevitable defeat. By 13 May, it had become clear that the government had not only accepted the necessity for wage reductions—it was Baldwin himself who suggested the figure of 10%—but the Cabinet's conception of a National Wages Board for the industry did not in practice accept the principle of a national minimum, since its function was restricted to specifying *variations* for the districts and not the rates actually to be paid.[143] On 15 June, the government's decision to suspend the Seven Hours Act for a five-year period indicated its final abdication from any earlier commitment it may have had to finding a genuine compromise settlement. By November, the miners' resistance had all but collapsed and the lock-out notices were removed piecemeal, district by district. The eight-hour day was generally restored and wage reductions were imposed immediately in the export coalfields, although settlements were more favourable in the less depressed inland districts.[144] It was not until the Coal Mines Act of 1930 that voluntary schemes established after 1928 for fixing output quotas and restricting competition were given statutory force, and the subsequent implementation of the Samuel Commission's original proposals for 'rationalisation' during the 1930s led to heavy unemployment and short-time working in the coalfields. The wider significance of defeat on the scale of 1926 was that it became a symbol evoked to discredit the strategy of mass industrial action for political ends, with the result that crucial breathing space was provided for the rehabilitation of the British 'labourist' tradition along recognisably modern lines.

Notes

1. Gerd Hardach, *The First World War* (London: Allen Lane, 1977), Table 17, p. 143.

2. Ibid., Table 18, p. 148.

3. David Williams, 'The Evolution of the Sterling System' in C. R. Whittlesey and J. S. G. Wilson (eds.), *Essays in Money and Banking* (Oxford: Clarendon Press, 1968), pp. 280–3, 294–5.

4. For the background to the inflation of 1919–20 see Chapter 5.

5. Keith Hancock, 'Unemployment and the Economists in the 1920's', *Economica*, XXVII (1960), no. 108, pp. 305–6.

6. Susan Howson, 'The Origins of Dear Money, 1919–20', *Economic History Review*, 2nd series, XXVII (1974), no. 1; Rodney Lowe, 'The Erosion of State Intervention in Britain, 1917–24', *Economic History Review*, 2nd series, XXXI (1978), no. 2.

7. A major problem during 1919–20 was that the floating of sterling had led to a rapid depreciation of the imperial currencies that were tied to sterling, which resulted in a general destabilisation of exchange relations between sterling bloc countries and the rest of the world. It was felt that a return to the gold standard was the only way of restoring monetary stability throughout the Empire and its relations with non-sterling bloc countries, upon which the prosperity of London's bankers, merchants and traders depended. See L. S. Pressnell, '1925: The Burden of Sterling', *Economic History Review*, 2nd series, XXXI (1978), no. 1.

8. K. J. Hancock, 'The Reduction of Unemployment as a Problem of Public Policy, 1920–29', *Economic History Review*, 2nd series, XV (1962), no. 2, pp. 331–2.

9. Sidney Pollard, *The Development of the British Economy 1914–1967* (London: Edward Arnold, 1969), p. 217.

10. Ibid.

11. Sidney Pollard (ed.), *The Gold Standard and Employment Policies between the Wars* (London: Methuen, 1970), pp. 13–14.

12. David Williams, 'Montagu Norman and Banking Policy in the Nineteen-Twenties', *Yorkshire Bulletin of Economic and Social Research*, XI (1959), no. 1, pp. 39–40 ff.

13. Ibid., pp. 46–7.

14. See L. J. Hume, 'The Gold Standard and Deflation: Issues and Attitudes in the Nineteen-Twenties', *Economica*, XXX (1963), no. 119, pp. 233–4, for the views of *The Economist* and the *Statist*.

15. See *Committee on Industry and Trade* (Balfour Committee), *1924–1927, Minutes of Evidence*, v. I, pp. 70 ff.

16. Ibid., v. III, pp. 1,578, 1,596; v. I, p. 358. ·

17. Ibid., v. II, p. 1,071.

18. Hume, 'Gold Standard', p. 242.

19. *Balfour Committee*, v. II, p. 1,062.

20. Maurice Dobb, *Studies in the Development of Capitalism* (London: Routledge & Kegan Paul, 1963), pp. 366–8.

21. J. A. Dowie, '1919–20 is in Need of Attention', *Economic History Review*, 2nd series, XXVIII (1975), no. 3, pp. 442, 449; for contemporary evidence of employers' complaints see *Balfour Committee*, v. I, p. 20—Chambers of Commerce; pp. 534, 539–40, 547, 549, 553—engineering employers; pp. 359, 362, 385, 389, 397—iron and steel makers; pp. 473–4, 480–4, 495–6—cotton manufacturers; v. II, p. 870—electrical manufacturers.

22. The impact of fixed overhead charges of this kind was not uniform throughout industry. It appears to have been most significant, for example, in the American section of the cotton industry—see G. W. Daniels and J. Jewkes, 'The Post-War Depression in the Lancashire Cotton Industry', *Journal of Royal Statistical Society*, 91 (1928), pt II, pp. 180–1; *Balfour Committee*, v. I, pp. 479–80, 489–90; the iron and steel industry was also affected to a lesser extent—see Ibid., v. I, pp. 277, 292, 309, 359, 385; as was also engineering—p. 570; and electricals—v. II, pp. 867–9.

23. Ibid. See also Dobb, *Capitalism*, pp. 367–8.

24. E. H. Phelps Brown and Margaret H. Browne, *A Century of Pay* (London: Macmillan, 1968), Fig. 43, p. 254; Sir Josiah Stamp, 'Industrial Profits in the Past Twenty Years—A New Index Number', *Journal of Royal Statistical Society*, 95 (1932), pt IV, Table III, p. 671.

25. Brown and Browne, *Century of Pay*, Appendix 2, p. 414.

26. E. H. Phelps Brown and Bernard Weber, 'Accumulation, Productivity and Distribution in the British Economy 1870–1938', *Economic Journal*, LXIII (1953), Figs. 6–7.

27. Pollard, *Development of Economy*, pp. 166–7, where it is estimated that 1,000 to 1,200 were in existence by the late 1930s.

28. Dobb, *Capitalism*, p. 323.

29. Brown and Browne, *Century of Pay*, Appendix 2, p. 414.

30. L. Hannah, 'Managerial Innovation and the Rise of the Large-scale Company in Inter-war Britain', *Economic History Review*, 2nd series, XXVII (1974), no. 1, pp. 252–3; for a detailed contemporary account see Patrick Fitzgerald, *Industrial Combination in England* (London: Pitman & Sons, 1927).

31. D. H. Macgregor, *et al.*, 'Problems of Rationalisation: A Discussion', *Economic Journal*, 40 (1930), p. 358; *Balfour Committee*, v. II, p. 733, for the consequences of 'rationalisation' in woollen textiles.

32. C. H. Feinstein, *Domestic Capital Formation in the United Kingdom 1920–1938* (Cambridge: University Press, 1965), Tables 3.20, 3.21, p. 36.

33. J. A. Dowie, 'Growth in the Inter-war Period: Some More Arithmetic', *Economic History Review*, 2nd series, XXI (1968), no. 1, p. 95.

34. Dobb, *Capitalism*, pp. 336–7.

35. Feinstein, *Domestic Capital*, Table 3.42, p. 50.

36. See Brown and Browne, *Century of Pay*, Fig. 36, p. 230, Fig. 37, p. 231, for an international comparison of changes in industrial unit costs and productivity during the inter-war period.

37. For contemporary evidence see *Balfour Committee*, v. III, p. 1,476, 1,479—information supplied by Margaret Bondfield representing the National Union of General and Municipal Workers.

38. Sean Glynn and John Oxborrow, *Interwar Britain. A Social and Economic History* (London: Allen & Unwin, 1976), pp. 24–5, 189–91 ff.

39. Dobb, *Capitalism*, pp. 348–9; Agatha L. Chapman and Rose Knight, *Wages and Salaries in the United Kingdom 1920–1938* (Cambridge: University Press, 1953), Table 1, p. 18.

40. Dobb, *Capitalism*, pp. 348 ff.

41. For the background to the growth of selective company welfare schemes during the 1920s see the forthcoming PhD thesis of Joseph Melling, 'Employers and Industrial Welfare in Britain: A Regional and Industrial Comparison, c. 1880–1920', Department of Economic History, University of Glasgow.

42. Bernard Waites, 'The Effects of the First World War on the Economic and Social Structure of the English Working Class', *Journal of Scottish Labour History Society*, 12 (February 1978), pp. 3–4, 6–8; P. Sargent Florence, *Investment, Location, and Size of Plant. A Realistic Inquiry into the Structure of British and American Industries* (London: Macmillan, 1948), Table VIE, p. 143.

43. Waites, 'Effects of War'; K. G. J. C. Knowles and D. J. Robertson, 'Differences Between the Wages of Skilled and Unskilled Workers, 1880–1950', *Bulletin of Oxford Institute of Statistics*, 13 (1951), no. 4, Table I, p. 111.

44. *Balfour Committee*, v. III, pp. 1,468, 1,471–2, 1,475, for the evidence of Margaret Bondfield.

45. E. J. Hobsbawm, 'Trends in the British Labour Movement since 1850', in the same author's *Labouring Men. Studies in the History of Labour* (London: Weidenfeld & Nicolson, 1968), pp. 301–2.

46. Florence, *Investment*.

47. Harry Braverman, *Labor and Monopoly Capital* (New York: Monthly Review Press, 1974), pp. 216–19; this was the essence of 'Fordism' as applied, for example, to the mass-production of automobiles—see L. T. C. Rolt, *A Short History of Machine Tools* (Cambridge: Massachusetts Institute of Technology Press, 1965), pp. 237–8.

48. A. Touraine, *et al.*, *Workers' Attitudes to Technical Change* (Paris: OECD Press, 1965), pp. 32–3.

49. Ibid., p. 122; for the extent of this migration see Brinley Thomas, 'The Movement of Labour into South-East England, 1920–1932,' *Economica*, new series, I (1934), no. 2.

50. Touraine, *et al.*, *Workers' Attitudes*, p. 48; for the expansion of public entertainment during the inter-war period see Richard Stone and D. A. Rowe, *The Measurement of Consumers' Expenditure and Behaviour in the United Kingdom 1929–1938* (Cambridge: University Press, 1966), v. II, Table 38, p. 92.

51. W. G. Runciman, *Relative Deprivation and Social Justice* (London: Routledge & Kegan Paul, 1966), pp. 57–9.

52. A. B. Atkinson and A. J. Harrison, *Distribution of Personal Wealth in Britain* (Cambridge: University Press, 1978), Ch. 6, discusses the problems associated with time-series comparisons.

53. L. R. Connor, 'On Certain Aspects of the Distribution of Incomes in the United Kingdom in 1913 and 1924', *Journal of Royal Statistical Society*, 91 (1928), pt I, Table C, p. 15.

54. Ibid.

55. Waites, 'Effects of War', Table 3, p. 15; for a calculation of the effect of unemployment on wages see Jürgen Kuczynski, *A Short History of Labour Conditions Under Industrial Capitalism* (London: Muller, 1972), p. 104.

56. Brown and Browne, *Century of Pay*, Fig. 33, p. 219.

57. Chapman and Knight, *Wages*, e.g. Tables 50–1, pp. 113–4; Stone and Rowe, *Measurement of Behaviour*, v. II, p. 41.

58. Brown and Browne, *Century of Pay*, Table 45, p. 258.

59. Glyn and Oxborrow, *Interwar Britain*, Table 5.1, p. 145.

60. See, for example, Stuart MacIntyre, 'Unemployment Policy in the Vale of Leven, 1918–1939', paper presented to a conference on the Local Implementation of Social Policy in Britain since 1880, University of Glasgow, May 1978, pp. 4–6.

61. Alan Deacon, 'Concession and Coercion: the Politics of Unemployment Insurance in the Twenties' in Asa Briggs and John Saville (eds.), *Essays in Labour History* (London: Croom Helm, 1977), p. 30.

62. Ibid., p. 16.

63. Glyn and Oxborrow, *Interwar Britain*, p. 217.

64. Bentley B. Gilbert, *British Social Policy 1914–1939* (London: Batsford, 1970), p. 147.

65. Only about one-quarter of the money borrowed by local authorities under the Addison Act was in the form of short-term loans that would have enabled them to benefit from any subsequent decline in interest rates.

66. Marian Bowley, 'Some Regional Aspects of the Building Boom, 1924–36', *Review of Economic Studies*, V (1937–38); Glyn and Oxborrow, *Interwar Britain*, p. 223–4.

67. A. L. Bowley and Margaret M. Hogg, *Has Poverty Diminished?* (London: P. S. King, 1925).

68. Waites, 'Effects of War', pp. 25 ff.

69. In the Vale of Leven, for example, it was not until the 1930s that the development of so-called 'Little Moscows' posed an effective challenge to national social policy—see MacIntyre, *Vale of Leven*, pp. 15 ff.

70. John Foster, 'British Imperialism and the Labour Aristocracy' in Jeffrey Skelley (ed.), *The General Strike 1926* (London: Lawrence & Wishart, 1976), pp. 28–9; James Hinton, *The First Shop Stewards' Movement* (London: Allen & Unwin, 1973), pp. 308–10.

71. G. A. Phillips, *The General Strike. The Politics of Industrial Conflict* (London: Weidenfeld & Nicolson, 1976), p. 9.

72. Foster, 'Imperialism', Fig. 4, p. 14.

73. P. S. Bagwell, 'The Triple Industrial Alliance, 1913–1922' in Asa Briggs and John Saville (eds.), *Essays in Labour History, 1886–1923* (London: Macmillan, 1971), pp. 110–11, 116–17; Ralph Desmarais, 'Lloyd George and the Development of the British Government's Strike-breaking Organization', *International Review of Social History*, XX (1975), pt 1, pp. 9–13.

74. Chapman and Knight, *Wages*, Table 9, p. 27; Bagwell, 'Triple Alliance', p. 118.

75. Bagwell, 'Triple Alliance', pp. 121–2; Dr Bagwell notes the absence of a verbatim report of the meeting of the Triple Alliance Executive on 15 April, which makes an assessment of their motives in refusing support for the miners a matter of conjecture. In militant areas like South Wales, there is definite evidence on the willingness of local railwaymen to take sympathetic industrial action in support of the miners—see M. G. Woodhouse, 'Rank and File Movements Among the Miners of South Wales, 1910–1926', unpublished DPhil thesis, University of Oxford, 1970, p. 206.

76. Phillips, *General Strike*, pp. 33 ff.

77. Ibid. For a critique of the economics of 'rationalisation' in the coal industry during the 1920s see N. K. Buxton, 'Entrepreneurial Efficiency in the British Coal Industry Between the Wars', *Economic History Review*, 2nd series, XXII (1970), no. 3.

78. Woodhouse, 'Rank and File', pp. 220–1, 226–7.

79. Ibid., pp. 251–2.

80. *Balfour Committee*, v. I, pp. 566–7, 609.

81. Chapman and Knight, *Wages*, Table 47, p. 105.

82. J. B. Jefferys, *The Story of the Engineers* (London: Lawrence & Wishart, 1946), pp. 223–7; Eric Wigham, *The Power to Manage. A History of the Engineering Employers' Federation* (London: Macmillan, 1973), pp. 117–24.

83. *Balfour Committee*, v. I, p. 538, for the evidence of Sir John Dewrance, President of the Engineering Employers' Federation.

84. Jefferys, *Engineers*, p. 227.

85. H. A. Clegg, A. J. Killick and Rex Adams, *Trade Union Officers* (Oxford: Blackwell, 1961), Table 7, p. 40.

86. V. L. Allen, 'The Reorganization of the Trades Union Congress, 1918–1927' in the same author's *The Sociology of Industrial Relations. Studies in Method* (London: Longmans, 1971), p. 168.

87. Phillips, *General Strike*, pp. 15–16.

88. Allen, *Sociology of Industrial Relations*, p. 184.

89. L. J. Macfarlane, *The British Communist Party. Its Origins and Development Until 1929* (London: Macgibbon & Kee, 1966), p. 80.

90. Ibid., p. 287; this is also the view of James Hinton and Richard Hyman, *Trade Unions and Revolution. The Industrial Politics of the Early British Communist Party* (London: Pluto Press, 1975), p. 9.

91. B. A. Waites, 'The Effect of the First World War on Class and Status in England', *Journal of Contemporary History*, 11 (1976), no. 1, p. 45.

92. *Cotton Factory Times*, 20 June 1919; cited in Waites, 'Effects of War', p. 9.

93. Trevor Wilson, *The Downfall of the Liberal Party 1914–1935* (London: Fontana, 1968), pp. 225 ff.

94. Bernard Barker, 'Anatomy of Reformism: The Social and Political Ideas of the Labour Leadership in Yorkshire', *International Review of Social History*, XVIII (1973), p. 16.

95. Martin Jacques, 'Consequences of the General Strike' in Skelley, p. 377.

96. Ross McKibbin, *The Evolution of the Labour Party 1910–1924* (Oxford: University Press, 1974), p. 244.

97. C. L. Mowat, 'Ramsay MacDonald and the Labour Party' in Briggs and Saville, p. 148.

98. Macfarlane, *Communist Party*, Ch. IV.

99. Wilson, *Liberal Party*, pp. 272–5; Ralph Miliband, *Parliamentary Socialism. A Study of the Politics of Labour* (New York: Monthly Review Press, 1964), pp. 98–9, 100.

100. Miliband, *Parliamentary Socialism*, p. 101.

101. Ibid., pp. 101 ff.

102. For a discussion of the formation of an 'integrated' working-class culture as the basis for revolutionary social change see Gwyn A. Williams, 'The Concept of "Egemonia" in the Thought of Antonio Gramsci: Some Notes on Interpretation', *Journal of History of Ideas*, XXI (1960), no. 4, pp. 592–4.

103. Cited in W. L. Guttsman, *The British Political Elite* (London: Macgibbon & Kee, 1965), p. 368.

104. Stamp, 'Industrial Profits', Table III, p. 671; *Balfour Committee*, v. I, pp. 366, 578.

105. Foster, 'Imperialism', Fig. 2, p. 13; see also Chapman and Knight, *Wages*, especially Table 88, p. 225.

106. *Balfour Committee*, v. I, evidence of Henry Cromwell Field, Chairman of the Association of British Chambers of Commerce, p. 20; Sir John Dewrance, President of the Engineering Employers' Federation, pp. 536, 543–6, 554; Arthur Pugh, Iron and Steel Trades' Federation, p. 294.

107. Interest rates were generally hardening at this time, particularly during the latter half of 1924.

108. Phillips, *General Strike*, Table 3, p. 52.

109. Ibid., pp. 52, 54–5; see also the evidence presented to the Balfour Committee referred to in Note 106 above. The warnings of Keynes that the return to gold in April would require widespread wage reductions were also reported in the national press at this time.

110. Roderick Martin, *Communism and the British Trade Unions 1924–1933. A Study of the National Minority Movement* (Oxford: Clarendon Press, 1969), p. 64.

111. J. T. Murphy, *Preparing for Power. A Critical Study of the History of the British Working-Class Movement* (London: Pluto Press, reprint, 1972), p. 214; this was first published in 1934.

112. Phillips, *General Strike*, pp. 55 ff.

113. A. Mason, 'The Government and the General Strike, 1926', *International Review of Social History*, 14 (1969), pt 1, p. 7.

114. Phillips, *General Strike*, p. 98.

115. Foster, 'Imperialism', Fig. 7, p. 47.

116. The other members of the Samuel Commission were Sir Herbert Lawrence, once General Haig's Chief of Staff and at the time a director of the banking house, Glyn Mills; Kenneth Lee of the prominent Manchester-based textile firm of Tootal's, and also connected with the District Bank; and W. H. Beveridge, one of the leading architects of Liberal welfarism who was at the time Director of the London School of Economics and Political Science.

117. Alan Bullock, *The Life and Times of Ernest Bevin, vol. I. Trade Union Leader 1881–1940* (London: Heinemann, 1960), pp. 282 ff.

118. TUC (General Council), *Mining Dispute. National Strike, Report of the General Council to the Conference of Executives of Affiliated Unions 25th June, 1926*, p. 4.

119. John Lovell, 'The TUC Special Industrial Committee, January–April 1926' in Briggs and Saville, p. 39.

120. See Phillips, *General Strike*, pp. 75–9, for an especially perceptive analysis of the Samuel Report.

121. Ibid., p. 83.

122. Lovell, 'TUC Committee', pp. 48–9.

123. Ibid., p. 53.

124. Phillips, *General Strike*, p. 113.

125. Bullock, *Bevin*, pp. 305–6.

126. See Phillips, *General Strike*, pp. 206–19, for the most recent detailed assessment of the extent of the strike.

127. Excerpts from the government's *British Gazette* are reproduced in James Klugmann, 'Marxism, Reformism and the General Strike' in Skelley, pp. 83–4.

128. Phillips, *General Strike*, p. 170.

129. Ibid., pp. 183–8.

130. Ibid., p. 213.

131. Macfarlane, *Communist Party*, pp. 163–4; Klugmann, 'Marxism', pp. 78–9.

132. This is suggested by the essays on local conditions contained in Skelley, *Strike 1926*. The problems faced in organising the strike in areas lacking a tradition of militancy are highlighted in J. H. Porter, 'Devon and the General Strike, 1926', *International Review of Social History*, XXIII (1978), pt 3. The ongoing research on the General Strike in East Anglia, undertaken currently by Mr Gerald Crompton, Department of Economic History, University of East Anglia, may mean, however, that this view will have to be revised.

133. Klugmann, 'Marxism', p. 86.

134. Paul Carter, 'The West of Scotland', and Hywel Francis, 'South Wales' in Skelley.

135. Glasgow Trades Council, *1926: Glasgow Strike Committee Reports*, 5 May 1926, p. 2.

136. John Attfield and John Lee, 'Deptford and Lewisham' in Skelley, p. 263.

137. See Phillips, *General Strike*, pp. 140–1, for unofficial discontent with the circumscribed coverage of the strike.

138. See, for example, Carter, 'West of Scotland', p. 135; John McLean, *The 1926 General Strike in Lanarkshire* (London: CPGB History Group Pamphlet 65, Spring 1976), pp. 16–17; Ian MacDougall, 'Some Aspects of the 1926 General Strike in Scotland' in the same author's edited volume, *Essays in Scottish Labour History* (Edinburgh: John Donald, 1979), pp. 190–2.

139. See, for example, the official organ of the Scottish TUC, the *Scottish Worker*, 13 May 1926.

140. Bullock, *Bevin*, pp. 332 ff. Alan Anderson, 'The Labour Laws and the Cabinet Legislative Committee of 1926–27', *Bulletin of Society for the Study of Labour History*, 23 (Autumn 1971), p. 40.

141. Ibid.; Phillips, *General Strike*, p. 146, notes that the TUC General Council deliberately refused an offer of Russian financial assistance, in the knowledge that if it had accepted, the payment of the money would have been withheld under the government's emergency regulations.

142. See, for example, Phillips, *General Strike*, pp. 244–8, for the extent of victimisation and worsening of conditions after the strike.

143. Ibid., pp. 253–4.

144. Ibid., p. 257.

CHAPTER 7

Post-1926: Labourism Rehabilitated

The termination of the General Strike on the employers' terms completed the task of depoliticising labour unrest begun in the early 1920s, following the confrontations of the previous period. The burden of defeat bore especially hard on groups like the miners who had been most attracted to the idea of industrial action for political ends. Trade union membership in coal-mining fell by more than 33 % during the years 1925–8, which was a greater reduction than was experienced by any other comparable industrial group.[1] This reflected the impact of rising unemployment, particularly in the export districts, and a general disillusionment among the rank and file with their union officials. It was only the threat of starvation that in many districts finally drove the miners back to work, after they had rejected the government's last offer in November 1926 against the advice of the Executive of the Miners' Federation, and even in a relatively moderate area like Durham the membership refused to accept the terms negotiated by their local official leaders at the end of November.[2] Thus the Miners' Federation was in no position to maintain its role as a radical force inside the TUC after 1926. In fact, its leaders had to devote all their energies in keeping intact at least some semblance of national organisation, in the face of breakaway 'non-political' miners' unions in the Midlands and South Wales.[3]

It was in this context that the government now regarded the time as propitious for intervention in the coal industry. The timing of this action is itself significant. In the early 1920s, government had sought to withdraw from its earlier involvement in the industry because state control was represented as a socialist demand in the political climate of the period, and thus had to be energetically resisted. After 1926, however, the miners were in no position to *demand* anything, including state control of the industry, hence the government was on safe ground to introduce limited instalments of assistance, without fear of being seen to give way to militant pressure emanating from below. The measures subsequently adopted indicated the government's priorities, which were to protect existing capitals in the industry. Their main aim was to raise coal prices by regulating output, in the hope that higher prices and profits would encourage modernisation. This left the government with the intractable problem of the large numbers of miners who were consequently surplus to the requirements of profitable production. A special Industrial Transference Board was set up and it reported in June 1928 that there was a permanent labour surplus of more than 200,000 workers in the coal industry. A scheme for the transfer of labour from mining areas was later organised by the employment exchanges, which were authorised to make contributions to removal and maintenance expenses. By the end of 1929, about 42,000 miners had been transferred, but the onset of the world depression led to rising unemployment, even in regions to which they were being moved, and the numbers leaving began to dwindle, with the result that a hard core of permanent unemployed remained in the coalfields until the rearmament boom of the late 1930s.[4]

In the meantime, the Coal Mines Act of 1930 gave statutory authority to earlier voluntary schemes for allocating output quotas and fixing minimum prices, although these were still to be implemented by the coal-owners themselves.[5] The outcome was that gross fixed capital formation in the industry, which had recovered during 1929–30, remained low throughout the 1930s when it was depreciation rather than capital additions that was responsible for a large measure of the modernisation undertaken.[6] Productivity was only 10% higher in 1936 than it had been in 1913, and by international standards the British coal industry continued to fall behind its foreign rivals.[7] Thus the miners' sacrifices had been in vain, justified neither by the General Strike and lock-out, nor by the terms of settlement they subsequently had to endure.

A comparison of coal-mining with other industries after the 1926 General Strike emphasises, again, the uneven character of Britain's economic development. This was to provide an objective basis for the rehabilitation of an identifiably labourist outlook, characterised by its acceptance of strictly separate spheres of industrial and political action. The export industries suffered from similar problems but the wage reductions endured were not of the same magnitude as in coal-mining, and they were imposed later in a different context. In cotton textiles, for example, it was not until 1929 that wages were cut by 6%, to be followed by a further reduction of 8%

in 1931; while in woollen textiles, it was not until 1930 that there were reductions of 5–9%, followed by another 11–12% in 1931.[8] In contrast, only temporary reductions of 2½–5% were made in railwaymen's wages after 1926, and there were no cuts at all in basic rates in the engineering industry. The continuing decline in the cost of living meant that average annual *real* earnings of employees in all industries rose by slightly less than 5% between 1925 and 1930, and this increase was undoubtedly greater in the relatively sheltered sectors.[9] Even in a heavy industry like iron and steel, average wages rose as traditional differentials were reduced by upgrading, made possible by technological change.[10]

At the same time, the heavy financial cost of the General Strike made trade union leaders wary of large-scale industrial action.[11] Thus only 4.3 million working days were lost on average during the period 1927–34, in contrast to an average of 28 million working days lost during the years 1919–25, since in both periods industry-wide disputes accounted for the bulk of the days lost in strikes or lock-outs.[12] The general hostility of trade union leaders to industrial action that would drain union funds was not shared to the same extent by the rank and file. Hence the actual number of disputes in the decade 1929–39, as distinct from the aggregate days lost in disputes, was on average considerably greater than during the year of the General Strike.[13] Many of these were local and 'unofficial', not sanctioned by the union executive. In this respect, therefore, the aftermath of the General Strike had not totally discredited the appeal of 'direct action', although the terms of reference were now defined along 'economistic' lines and lacked the political overtones of the pre-1926 period.

The effect of the Trade Disputes and Trade Unions Act of 1927 was to vindicate the outlook and practices of labourism that were reimposed upon labour in the aftermath of the General Strike. Although its impact on the practical conduct of industrial relations was to prove of only marginal significance, the 1927 legislation did have a symbolic importance, especially in the eyes of trade union leaders. It was clearly not simply a punitive measure or act of revenge, inspired by the trade unions' 'unconstitutional' challenge to a Conservative government. What the latter sought was to redefine and clarify the 'proper' functions of trade unionism, in such a way that it could never again be used as a vehicle for intimidating the existing order of the state. During the deliberations on the form the government's legislation should take, its motives are revealed in the

following memorandum submitted in November 1926 by the
Minister of Labour, Arthur Steel-Maitland:[14]

> There has been a marked trend in the trade union movement in
> recent years towards political action. The pernicious doctrine of
> class war, and the activities of the Minority Movement are
> helping to push it in this direction, and should be combated by all
> legitimate means... In my view the policy of the Conservative
> party towards trade unionism should be in substance, and not
> merely in profession, 'constructive' and not vindictive. It should
> be made capable of being appreciated by the rank and
> file... Some element of coercion, or of apparent coercion, is
> inevitable in any legislative proposals, but it ought to be as small
> as possible... If we can adopt or show convincingly that we have
> adopted, a policy which is neither hostile nor avoidably coercive,
> but is designed to help trade unions so to organize themselves
> that they can conduct a consistent and dignified policy com-
> patible with the interests of other classes and the state, we may be
> able to avoid the danger of pushing the rank and file wholly into
> the arms of the socialist party.

It was with this purpose in mind that led the government to resist
the more extreme proposals of some leading employers, including
the demand made by the Shipbuilding Employers Federation for all
sympathetic strikes to be withdrawn from the protection of the 1906
Trade Disputes Act.[15] Thus Section I of the 1927 Trade Disputes
and Trade Unions Act prohibited all strikes whose object was not to
further a dispute within the trade or industry where the strikers were
employed, and included within its remit all strikes 'designed or
calculated to coerce the Government'. Section II stipulated that
non-participants in such illegal strikes should not be deprived of
union membership or benefits. Section III was aimed at mass
picketing and extended the meaning of 'intimidation' to include a
new offence of 'watching and besetting, if the numbers involved were
calculated to intimidate'; and 'injury' likely to arise from intimidation was broadly defined to include the watching and besetting of
residences, as well as property, business or other sources of income.
Section IV, which attracted the most publicity, reversed the legislation of 1913 by requiring that trade union members had to
'contract in' to the political levy made by their organisation, rather
than 'contract out' of this commitment. This section most directly

fulfilled the spirit of Steel-Maitland's memorandum, which had wanted the trade unions to be 'dignified', i.e. non-political. Finally, Sections V and VI prevented established civil servants from joining 'outside' organisations, meaning TUC-affiliated bodies rather than the usual staff associations, and other public authority unions were not allowed to insist on membership as a condition of employment. These sections were designed explicitly to ensure the loyalty of state employees to the civil power and prevent the danger of 'divided allegiance'. Thus the spirit if not the letter of the 1927 labour legislation was clearly not aimed at 'smashing' the trade unions, but sought to circumscribe their activities along labourist lines.

Whilst the motives behind the 1927 labour laws may be regarded as negative rather than deliberately punitive, more positive moves were being made at the same time to establish a more 'constructive' *modus vivendi* between capital and labour. The determination of trade union leaders to avoid large-scale disputes was reciprocated on the employers' part by a new willingness to collaborate with them on issues like union recognition, bargaining procedures, and plans for rationalisation to promote greater efficiency. Influential union leaders like Arthur Pugh had in the mid-1920s argued that the interests of both employers and workers as 'producers' could be served by improved procedures for collective bargaining, including the creation of statutory industrial councils, which would not only ameliorate labour unrest but form the basis for controlling 'self-governing' industries embodied, for example, in schemes for rationalisation.[16] This reasoning was echoed by leading industrialists like Sir Alfred Mond of ICI, and was later to develop into what has been called the 'ideology of corporatism'.[17] The organising function the latter assigns to the state in the regulation of self-governing industries is illustrated by the provisions of the Coal Mines Act of 1930, and the prominent role it implies for the trade union leadership made corporatism attractive to a rising generation of union leaders like Ernest Bevin, who had become disillusioned with 'direct action'.[18] Corporatism also represents a reformulation of the labourist assumption that political and industrial questions should be kept separate, since the motion of self-governing industries run by national committees implies that the organising function of government in this process of administration *defines* the content of 'politics' in light of an acceptance of the capitalist social order.

This changing climate of ideas was the background to the invitation made by Sir Alfred Mond and 21 other employers to the TUC General Council in November 1928, proposing joint discussions with a view to 'rationalising' their relationship. The employers regarded their initiative as potentially invaluable in helping to educate labour in the facts of economic reality, as they conceived it, and formed part of their wider aim of harnessing the unions in a partnership designed to control the economy rather than be controlled by it.[19] The timing of the invitation had itself been carefully planned. At the Edinburgh TUC in September 1927, the General Council's report had approved in principle the idea of joint discussions with employers, and this had been the outcome, in turn, of the positive moves made by the government to get talks going during 1926–7.[20] Steel-Maitland, the Minister of Labour, was convinced of the need for an 'Industrial Concordat' between organised capital and the trade unions, Sir Alfred Mond was himself a Tory MP, and the informal meetings arranged subsequently including Bevin and Lord Weir testified to the interest of major industrialists and trade union leaders alike in co-operating to create a climate of opinion that would be conducive to greater 'flexibility'. Items for discussion included such practical issues as payments systems, demarcation problems, labour productivity and 'restrictive practices'. There were precedents for this kind of discussion, like the Whitley scheme for industrial councils during the First World War, yet the context of the post-1926 period was quite different. There was now no strong workers' rank-and-file movement or influential socialist left, which had previously aborted plans for industrial co-operation during the 1918–20 period. What motivated the employers was that unless positive initiatives were undertaken on a voluntary basis the state might be forced to encroach more and more upon the prerogatives of private capital.[21] At the same time, the trade union leaders wanted to retrieve something positive from the aftermath of defeat in 1926, and the humiliation of the 1927 labour legislation with its implication that union leaders could not be left to themselves to look after workers' interests. They also viewed the prospect of joint discussions with employers as a means of legitimating their abandonment of a militant posture in regard to industrial relations, which was confirmed during 1926–7 by the TUC General Council's concerted campaign to discredit Communist Party industrial policies.[22]

In the event, three conferences were held between January 1928 and March 1929, with Mond leading the employers' delegation and the trade union representatives led by Ben Turner, President of the National Union of Textile Workers. The employers present included many famous names like Sir Herbert Austin (motor vehicles), Sir John Cadman (Anglo-Persian Oil), Samuel Courtauld, Lord Londonderry (coal), Sir Charles Parsons and Lord Weir. It is significant that a majority of the employers came from expanding 'science-based' industries, possessing either an oligopolistic dominance of world markets (Cadman and Mond), or a secure base in a growing home market (Austin and Courtauld). Moreover, policy-making for the employers was delegated to a special seven-member subcommittee, four of whom were ICI directors.[23] It is clear, therefore, that the employers present at the conferences of 1928–9 were not representative of British capital as a whole, but were drawn mostly from large-scale capital-intensive and expanding industry where trade unionism was relatively weak, and which had been comparatively unaffected by the labour unrest of the pre-1926 period. There was thus no precise analogue between the sectors represented by the employers and the industries where union membership was most heavily concentrated or where industrial relations had been long established. This fact was to bear directly on the content of the ensuing discussions and was to shape their outcome.

Reports were published for each of the conferences that took place. Agreement was reached on the following issues: trade union recognition, victimisation, industrial relations machinery, rationalisation, unemployment and the gold standard.[24] This meant in effect that the employers had conceded the right of union leaders to negotiate collectively on behalf of their members, and was embodied in the recommendation for the setting up of a National Industrial Council (NIC), composed of representatives from the TUC, FBI and the National Confederation of Employers' Organisations. The last-mentioned was an all-embracing body including smaller firms affiliated to employers' associations, as well as big industrial capital. The proposed NIC was authorised to appoint a Joint Conciliation Board of employers and union leaders, in the event of a dispute that threatened to escalate into a major stoppage. In return for this recognition of their position and power, the trade union leadership agreed to 'co-operate' in assisting amalgamation and general re-organisation, particularly if this promised improved efficiency and higher wages. Thus a result of the conferences that was especially novel was the assumption that the representatives of organised labour should have an influential voice in high policy-making, with the view to modernising and 'rationalising' the British economy. This implied a commitment, for example, to co-operate with employers in removing restrictive practices, when these interfered with flexible manning arrangements, and an acceptance of methods to improve labour productivity like scientific management. The managerialist premiss of the employers is reflected in the conference resolution on the gold standard, which wanted the latter substituted by a more flexible system for controlling the currency and regulating credit, in accordance more with the requirements of industry than the priorities of London bankers. This resolution was clearly designed to allay the fears of organised labour that rising and permanent unemployment would result if proposals for amalgamation and rationalisation were implemented.

The recommendations of the joint discussions of 1928–9 were thus not in themselves new. They had been anticipated earlier, for example, by the arguments presented by some industrialists and union leaders to the Balfour Committee inquiry.[25] What was novel was the recognition that these aims could only be achieved by co-operation between organised capital and organised labour—a difference in emphasis, perhaps, but still noteworthy. The resolution on the gold standard indicated, moreover, that government co-operation was also required. Yet those optimists like Mond and Pugh who hoped that this corporatist-style solution to Britain's economic ills would be readily acceptable were to be proved sadly mistaken. The climate of opinion prevailing during the 1920s was not favourable to bold experimentation, except in limited instalments when conditions of dire need justified government intervention in the coal industry. The representatives at the 1928–9 conferences did not accord with the balance of class relations in Britain, and the fact that joint discussions took place at all is indicative of their unrepresentative character. The numerical predominance of smaller firms, including those in the more labour-intensive, staple-export trades, explains the refusal of employers' organisations to adopt the Mond–Turner proposals, which they regarded as a threat to their independence and existing industrial relations machinery.[26] They preferred the disciplines of the market to the dubious benefit of centralised organisation administered, on the one hand, by oligopolistic industrial capital and, on the other, by a trade union leadership still tarnished by the confrontation of 1926. On the trade union side, Bevin and company reckoned without the hostility of powerful unions like the AEU, with their traditions of militancy and rank-and-file democracy, to proposals for 'class collaboration'. Support for this opposition within the TUC increased after the Mond–Turner proposals had been rejected by the employers.[27] Finally, and perhaps most important of all, the Conservative government refused to accept any responsibility for 'managing' the economy as envisaged by industrialists like Mond himself, and union leaders like Bevin and Pugh, as well as by outside experts like Keynes. Its experience of state intervention during the period of labour unrest prior to 1926 had taught the Conservative Party that experiments in government control were not compatible with social stability, based upon labour's acceptance of capitalist social relations.

In a more fundamental sense, the Mond–Turner talks were a failure because the aims of their protagonists were mutually incompatible. Ambitious union leaders like Bevin wanted to play a part in national policy-making; but what were to be the terms of reference for policy-making? The conception of rationalisation adhered to by industrialists like Weir was not likely to appeal to many trade unionists who were to be most directly affected, hence the AEU's opposition to the talks from their inception. Workers in areas of export industry like Clydeside could not be expected to welcome the prospect of even higher unemployment and the sacrifice of what remained of their 'restrictive practices'. The significance of the Mond–Turner discussions arises from their contribution in helping to shape a new climate of opinion that began to emerge during the 1930s, based upon a different alignment of class interests. In this respect, a rising generation of trade union leaders like Ernest Bevin, for example, had been impressed by the arguments put forward during the talks by the spokesmen for big industrial capital, and this was crucial in anticipating Bevin's later conversion to Keynesian economic policies and corporatist industrial strategies.[28] The extent to which the TUC as a whole was won over to these ideas between 1929 and 1935 marked the final stage in the containment of the challenge of labour to the existing social order. This conversion was the key to the subsequent consolidation of labourism on the basis of the political consensus expressed in the concept of 'social democracy'.

.In the meantime, the defeat of the General Strike in discrediting the tactics of direct action for political ends produced a marked shift to the 'left' in the policy orientation of the Communist Party of

Great Britain. The ambiguities of the party's propaganda prior to 1926, which oscillated between the slogan 'All Power to the General Council' and its call for the setting up of local Councils of Action, had inhibited the development of alternative forms of working-class leadership in the localities once the strike had begun. Only these would have been capable of transforming the defensive apparatus of 'dual power' into an offensive weapon that would have allowed Councils of Action to defy the TUC General Council's instructions to return to work.[29] The party had been slow to realise that what had begun as an 'industrial' stoppage could only be pressed home to a successful conclusion by challenging the political authority of the capitalist state, and it did not fully appreciate the extent to which workers' consciousness remained constrained within official union structures.[30] It was not until the Party Congress in October 1926 that it was formally admitted that 'every mass strike' was necessarily *political*, while the inadequacy of the General Council's preparations was emphasised as the cause of defeat. There was still little realisation of the fact that the role of the trade union bureaucracy made it inherently 'anti-revolutionary'.

This was the background to intensifying rivalry within the CPGB. A vocal minority led by Palme Dutt argued that the working class had been 'revolutionised' by the General Strike, only to be betrayed by its leaders and especially the 'pseudo-lefts' on the TUC General Council. Yet the willingness of most trade unionists to return to work on instructions from their leaders indicated to a majority in the party that the union leadership could not be attacked outright, without quickly isolating revolutionary activists, and the illusions the party had itself continued to retain concerning the value of 'left' union leaders made any such sudden change in policy undesirable. Thus Communists continued to adhere to the slogan 'All Power to the General Council' in the period just after the General Strike, but there was a change in emphasis reflected in their call for 'unity from below' and the criticism they directed at existing union leaders. The latter responded by curbing Communist-inspired activities, with some unions deciding that party membership was 'inconsistent' with the principles of trade unionism.[31] At the same time, the earlier localisation of the party's strength in areas of export industry, particularly in the coalfields, meant that its capacity to intervene effectively in industrial disputes dwindled in the face of persistent unemployment and workplace demoralisation. Yet despite these objective difficulties confronting the party in Britain, it was events in the Soviet Union that were to complete the transformation of the CPGB into a substitute form of working-class activity during the 1930s, in all but a few exceptional instances. This followed as a result of the triumph of the bureaucratic faction inside the Russian Communist Party led by Stalin, and the ousting of his critics, including Trotsky.

Stalin argued that capitalism was now entering a third post-war period of crisis, following the stabilisation of 1923–6. This implied that the revolutionary potential of the masses had to be mobilised along strictly Bolshevik lines, in opposition not only to reformist labour leaders but against the apparatus of trade unionism itself. This analysis may have served Stalin's ambitions in discrediting his rivals, but in the British context it could not have been more misconceived. Its implications manifest in the doctrine of 'class against class' and the exhortation to form 'revolutionary' breakaway trade unions were anathema to British traditions of industrial militancy. By 1929, the CPGB had been forced to accept the 'new line' despite substantial opposition, and its Executive was subsequently purged with the result that the party lost many of its most able and experienced leaders. Its membership that had approached 12,000 at the end of 1926 fell steadily thereafter, until it was no more than 3,200 by the end of the decade.[32] Most of the breakaway unions it sought to set up were short-lived, obliterated with the beginnings of the world depression. In the meantime, bitterness and sectarian rivalry became the hallmark of a now divided revolutionary left, marked by the periodic expulsion from the party of dissident elements accused of 'Trotskyist' tendencies.[33] Lenin's original plan to create one mass revolutionary party in Britain had thus degenerated into surrogate forms of working-class activity that came to share all the characteristics of quasi-religious sects.

There were also, of course, significant economic reasons why the influence of the socialist left collapsed after 1926. The aftermath of the General Strike allowed breathing space for the rehabilitation of labourism in its economic as well as ideological and political aspects. The continuing upward trend in real wages after 1926, for example, was based on a recovery in the British economy's profitability between 1926 and 1929, in addition to reflecting the decline in the cost of living. Particular sectors that benefited included not only growing home-based industries like commercial vehicles, but also some traditional export trades like shipbuilding and even coal-mining where the implementation of corporatist strategies helped

increase profits, if at the expense of levels of employment.[34] It is true
that the beginning of the world depression caused a rapid fall in
overall levels of profitability, but this was not experienced to the
same degree throughout British industry. The capital goods and
especially the export trades suffered, while profits remained comparatively buoyant in the durable consumer goods industries, and
even more so in sectors producing non-durable consumer goods.[35]
By 1935, there was a marked disparity in the rate of profit between
industries manufacturing consumer goods for the home market and
the export trades. Even so, during the depression years of 1930–5, in
comparison with the period 1924–9, unprofitable sectors were still
able to maintain dividend payments by drawing upon reserves, thus
assisting the shift of investors' income to the more profitable and
rapidly growing sectors of the economy.[36] The multiplier effect of
the spectacular rise in housebuilding between 1928 and 1934 was
particularly important in supporting profitability, as was the growth
of fixed capital formation in the public and semi-public sectors.[37] In
practice, therefore, British capitalism was putting Keynesianism into
effect before its theory had become widely known or accepted.

The factors making for growth in the economy during the 1920s
received additional impetus after 1929 because the world depression
affected primary producers far more than it did the industrial
economies. This produced an even more violent swing in the terms
of trade in Britain's favour. Its effect was to intensify the disparity
evident by 1935 between the rate of profit in the export trades, which
suffered from the poverty of primary producers, and industries
manufacturing consumer goods for the home market that benefited
from falling costs as well as rising real incomes.[38] Thus the gains in
real wages made in Britain during the late 1920s were retained and
improved upon further during the 1930s.[39] Another contributing
factor was the growing bargaining strength of the general unions
like the TGWU and the National Union of General and Municipal
Workers. They were able to obtain wage increases, or at least resist
reductions, for workers employed in the sheltered trades and the
rising numbers engaged in public authority occupations where
investment was relatively high.[40]

The trend of consumer expenditure shows that the quantities of
many basic food products purchased continued to rise during the
depression of the 1930s, and this is confirmed by evidence of
improving nutritional standards, whilst expenditure on consumer
durables did not fall but in many cases actually rose between 1930

and 1935.[41] This had the effect of reducing labour's sense of 'relative deprivation' that had been extreme in the early 1920s. The uneven impact of the world depression, indicated by the wide regional variations in unemployment, meant that working-class terms of reference for comparability in terms of living standards tended to focus on the improving lifestyles of workers in centres of expanding industry, on the basis of intra-class criteria. The capacity of a distinctively labourist subculture to survive and reproduce itself was thus grounded on solid economic foundations, and this effectively insulated the working class from the blandishments of a dwindling number of revolutionary socialists whose activities became for many only a source of mild amusement.

In the political sphere, it might have been expected that the effect of economic change in the context of the post-1926 period would produce a coalescing of working-class allegiances in support of the reformist 'umbrella' represented by the Parliamentary Labour Party. Although this had been taking place almost imperceptibly since 1918, the extremely limited achievements of the first Labour government and its continued adhesion to economic orthodoxy did not result in any sudden increase in the party's credibility as an alternative to the dominance of Conservatism. Most Labour politicians had remained aloof from the industrial struggles of the 1920s, and the undisguised hostility shown by the party's leadership to the General Strike had angered union leaders like Ernest Bevin.[42] Yet the latter resented even more the Conservative government's 1927 labour legislation, and the dependence of the Labour Party on financial support from the TUC naturally led the unions to seek redress by asserting their authority inside the Labour Party. After all, the TUC was now much more powerful than it had been in the early 1900s when its electoral bargain with the Liberals had extracted a major concession in the form of the 1906 Trade Disputes Act. The impact of the failure of the General Strike and the government's subsequent labour legislation thus imposed a degree of unity on the labour movement, if only for instrumental reasons. The closer links this created between the TUC and the Labour Party were consolidated by the activities of propaganda bodies like the National Trade Union Defence Committee, set up in April 1927 as an alliance of groups including the Labour Party Executive, with the aim of campaigning for the repeal of the 1927 Trade Union and Trade Disputes Act.[43]

The steady shift to the right in the policy orientation of the

Labour Party since the early 1920s reflected the willingness of some of its leaders like Snowden to enter into a new pact with the Liberals.[44] Informal discussions had taken place with this end in view during 1925–6, involving Snowden and Lloyd George, but the ambitions of most leading Labour politicians made them reluctant to harness their aspirations to the expiring body of Liberalism; and the more astute among them realised, moreover, that this would not be acceptable either to the trade unions or to party activists in the constituencies. On the other hand, the task of making Labourism a popular alternative to Conservatism required the development of recognisably different policies, which would represent the party as the agent for social progress to be pursued by constitutional means. The almost uninterrupted domination of British politics by the Conservatives throughout most of the inter-war period indicates that this was to prove an especially slow and painful process. In the event, the circumstances that paved the way for the Labour Party's gradual conversion to Keynesian principles of demand management followed from a growing awareness of the party's continued electoral impotence. It came subsequently to abandon economic orthodoxy only with great reluctance, and in this the Labour Party owed more to the pressure of the trade unions and the example of the Liberal's flirtation with Keynesian ideas in the late 1920s, rather than to any originality of its own.[45]

The Labour Party's redefinition of 'socialism' in terms of state intervention in economic and social affairs had become apparent by 1927 when it published a new programme entitled *Labour and the Nation*.[46] This was to launch the party on the path towards corporatist-style policies that were subsequently to owe much to the insights of Keynes, although there was little explicitly Keynesian about the document itself. It advocated taking over 'the great foundation industries', to be administered by the state in the interests of 'the whole community'. But since this implied that the bulk of private capital still remained in the hands of its existing owners, how state control might benefit the whole community was not made clear. There was no mention, for example, of earlier proposals to nationalise the financial institutions, with the purpose of redirecting capital according to the criterion of social need rather than private profit. What the document did propose was to change the banking system so as to make available funds for enterprises of 'national advantage'. This seemed to imply an acceptance of a corporatist solution to the problem of the depressed areas by resort to some form of state holding company, probably along the lines of a reorganised Bank of England acting as a 'public corporation'. This promise was suitably vague and was strictly a long-term objective. What gave *Labour and the Nation* immediate electoral appeal was its specific demands, which included the repeal of the 1927 labour legislation, a pledge to increase unemployment benefits and restore the seven-hour day in the coal industry, and establish a statutory maximum of 48 hours as the normal working week.

It was on the basis of this new programme that the Labour Party made important gains in the 1929 General Election, becoming for the first time the largest single party, although lacking an overall majority. The experience of a second Labour government, however, served only to repeat the pattern of its first administration, and MacDonald's handling of the world depression emphasised the government's unwillingness to challenge existing orthodoxy. The result was that the ambitious plans for state intervention suggested in *Labour and the Nation* were sacrificed on the altar of the balanced budget.[47] It is a fitting obituary to his career as a Labour politician that MacDonald subsequently agreed to serve as a member of the Tory-dominated 'National Government', after the second Labour administration collapsed during the financial crisis of 1930–1. Thereafter, it was again the trade unions and the Liberals who made the running in developing Keynesian ideas for managing the economy, which did not entail total nationalisation let alone 'socialism'.[48] In the process, the trade union leadership came to appreciate the common ground it shared with some prominent employers, particularly in the relatively expansive home-based industries.[49] What would have appeared an unlikely alignment of interests before 1920 was to become an increasingly likely possibility during the 1930s. It was only as a consequence of the experience of the Second World War, however, that this new alignment found political expression in the form of a revitalised Labour Party. Yet an expectation grew in the 1930s that a combination of Keynesian principles and corporatist strategies might well produce the 'New Social Order', which had been promised during 1918–20, and the 1945 landslide to the Labour Party must be seen in this context. It remains a testimony to the illusory hopes entertained by many on the left at the time that the outcome would necessarily be a 'socialist society' as they conceived it.[50]

The aftermath of the 1926 General Strike was thus decisive in strengthening the forces making for social stability during the inter-war period. The economic recovery of the late 1930s, initiated and sustained to a large extent by rearmament, pointed to a new period of growth and stability that was to last until the late 1960s. In consequence, a new 'power bloc' was established in British society, analogous to the alliance of dominant groups of factions of the mid-Victorian period. This consisted, first of all, of the more 'progressive' sections of big industrial capital, represented by employers in the growing home-based industries and including huge combinations like ICI with their oligopolistic control of world markets. There was, in addition, the expanding body of salaried employees who phased into a new managerial elite at the highest echelons of administration in commerce, industry and government. There also remained, of course, a powerful and influential rentier bourgeoisie centred on London, which continued to benefit from Britain's imperial connections, although its more dynamic elements were establishing direct links with industry itself via interlocking directorships. And, finally, there was an increasingly influential labourist bureaucracy, consisting of the leaders of the union amalgamations formed in the early 1920s and an emerging cadre of career politicians in the Parliamentary Labour Party.

Again, the concept of a power bloc should not be interpreted in this context as denying the existence of conflict among its component parts, nor as an alliance of groups did it speak with one voice. What drew together its various constituents, especially during the late 1920s and 1930s, was their overriding determination to avoid in the face of economic adversity the confrontations of the period 1914–26, and search for the conditions that would guarantee their power and influence. There was thus considerable variety in the policy proposals subsequently put forward to achieve this end, yet by 1939 it had become generally accepted that the problems of British capitalism justified a degree of state intervention and control unthinkable in the early 1920s. What made this increasingly acceptable during the 1930s was that labour was now being educated on the basis of a quite different climate of opinion, which no longer regarded state control as necessarily socialist. The steady diffusion of Keynesian ideas, and the success of corporatist schemes for reorganisation and rationalisation, emphasised that government intervention was not only compatible with the interests of private capital but could also be more positively beneficial.

It was the expanding managerial elite in commerce, industry and especially government itself who were to become the most active protagonists of this 'ideology of corporatism'. They were to become, therefore, the hegemonic faction of the new power bloc, analogous to the industrial bourgeoisie who had diffused its own way of life and thought throughout mid-Victorian society. Yet, in one crucial respect, the basis for this new hegemony rested on a more fragile foundation. The resolution of conflicting class interests now ultimately depended not so much on a shared ideology, which overlay social divisions however much it might have to be reformulated or reified; but upon the capacity of the state to manipulate the *organisations* of capital and labour, acting by itself in the interests of the whole. This mode of control has proved successful so long as economic conditions were sufficiently favourable to allow the state to pursue and, above all, to *represent* the conflicting interests of the whole in this way. But events since the late 1960s have indicated that the assumptions of the 1930s and 1940s may no longer be adequate to resolve social conflict, *without* imposing sacrifices that either organised labour or capital might come to regard as unbearable. There is clearly no end in sight, therefore, to the continuing dialectic between the challenge *of* and the challenge *to* labour.[51]

Notes

1. G. A. Phillips, *The General Strike. The Politics of Industrial Conflict* (London: Weidenfeld & Nicolson, 1976), Table 15, p. 283.

2. Ibid., pp. 259–60.

3. A. R. and C. P. Griffin, 'The Non-Political Trade Union Movement' in Asa Briggs and John Saville (eds.), *Essays in Labour History 1920–1939* (London: Croom Helm, 1977).

4. K. J. Hancock, 'The Reduction of Unemployment as a Problem of Public Policy, 1920–29', *Economic History Review*, 2nd series, XV (1962), no. 2, pp. 340–1.

5. W. H. B. Court, 'Problems of the British Coal Industry between the Wars', *Economic History Review*, XV (1945), no. 1, pp. 13–17.

6. C. H. Feinstein, *Domestic Capital Formation in the United Kingdom 1920–1938* (Cambridge: University Press, 1956), Table 6.10, pp. 82–3.

7. Court, 'Coal Industry', p. 21.

8. H. A. Clegg, 'Some Consequences of the General Strike', *Transactions of Manchester Statistical Society*, 1953–4, p. 6.

9. Agatha L. Chapman and Rose Knight, *Wages and Salaries in the United Kingdom 1920–1938* (Cambridge: University Press, 1953), Table 11, p. 30.

10. Frank Wilkinson, 'Collective Bargaining in the Steel Industry in the 1920s' in Briggs and Saville.

11. See, for example, Bevin's attitude in Alan Bullock, *The Life and Times of Ernest Bevin, vol. I. Trade Union Leader 1881–1940* (London: Heinemann, 1960), pp. 351–4.

12. Clegg, 'General Strike', p. 4.

13. Ibid., p. 29.

14. Alan Anderson, 'The Labour Laws and the Cabinet Legislative Committee of 1926–27', *Bulletin of Society for the Study of Labour History*, 23 (Autumn 1971), cited in Appendix I, pp. 53–4.

15. Ibid., p. 41.

16. *Balfour Committee*, v. I, pp. 280–1, 304–5.

17. L. P. Carpenter, 'Corporatism in Britain, 1930–45', *Journal of Contemporary History*, 11 (1976), no. 1, p. 3, where corporatism is defined as 'the unification of self-governing industries by a national committee representing them and other interests, including the state'.

18. Bullock, *Bevin*, pp. 394–6.

19. Rodger Charles, *The Development of Industrial Relations in Britain, 1911–1939* (London: Hutchinson, 1973), p. 263.

20. G. W. McDonald and H. F. Gospel, 'The Mond-Turner Talks, 1927–33: A Study in Industrial Co-operation', *The Historical Journal*, XVI (1973), no. 4, pp. 810–13.

21. Ibid., p. 816.

22. Roderick Martin, *Communism and the British Trade Unions 1924–1933. A Study of the National Minority Movement* (Oxford: Clarendon Press, 1969), pp. 96–8.

23. Martin Jacques, 'Consequences of the General Strike' in Jeffrey Skelley (ed.), *The General Strike, 1926* (London: Lawrence & Wishart, 1976), pp. 391–2.

24. McDonald and Gospel, 'Mond-Turner', pp. 819 ff.

25. See Ch. 6, Note 106.

26. McDonald and Gospel, 'Mond-Turner', pp. 822–4.

27. Ibid., pp. 821–2, 826–8; Phillips, *General Strike*, pp. 292–3.

28. Bullock, *Bevin*, pp. 425–34.

29. James Hinton and Richard Hyman, *Trade Unions and Revolution. The Industrial Policies of the Early British Communist Party* (London: Pluto Press, 1975), pp. 42–5.

30. Phillips, *General Strike*, pp. 360–1 (footnote).

31. L. J. Macfarlane, *The British Communist Party. Its Origins and Development Until 1929* (London: Macgibbon & Kee, 1966), pp. 185–6.

32. James Klugmann, 'Marxism, Reformism and the General Strike' in Skelley, p. 80.

33. See Reg Groves, 'Against the Stream. Part Six', *International Socialism*, 59 (June 1973), pp. 18–21, for the instance when the so-called 'Balham Group' was expelled from the CPGB in 1932.

34. R. S. Hope, 'Profits in British Industry from 1924 to 1935', *Oxford Economic Papers*, new series, I (1949), no. 2, Table I, p. 162.

35. Ibid., pp. 161–3.

36. Ibid., Table VI, p. 177: this was reflected in the sums paid to directors of private companies during the years 1930–5, which exceeded those paid in the period 1924–9—see Chapman and Knight, *Wages*, Table 88, p. 225.

37. Feinstein, *Capital Formation*, Table 3.34, p. 47.

38. E. H. Phelps Brown and Margaret H. Browne, *A Century of Pay* (London: Macmillan, 1968), Table 44, p. 256.

39. Ibid., Fig. 45, p. 258.

40. Clegg, 'General Strike', p. 7; Chapman and Knight, *Wages*, Table 9, p. 27.

41. Richard Stone, *The Measurement of Consumers' Expenditure and Behaviour in the United Kingdom 1920–1938*, vol. I (Cambridge: University Press, 1954), Ch. II, especially Table 62, p. 172; and vol. II (Cambridge: University Press, 1966), Table 8, p. 17.

42. Bullock, *Bevin*, pp. 348–50.

43. Phillips, *General Strike*, p. 279, where it is argued that this campaign like the 1927 legislation itself had little permanent impact. Yet it was at least of symbolic

significance in emphasising the mutual interdependence of the TUC and the Labour Party.

44. Michael Bentley, 'The Liberal Response to Socialism, 1918–29' in Kenneth D. Brown (ed.), *Essays in Anti-Labour History* (London: Macmillan, 1974), pp. 67–72.

45. Donald I. MacKay, David J. C. Forsyth and David M. Kelly, 'The Discussion of Public Works Programmes, 1917–1935: Some Remarks on the Labour Movement's Contribution', *International Review of Social History*, XI (1966), pt 1, especially pp. 12–17; S. Pollard, 'Trade Union Reactions to the Economic Crisis', *Journal of Contemporary History*, 4 (1969), no. 4, pp. 102–4.

46. A concise discussion of this document is contained in Ralph Miliband, *Parliamentary Socialism. A Study in the Politics of Labour* (New York: Monthly Review Press, 1964), pp. 155–8.

47. Ibid., pp. 159–64.

48. Pollard, 'Union Reactions', pp. 114–15; A. Marwick, 'The Labour Party and the Welfare State in Britain 1900–1948', *American Historical Review*, LXXIII (1967), no. 2, pp. 394–5.

49. Bullock, *Bevin*, pp. 425–34; Carpenter, 'Corporatism', pp. 15–18.

50. For an especially penetrating analysis of socialist thought and activity during the 1930s, see John Saville, 'May Day 1937' in Briggs and Saville.

51. There is, needless to say, a vast literature on the origins and character of the 'crisis' of the 1970s. An especially readable account is Andrew Gamble and Paul Walton, *Capitalism in Crisis. Inflation and the State* (London: Macmillan, 1976).

A Guide to Further Reading

The intention of this guide is to highlight some of the more important and interesting literature that has appeared on the issues and themes treated in the narrative. It does not purport to be comprehensive and many of the detailed references have been left to the notes at the end of each of the chapters.

General and Introductory

There is a wealth of specialist work on the economic, social and political history of Britain between the 1850s and the 1930s. Yet concise textbooks remain thin on the ground and the reader would probably do as well to begin by looking at some of the more general surveys of particular aspects of this period. A stimulating analysis of the extent and causes of economic growth, for example, is David S. Landes, *The Unbound Prometheus* (Cambridge: University Press, 1969), and a more recent comparative survey of a shorter time period is W. Arthur Lewis, *Growth and Fluctuations, 1870–1913* (London: Allen & Unwin, 1978), although from a different perspective there is still much that can be learned from Maurice Dobb's *Studies in the Development of Capitalism* (London: Routledge & Kegan Paul, 1963). Aspects of British working-class history have been the subject of innumerable studies. A reading of the classics is still invaluable, like Sidney and Beatrice Webb's *Industrial Democracy* (London: Longmans, Green, 1897), and the same authors' *The History of British Trade Unionism* (London: Longmans, Green, 1920). The historical phasing of industrial conflict has been more recently analysed in James E. Cronin, *Industrial Conflict in Modern Britain* (London: Croom Helm, 1979), and accounts of trade unionism are to be found in Henry Pelling's *A History of British Trade Unionism* (Harmondsworth: Penguin Books, 1963), whilst particularly detailed although less comprehensive in terms of the period covered is H. A. Clegg, Alan Fox and A. F. Thompson, *A History of British Trade Unions since 1889, vol. I, 1889–1910* (Oxford: University Press, 1964). These should be read in conjunction with E. H. Phelps Brown and Margaret H. Browne, *A Century of Pay* (London: Macmillan, 1968). Another study that is especially useful since it deals with community as well as workplace aspects of working-class life is David Kynaston's *King Labour. The British Working Class 1850–1914* (London: Allen & Unwin, 1976). Working-class ideology has been discussed in an influential article by John Saville, 'The Ideology of Labourism' in R. Benewick, R. N. Berki and B. Parekh (eds.), *Knowledge and Belief in Politics: the Problem of Ideology* (London: Allen & Unwin, 1973), and in David E. Martin and David Rubinstein (eds.), *Ideology and the Labour Movement* (London: Croom Helm, 1978). The attention of readers is also drawn to a new book by Eric Hopkins, *A Social History of the English Working Classes 1815–1945* (London: Edward Arnold, 1979), which is complemented by James D. Young's *The Rousing of the Scottish Working Class* (London: Croom Helm, 1979). Important collections of essays that have located the areas of much recent research include E. J. Hobsbawm's *Labouring Men. Studies in the History of Labour* (London: Weidenfeld & Nicolson, 1968), and the series of three volumes edited by Asa Briggs and John Saville: *Essays in Labour History* (London: Macmillan, 1967); *Essays in Labour History 1886–1923* (London: Macmillan, 1971); and *Essays in Labour History 1920–1939* (London: Croom Helm, 1977).

Chapter One. The Accommodation of Labour, 1850s–70s

The literature on this period is particularly extensive. A good synthesis of recent work on the development of the British economy during this period is provided by R. A. Church's *The Great Victorian Boom 1850–1873* (London: Macmillan, 1975), and a wider interpretation of social relations that is especially provocative is Robert Gray's 'Bourgeois Hegemony in Victorian Britain' in Jon Bloomfield (ed.), *Class, Hegemony and Party* (London: Lawrence & Wishart, 1977). A more ambitious attempt to understand Victorian society is Harold Perkin's *The Origins of Modern English Society* (London: Routledge & Kegan Paul, 1969), whilst E. J. Hobsbawm's *The Age of Capital 1848–1875* (London: Weidenfeld & Nicolson, 1975) establishes the international context for comparison. Debates on particular aspects and issues as well as detailed studies of the period are legion. The growth of trade unions and collective bargaining, for example, is examined in Keith Burgess, *The Origins of British Industrial Relations. The Nineteenth Century Experience* (London: Croom Helm, 1975). A major debate has arisen concerning the usefulness of the concept of the 'labour aristocracy', much of which derives from E. J. Hobsbawm's seminal article, 'The Labour Aristocracy in Nineteenth-century Britain', contained in the same author's *Labouring Men*. Readers who wish to pursue this further are advised to consider two important regional studies, Robert Q. Gray's *The Labour Aristocracy in Victorian Edinburgh* (Oxford: Clarendon Press, 1976), and Geoffrey Crossick's *An Artisan Elite in Victorian Society: Kentish London* (London: Croom Helm, 1978). Several journal articles illustrate the value as well as the limitations of academic polemic: A. E. Musson, 'Class Struggle and the Labour Aristocracy, 1830–60', and John Foster, 'Some Comments on "Class Struggle and the Labour Aristocracy, 1830–60"', both contained in *Social History*, I (1976), no. 3. The literature on this debate has been critically-reviewed by H. F. Moorhouse in 'The Marxist Theory of the Labour Aristocracy', *Social History*, III (1978), no. 1. That there seems no end in sight to argument on this subject is shown by Alastair Reid's 'Politics and Economics in the Formation of the British Working Class: A Response to H. F. Moorhouse', *Social History*, III (1978), no. 3. Other studies of working-class politics include an old but still valuable book by Frances Elma Gillespie, *Labor and Politics in England 1850–1867* (Durham, North Carolina: Duke University Press, 1927), and more recently Royden Harrison's very influential *Before the Socialists: Studies in Labour and Politics, 1861–1881* (London: Routledge & Kegan Paul, 1965).

Chapter Two. The Challenge of the 1880s

The decade of the 1880s has proved a particularly controversial period. Much of the writing on the economy during these years has centred on the utility or otherwise of the concept of the 'Great Depression'. This is reviewed in S. B. Saul's *The Myth of the Great Depression, 1873–96* (London: Macmillan, 1969), although the interpretation presented reflects the author's own views that are not necessarily consistent with all the sources cited, and should be read together with the previously noted *Growth and Fluctuations, 1870–1913* by W. Arthur Lewis. The reader is on more secure ground in the collection of industrial case-studies edited by Derek H. Aldcroft, *The Development of British Industry and Foreign Competition, 1875–1914* (London: Allen & Unwin, 1968). Helen Merrell Lynd's *England in the Eighteen-Eighties. Toward a Social Basis For Freedom* (London: Frank Cass, reprint, 1968) still remains of interest as an attempt at an overall social analysis of the period, but its interpretation is contentious and is not compatible with some more recent research, and should be read in conjunction with the latter sections of Harold Perkin's *The Origins of Modern English Society* and Elie Halevy's classic study, *Imperialism and the Rise of Labour* (London: Ernest Benn, 1961). An important article by W. D. Rubinstein, 'Wealth, Elites and the Class Structure of Modern Britain', *Past and Present*, 76 (1977), challenges some existing views of the changing character of the British 'ruling class' during the late nineteenth century. The implications of wider economic and social changes for working-class attitudes and activity have been examined by E. J. Hobsbawm in *Labouring Men*, especially his essay, 'Trends in the British Labour Movement since 1850', and by E. P. Thompson in his perhaps misleadingly entitled article, 'Homage to Tom Maguire', in the first volume of the series edited by Asa Briggs and John Saville, *Essays in Labour History*. The phenomenon of the so-called 'New Unionism' is dealt with by several of the contributions in *Labouring Men*, and in great detail by Clegg, Fox and Thompson's *A History of British Trade Unions since 1889*, although A. E. P. Duffy's 'New Unionism in Britain, 1889–1890: A Reappraisal', *Economic History Review*, 2nd series, XIV (1961–2), no. 2, is a useful corrective to the view that the 1880s marked a sharp break with previous developments. One of the outstanding works on this period to appear in the last decade remains Gareth Stedman Jones, *Outcast London. A Study in the Relationship Between Classes in Victorian London* (Oxford: Clarendon Press, 1971), which is in many respects a pioneering study in the 'history of society' approach to research on working-class attitudes and activity, and as a regional study it can be taken together with the more specifically political orientation of Paul Thompson's *Socialists, Liberals and Labour. The Struggle for London, 1885–1914* (London: Routledge & Kegan Paul, 1967). The changing climate of opinion in regard to 'the condition of the working class' is suggestively handled by E. P. Hennock's 'Poverty and Social Theory in England: The Experience of the Eighteen-eighties', *Social History*, I (1976), and how this affected the practical implementation of social policy is examined by the case studies contained in Pat Thane (ed.), *The Origins of British Social Policy* (London: Croom Helm, 1978). Finally, the variety of 'left' alternatives to Liberalism taking root during the 1880s is demonstrated by a comparison of C. Tsuzuki's *H. M. Hyndman and British Socialism* (Oxford: University Press, 1961), and the rather different interpretations offered in Henry Pelling's *Popular Politics and Society in Late Victorian Britain* (London: Macmillan, 1968).

Chapter Three. The Struggle for Control, 1890–1906

Much of the recent debate on the economic character of this period has been couched in increasingly theoretical terms following the publication of Donald N. McCloskey's provocatively entitled article, 'Did Victorian Britain Fail?' in *Economic History Review*, 2nd series, XXIII (1970), no. 3. The latter and subsequent contributions to this debate are critically assessed in W. Arthur Lewis, *Growth and Fluctuations, 1870–1913*. How institutional and social as well as economic factors helped shape business behaviour in these years are discussed in S. G. Checkland, 'The Mind of the City, 1870–1914', *Oxford Economic Papers*, new series, 9 (1957), no. 3, and in D. C. Coleman, 'Gentlemen and Players', *Economic History Review*, 2nd series, XXVI (1973), no. 1. And how these affected, in turn, the industrial relations climate of the 1890s is dealt with in Clegg, Fox and Thompson, *A History of British Trade Unions since 1889*, and in Keith Burgess, *The Origins of British Industrial Relations*. Their political implications have been examined in a number of studies, including John Saville's authoritative article, 'Trade Unions and Free Labour: The Background to the Taff Vale Decision' in Asa Briggs and John Saville (eds.), *Essays in Labour History* (London: Macmillan, 1967), and more extensively in Frank Bealey and Henry Pelling, *Labour and Politics 1900–1906* (London: Macmillan, 1958). The conflict of interest underlying government policy-making in response to labour unrest is stressed in H. V. Emy's *Liberals, Radicals and Social Politics, 1892–1914* (Cambridge: University Press, 1973), whilst an especially crucial area of social policy-making is explored by José Harris in her book *Unemployment and Politics. A Study of English Social Policy, 1886–1914* (Oxford: University Press, 1972). The recent shift in the focus of research away from the details of government decision-making to the wider forces affecting it is illustrated by Roy Hay's 'Employers and Social Policy in Britain: The Evolution of Welfare Legislation, 1905–1914', *Social History*, II (1977), no. 4, whilst the need to locate it in the context of the changing climate of ideas is emphasised by Bernard Semmel in *Imperialism and Social Reform* (London: Allen & Unwin, 1968). In this latter respect, the popular appeal of imperialism as an antidote to socialism at the time of the Boer War is assessed in Richard Price's *An Imperial War and the British Working Class* (London: Routledge & Kegan Paul, 1972).

Chapter Four. The Edwardian 'Crisis', 1906–14

The applicability of the term 'crisis' to this period acquired popular currency as a result of George Dangerfield's now famous study, *The Strange Death of Liberal England* (London: Constable, 1935). Although the vast body of research undertaken since its publication makes this book appear now to be rather slight and impressionistic, the appeal of Dangerfield's original hypothesis continues to fascinate historians, hence Standish Meacham's article, ' "The Sense of an Impending Clash": English Working-Class Unrest before the First World War', *American Historical Review*, 77 (1972), no. 5. The literature on this period leaves no doubt about the extent of labour unrest, even if there is little agreement as to its significance. The standard industrial relations text for this period remains E. H. Phelps Brown, *The Growth of British Industrial Relations. A Study from the Standpoint of 1906–14* (London: Macmillan, 1959), and this should be taken together with the more recent study of E. H. Phelps Brown and Margaret H. Browne, *A Century of Pay*, which provides a solid statistical understanding of the period. Works of special interest include Bob Holton's *British Syndicalism 1900–1914* (London: Pluto Press, 1976), which is the most recent major study of this subject, although the reader should also be aware of conflicting interpretations of the pre-war labour unrest like G. A. Phillips, 'The Triple Industrial Alliance in 1914', *Economic History Review*, 2nd series XXIV (1971), no. 1. This was also the period of the Liberal welfare reforms, analysed most concisely in J. R. Hay's *The Origins of the Liberal Welfare Reforms 1906–1914* (London: Macmillan, 1975), and examined more particularly in Pat Thane (ed.), *The Origins of British Social Policy*, and in the forthcoming volume edited by Joseph Melling, *Housing, Social Policy and the*

State, 1880–1939 (London: Croom Helm, 1979). José Harris in her study of *William Beveridge: A Biography* (Oxford: Clarendon Press, 1977), provides insight into the climate of ideas prevailing at the time, while the popular appeal of Liberal welfarism is assessed in P. F. Clarke's definitive case-study, *Lancashire and the New Liberalism* (Cambridge: University Press, 1971). The extent and character of the growth of support for independent labour politics during these years has been widely debated. Ross McKibbin's *The Evolution of the Labour Party 1910–1924* (Oxford: University Press, 1974) has proved very influential, but it has not found universal acceptance and should be taken together with case-studies like Roy Gregory's *The Miners and British Politics, 1906–1914* (Oxford: University Press, 1968), which focus more on conditions in the constituencies, whilst the growth of the extraparliamentary socialist presence has been treated sympathetically in Walter Kendall's *The Revolutionary Movement in Britain 1900–21* (London: Weidenfeld & Nicolson, 1969), and in the more openly partisan study by Raymond Challinor, *The Origins of British Bolshevism* (London: Croom Helm, 1978). The lack of agreement among historians in regard to the character of this period reflects their selectivity in the sources they have used, as well as their conflicting interpretations of the evidence that is available. In this respect, Paul Thompson's *The Edwardians. The Remaking of British Society* (London: Weidenfeld & Nicolson, 1975) examines evidence drawn from oral history sources and provides a useful corrective to those studies that assume the written records left by working-class leaders necessarily represent the outlook of the 'voiceless' majority.

Chapter Five. 1914–20: A New Social Order?

The significance of this period is attracting an increasing body of new research. There are numerous texts seeking to provide an overview of these years. Gerd Hardach's *The First World War* (London: Allen Lane, 1977) is particularly useful since it sets out the international context for an assessment of developments in Britain. Sidney Pollard's *The Development of the British Economy 1914–1967* (London: Edward Arnold, 1969) remains the best general treatment of the economic changes of the period, while A. J. P. Taylor's *English History 1914–1945* (Oxford: University Press, 1965) is beautifully written although it is less useful as a guide to the economic and

social developments of these years. More relevant in this respect is
W. J. Wrigley's *David Lloyd George and the British Labour
Movement* (Hassocks, Sussex: Harvester Press, 1976), yet the atten-
tion of readers is also drawn to older but still invaluable works like
E. M. H. Lloyd, *Experiments in State Control* (Oxford: Clarendon
Press, 1924), and Samuel J. Hurwitz, *State Intervention in Great
Britain. A Study in Economic Control and Social Response, 1914–1919*
(New York: Columbia University Press, 1949). James Hinton's
The First Shop Stewards' Movement (London: Allen & Unwin, 1973)
has proved extremely effective in reopening the debates on the
nature of working-class attitudes and activity during the First
World War, although many remain unconvinced by his interpre-
tation, including Iain McLean in 'Red Clydeside 1915–19' in R.
Quinault and J. Stevenson (eds.), *Popular Protest and Public Order.
Six Studies in British History 1790–1920* (London: Allen & Unwin,
1974). There are some readily available books by contemporaries
active during this period that are especially interesting in informing
an understanding of labour unrest like, for example, J. T. Murphy's
*Preparing for Power. A Critical Study of the History of the British
Working-Class Movement* (London: Pluto Press, reprint, 1972); and
Harry McShane (with Joan Smith), *Harry McShane—No Mean
Fighter* (London: Pluto Press, 1978). In respect to the making of the
modern 'constitutional' Labour Party, Ross McKibbon's *The
Evolution of the Labour Party 1910–1924* remains essential reading,
together with J. M. Winter's *Socialism and the Challenge of War.
Ideas and Politics in Britain 1912–18* (London: Routledge & Kegan
Paul, 1974). Significant aspects of the war, like for example its
impact on women, are treated in Norbert C. Soldon, *Women in
British Trade Unions 1874–1976* (Dublin: Gill & Macmillan, 1978),
and this subject is discussed together with some of the other long-
term effects of the conflict in a stimulating article by B. A. Waites,
'The Effect of the First World War on Class and Status in England',
Journal of Contemporary History, 11 (1976), no. 1. The importance
of the 'reconstruction' years of 1917–20 has been assessed by a
number of writers including R. H. Tawney's 'The Abolition of
Economic Control, 1918–1921', *Economic History Review*, XIII
(1943), and more recently by Susan Howson in 'The Origins of Dear
Money, 1919–20', *Economic History Review*, 2nd series, XXVII
(1974), no. 1, and Rodney Lowe, 'The Erosion of State Intervention
in Britain, 1917–24', *Economic History Review*, 2nd series, XXXI
(1978), no. 2. Finally, the fate of the revolutionary left during this

period has been dealt with by Raymond Challinor's *The Origins of British Bolshevism*, and in Walter Kendall, *The Revolutionary Movement in Britain 1900–21.*

Chapter Six. The 1920s: The Challenge Contained

A major problem that arises when writing on a particular period in history is that the literature tends to proliferate as contemporary times are approached. This poses special difficulties when considering Britain between the wars. The best general treatment of economic developments during this period is still probably Sidney Pollard's *The Development of the British Economy 1914–1967*, although more recent research completed since the publication of its latest edition has been taken into account in Sean Glynn and John Oxborrow, *Interwar Britain. A Social and Economic History* (London: Allen & Unwin, 1976), which also has the advantage of stressing aspects most relevant to my study like poverty and housing. B. W. E. Alford's *Depression and Recovery? British Economic Growth 1918–1939* (London: Macmillan, 1972) is also useful, and from a different perspective, the insights contained in Maurice Dobb's *Studies in the Development of Capitalism* continue to make it worthwhile reading. The climate of opinion prevailing during the 1920s is examined in a collection of articles by Sidney Pollard, *The Gold Standard and Employment Policies between the Wars* (London: Methuen, 1970), although one interesting article not included in the collection is David Williams, 'Montagu Norman and Banking Policy in the Nineteen-Twenties', *Yorkshire Bulletin of Economic and Social Research*, XI (1959), no. 1. How economic change affected working-class attitudes and activity has been looked at generally by E. J. Hobsbawm in his influential essay, 'Trends in the British Labour Movement since 1850', contained in *Labouring Men*, and by John Foster in 'British Imperialism and the Labour Aristocracy' in Jeffrey Skelley (ed.), *The General Strike 1926* (London: Lawrence & Wishart, 1976). The effect of the government's retreat from intervention in economic and social affairs, which underlay much of the labour unrest of the 1920s, has been exhaustively studied by Bentley B. Gilbert in *British Social Policy 1914–1939* (London: Batsford, 1970), and there is also much that is interesting in this respect in the perceptive study by W. G. Runciman, *Relative Deprivation and Social Justice* (London: Routledge & Kegan Paul, 1966). An especially crucial area of social policy is treated by Alan Deacon in 'Concession and Coercion: The Politics of Unemployment Insurance in the Twenties' in Asa Briggs and John Saville (eds.), *Essays in Labour History 1920–1939* (London: Croom Helm, 1977), whilst the importance of housing that has often rightly been regarded as central to the assumptions determining policy-making during this period has recently generated some thought-provoking scholarships like the forthcoming collection of articles edited by Joseph Melling, *Housing, Social Policy and the State, 1880–1939*. The labour unrest of the 1920s continues, of course, to attract the attention of historians. Of the many studies made of the 1926 General Strike, the best are probably G. A. Phillips, *The General Strike. The Politics of Industrial Conflict* (London: Weidenfeld & Nicolson, 1976), which is likely to become accepted as the definitive study, and the articles contained in Jeffrey Skelley (ed.), *The General Strike 1926* (London: Lawrence & Wishart, 1976), which provide an interesting insight into local conditions. There is also important material in Asa Briggs and John Saville (eds.), *Essays in Labour History 1920–1939*, whilst an understanding of the wider significance of the 1920s and 1930s would not be complete without a reading of Alan Bullock's monumental biography of one of the most influential labour leaders in British history, *The Life and Times of Ernest Bevin, vol. I. Trade Union Leader 1881–1940* (London: Heinemann, 1960). The failure of the revolutionary left to harness the labour unrest of the 1920s for its political ends has been dealt with in three major studies: L. J. Macfarlane, *The British Communist Party. Its Origins and Development Until 1929* (London: Macgibbon & Kee, 1966); Roderick Martin, *Communism and the British Trade Unions 1924–1933* (Oxford: Clarendon Press, 1969); and James Hinton and Richard Hyman, *Trade Unions and Revolution. The Industrial Politics of the Early British Communist Party* (London: Pluto Press, 1975). The consequences of this in terms of the subsequent consolidation of 'social democracy' have been delineated by Ralph Miliband in *Parliamentary Socialism. A Study in the Politics of Labour* (New York: Monthly Review Press, 1964).

Chapter Seven. Post-1926: Labourism Rehabilitated

Some of the most useful literature that is relevant to a study of this period can be found in the references made above to the previous chapter. Yet the background to the emergence of a new climate of opinion manifest in 'the ideology of corporatism' is illuminated further by references to the following: Alan Bullock, *The Life and Times of Ernest Bevin, vol. I. Trade Union Leader 1881–1940;* L. P. Carpenter, 'Corporatism in Britain, 1930–45', *Journal of Contemporary History,* 11 (1976), no. 3; Susan Howson and Donald Winch, *The Economic Advisory Council, 1930–39: A Study in Economic Advice during Depression and Recovery* (Cambridge: University Press, 1977); Ralph Miliband, *Parliamentary Socialism. A Study in the Politics of Labour;* Donald Winch, *Economics and Policy: A Historical Study* (London: Hodder & Stoughton, 1969). How the changing climate of opinion was perceived by activists in the labour movement during the 1930s is examined in the seminal article by John Saville, 'May Day 1937' in Asa Briggs and John Savilie (eds.), *Essays in Labour History 1920–1939.*

INDEX